CONTROVERSIES IN PHILOSOPHY

Each volume in this series deals with a topic that has been, and still is, the subject of lively debate among philosophers. The sort of issues that it embraces are only partially covered, if covered at all, by the usual collections of reprinted work.

The series consists largely but not entirely of material already published elsewhere in scattered sources. It is, as a series, distinguished by two guiding ideas. First, the individual editors of the various constituent volumes select and collect contributions to some important controversy which in recent years has been, and which still remains, alive. The emphasis is thus upon controversy, and upon the presentation of philosophers in controversial action. Second, the individual editors are encouraged to edit extensively and strongly. The idea is that they should act as firm, fair and constructive chairmen. Such a chairman gives shape to a discussion and ensures that the several contributors are not merely heard, but heard at the moment when their contributions can be most relevant and most effective. With this in mind, the contributions, as they appear in these volumes, are arranged neither in the chronological order of their first publication nor in any other possibly arbitrary sequence, but in such a way as to provide and to reveal some structure and development in the whole argument. Again, and for similar reasons, the editorial introductions are both substantial and forthcoming.

Although most of the contributions in each volume have been published before as articles in journals, the editors are asked not to confine themselves to this source. There will be a fair element of original material and, even more frequently, extracts will be taken from books.

CONTROVERSIES IN PHILOSOPHY

General Editor A. G. N. Flew

THE IS—OUGHT QUESTION

Edited by W. D. Hudson

THE MIND—BRAIN IDENTITY THEORY

Edited by C. V. Borst

PHILOSOPHY AND LINGUISTICS

Edited by Colin Lyas

WEAKNESS OF WILL

Edited by G. W. Mortimore

THE PRIVATE LANGUAGE ARGUMENT

Edited by O. R. Jones

The Mind–Brain Identity Theory

A COLLECTION OF PAPERS
COMPILED, EDITED AND FURNISHED
WITH AN INTRODUCTION BY

C. V. Borst

CONTRIBUTORS
D. M. Armstrong, Kurt Baier, Robert Coburn, James Cornman
Herbert Feigl, Paul Feyerabend, J. M. Hinton, Norman Malcolm
Thomas Nagel, U. T. Place, Richard Rorty, Jerome Shaffer
J. J. C. Smart, Ernest Sosa, J. T. Stevenson, Charles Taylor

ST. MARTIN'S PRESS   NEW YORK

Foreword by the General Editor

The series of which the present volume is the second member is to consist largely but not entirely of material already published elsewhere in scattered sources. It is as a series distinguished by two guiding ideas. First, the individual editors of the various constituent volumes select and collect contributions to some important controversy which in recent years has been, and which still remains, alive. The emphasis is thus upon controversy, and upon the presentation of philosophers in controversial action. Second, the individual editors are encouraged to edit extensively and strongly. The idea is that they should act as firm, fair, and constructive chairmen. Such a chairman gives shape to a discussion and ensures that the several contributors are not merely heard, but heard at the moment when their contributions can be most relevant and most effective. With this in mind the contributions as they appear in these volumes are arranged neither in the chronological order of their first publication nor in any other and arbitrary sequence, but in such a way as to provide and to reveal some structure and development in the whole argument. Again, and for similar reasons, the editorial introductions are both substantial and forthcoming.

They can be seen as representing a deliberate rejection, at least within this special limited context, of the 'throw-a-reading-list-at-them, send-them-away, and-see-next-week-whatever-they-have-made-of-it' tutorial traditions of some ancient British universities.

The problem to which the Mind–Brain Identity Theory is offered as a solution was set by Descartes. For it was Descartes who persuaded modern philosophy to put enormous weight upon a fundamental distinction between mind and matter, consciousness and stuff. The problem is to say how the two can be, and are, related. Among the traditional answers have been epiphenomenalism, parallelism, and interactionism. The first of these urges that consciousness is some sort of result or property of a certain sort of material thing, but is incapable of any reciprocal effect on matter. Among the analogies suggested are phosphorescence on water or – mischievously – 'the halo on the saint' (C. J. Ducasse). The second claims that states of consciousness and physical states run parallel with one another, but with neither affecting the other. The traditional analogy here is that of two ideal clocks, each keeping perfect time, but neither having the slightest effect on the other. The third, which seems to be the view of at any rate post-Cartesian commonsense, is that the two interact, each one upon the other. Descartes himself was such a two-way interactionist; since his own solution was, notoriously, in terms of mechanical transactions supposedly occurring in the pineal gland.

In recent years the thesis most often and most powerfully argued has been that being conscious is just being in a certain brain state, and the present volume presents the controversy provoked by this vigorous advocacy. For reasons which Mr Borst indicates in his introduction, the Mind–Brain Identity Theory was developed later than its three traditional rivals. But hindsight can enable us to discern anticipations in Spinoza, perhaps, and in Hobbes. Thus in the first chapter of *Leviathan* we can read: 'All which qualities called sensible are in the object that calleth them but so many several motions of the matter by which it preseeth our organs diversely. Neither in us that are pressed are they anything else but diverse motions; (for motion produceth nothing but motion.) But their appearance to us is fancy, the same waking, that dreaming. . . .'

Three further volumes in the present series are already in active preparation. As General Editor I shall be glad to consider other possibilities, whether the suggestions come from colleagues who would like to do the editorial work themselves or whether they are made by others who as teachers feel a need which they would like someone else to fill.

ANTONY FLEW

University of Keele,
Staffordshire,
England

Contents

Contents 9

Acknowledgements

I should like to express my sincere thanks to all the authors who have allowed me to use their papers in this collection. The sources in which the papers first appeared are as follows:

I. *Dimensions of Mind*, ed. Sidney Hook (New York University Press 1960). II. The *British Journal of Psychology*, XLVII (1956). III. *The Philosophical Review*, LXVIII (1959). IV. Inaugural lecture of the Challis Professor of Philosophy at the University of Sydney (1965). V. The *Philosophical Review*, LXIX (1960). VI. *The Philosophical Review* LXIX (1960). VII. The *Philosophical Review*, LXX (1961). VIII. The *Australasian Journal of Philosophy*, XL (1962). IX. The *Australasian Journal of Philosophy*, XL (1962). X. The *Journal of Philosophy*, LVIII (1961), XI. The *Journal of Philosophy*, LIX (1962). XII. The *Journal of Philosophy*, LX (1963). XIII. The *Journal of Philosophy*, LX (1963). XIV. The *Journal of Philosophy*, LX (1963). XV. The *Review of Metaphysics*, XVII (1963), XVI. The *Journal of Philosophy*, LX (1963). XVII. *Dialogue*, III (1964). XVIII. *Dialogue*, III (1965). XIX. *Dialogue*, III (1965). XX. The *Review of Metaphysics*, XIX (1965). XXI. The *Philosophical Review*, LXXIV (1965). XXII. The *Philosophical Review*, LXXVI (1967). XXIII. *Analysis*, 27 (Basil Blackwell 1967).

My thanks are due to the editors and publishers of all these publications for permission to reprint.

C. V. BORST

Department of Philosophy,
University of Keele

Editor's Introduction
C. V. Borst

I. CONTINGENT IDENTITY

The papers in this volume are all concerned with expounding and examining a certain view of the nature of the relation between mind and body, mental states and physiological states. The particular theory under discussion is commonly known as the Identity Theory, though at least some versions of it also go under the name of Central-state Materialism.

The view is, as the name suggests, that mental states are quite literally identical with brain states: any given mental state is, roughly, a brain state, brain process or feature of a process in the central nervous system. However, what is distinctive about the currently canvassed Identity Theory is that the proposed identity is put forward as a scientific discovery – or at least potential scientific discovery – and not as a truth concerning the meaning of mental terms or concepts. This explains a good deal.

At first sight it might seem strange that so apparently obvious a suggestion as this identification has not, until so recently, been much discussed by philosophers. The reason, though, is not hard to find. The suggestion has been thought open to insuperable objections. Philosophers, especially since Descartes, have usually defined the mental in terms incompatible with the physical; mind for Descartes was in essence unextended, matter in essence extended. Even at a more everyday level the mental is customarily contrasted with the physical – rather as hot is exclusively contrasted with cold, wet with dry, light with dark, abstract with concrete. Any suggestion, therefore, that the mental *is* physical inevitably carries with it an air of paradox, if not of outright contradiction; for it seems, on the face of it, to imply that the mental is not mental.

However it is certainly now common knowledge that the brain, even although a physical organ, bears some intimate relation to the mind; and this knowledge is manifestly embodied in common idiom. When referring to admittedly mental happenings or conditions we speak of racking one's brains, picking another's brains, having it on the brain, having a good brain or, contrariwise, being all brawn and no brain; and so on. Hence the question inevitably arises of just what the relation is between mind and brain. Few would want to dispute that the brain has a great deal 'to do' with the mind. Injuries to the former are known to impair functions associated with the latter; certain drugs are presumed to alter mental states by their effect on the electrochemical processes of the nervous system; psychologists and physiologists have discussed the localisation of mental functions in specific regions of the brain. Even Descartes was prepared to allow, with doubtful consistency, a special role, in relation to mental operations, to the brain and especially to the pineal gland.

An obvious enough proposal is that the relation is of a causal nature. Sensations are, perhaps, the effects of stimulation of the sensory areas of the brain; volition perhaps causes motion of the limbs by its effect on the motor areas. Since it only makes sense to speak of causal transactions between ontologically distinct phenomena, the result is a dualist point of view. The difficulties of attempting to explain the causal interaction of fundamentally unlike phenomena have, notoriously, led to various psycho-physical parallelist doctrines. An obtrusive feature of any proposal to *identify* the mental with the cerebral is, manifestly, a denial of any form of psycho-physical or more specifically of mind–brain dualism, and an assertion of some form of philosophical monism. If the mental is still, none the less, conceived as a special category it will be so only as a particular subclass of the physical. Indeed just such a point of view is characteristic of what can profitably be seen as the predecessor of the Identity Theory, an alternative monistic account, namely, Behaviourism.

II. Behaviourism

Significantly the two philosophers chiefly responsible for the introduction of the Identity Theory, Professor Herbert Feigl and U. T. Place, both take as starting points of their discussions some form of behaviourist doctrine. Behaviourism, in fact, started out as a psychological theory. It was originated in the second decade of the present century by J. B. Watson. Instead of the predominantly introspective study of states of consciousness, psychology was to become the scientific study of human and animal behaviour. What then becomes of states of consciousness? These can occur in the absence of observable behaviour, so it looks as if the two cannot simply be equated, at least on the face of it. One way of meeting this point was by means of the notion of *covert* behaviour. Thinking, for example, was equated with or replaced by minute movements of the larynx or laryngeal muscles, and perhaps also of other organs associated with speech. Yet it could hardly be maintained that what was commonly *meant* by 'thinking' consisted in, or indeed had anything at all to do with, laryngeal movements. Rather the suggestion was that what went under the name of 'thinking' was *as a matter of fact* nothing but certain minute movements of the larynx (or in the case of deaf mutes, of the muscles of the fingers). Less ambitiously, but more plausibly, it was alternatively maintained that for the purposes of psychological investigation thinking could best be *regarded as* larynx movement: thus conceived, Behaviourism was a methodological principle. Psychology should, in common with the established sciences, deal exclusively with intersubjectively observable phenomena and not rely on non-intersubjectively confirmable reports of occurrences 'in the minds' of its subjects.

In contrast to this methodological Behaviourism and to the bolder doctrine that might be called *Contingent* Behaviourism (but which is otherwise known as *Metaphysical* Behaviourism), was a doctrine developed by philosophers which is called *Logical* (or *Analytic*) Behaviourism. Here the viewpoint is one not of science but of logical or conceptual analysis. The contention was that the meaning of mental statements was analysable, without remainder, into statements about behaviour (possibly also about physiological changes) and about the observable circumstances in which such behaviour occurred. The previously mentioned objection that mental processes can occur in the absence of any overt behaviour was taken care of, not by invoking the notion of covert behaviour, so much as by the notion of unfulfilled disposition to behave. Thus someone may be angry whilst sitting apparently undisturbed in an armchair yet, it would be said, he is none the less necessarily disposed to act aggressively, and would do so but for willed or learned restraint. Such a doctrine, with very great refinements, is commonly associated with the names of Rudolf Carnap, Gilbert Ryle, and, some would contentiously add, Ludwig Wittgenstein. A close parallel as regards the type of thesis concerned is provided by Logical (or Analytic) Phenomenalism, to the effect that any statement about a physical object can be analysed into a set of statements about sense-impressions. In both cases the logical tool involved can be seen as Bertrand Russell's notion of a logical construction. The idea here is, roughly, that A's are logical constructions out of B's if and only if all statements about A's can be replaced, without loss of meaning, by concatenations of statements about B's. Physical objects become logical constructions out of sense-impressions, minds out of behaviour, somewhat as nations might be logically constructed out of individual citizens or universities out of their several colleges or departments. But in no case was any real entity to be postulated over and above the constituent entities. Russell's own principle was that where possible, logical constructions should replace inferred entities, on the ground that avoiding the unnecessary postulation of unobservable entities reduces the risk of being mistaken, provided that one does not explicitly deny that such entities may exist. However, this principle does tend to overlook the explanatory advantages of judicious entity-postulation and the fact that through technological advances one-time unobservable entities can become, at a later time, observed, in some sense or other.

III. Causal Explanations and the Identity Theory

U. T. Place begins his discussion by admitting that a dispositional analysis is fundamentally sound in the cases of our cognitive and volitional concepts, but he contends that there remains a number of our mental concepts, of consciousness, of sensation, and mental imagery where such an analysis fails, and an inner process account becomes unavoidable. Place was followed in this by Professor J. J. C. Smart, who originally applied the Identity Theory only to the case of sensations. Smart asserts that his 'Sensations and brain processes' takes its departure from Place's 'Is consciousness a brain process?' while also supplementing Feigl's 'The "Mental" and the "Physical"'. But it is in fact Smart's own article which seems more than any other to have caught the attention of philosophers and to be primarily responsible for putting the Identity Theory firmly on the current philosophical map. Since its publication in 1959 this relatively brief article has been veritably echoing through the pages of the journals in the form of discussion which it has engendered, and must, in addition, surely be near to creating a record as the most frequently reprinted article.

Feigl, also, in his mammoth essay 'The "Mental" and the "Physical"' (see Bibliography) develops his theory from a considera-tion of Behaviourism, though in this case the primary concern is with the molar behaviour theory of the psychologist (a résumé of his position is given in the included article, Paper I). Feigl points out that theoretical concepts are frequently employed by psychologists in the explanation of behaviour. Certainly there are some psychologists, of whom B. F. Skinner is a notable example, who wish to work solely in terms of observables. However Feigl's argument is that as soon as one passes, as he clearly believes should be done, beyond this *peripheralistic* Behaviourism and introduces *central* states in the explanation of overt behaviour, then the way is opened to a twofold identification. Firstly these central causes are identified with the referents of the phenomenal terms used by subjects in introspective descriptions of direct experience, and secondly these postulated central states are further identified with the referents of certain neurophysiological terms.

These postulated central states are in fact an example of the psychologists' so-called *hypothetical constructs* and as such are not definable in terms of observables, though they are logically related to such observables. Being thus ontologically distinct states they are able, as previously indicated, to feature in causal explanations of observable behaviour. The contrast is with the misleadingly called *intervening variables*, which are similar to the philosophers' logical constructions. Here there is no postulation since the meaning is restricted to observables, as the meaning of the term 'thirst' would be if it were taken to mean no more than, say, not having had a drink for a considerable time, and there thus subsisting a high probability of drinking-behaviour if presented with the opportunity.

Now one of the merits which proponents of the Identity Theory are wont to claim as against Logical Behaviourism is that their theory enables them to assign to mental states a genuinely causal explanatory role. This, they contend, accords with the role that such states carry in ordinary thought and speech. Take again the case of anger. As conceived by the Identity Theory, anger is thought of as an inner state over and above and standing behind angry-behaviour and bringing it about, so that it then becomes possible to construe such everyday remarks as 'He shouted *because* he was angry' or 'His anger made him go red in the face' in a genuinely causal sense. Whereas if anger is conceived as a logical construction out of angry-behaviour the explanatory force of such remarks is confined to being of a generalisatory nature. To put it briefly, he shouted or turned red because he was in a state constituted by being disposed, or possessing a tendency, to shout, turn red, and generally act aggressively: and not because he had difficulty in making himself heard, was blushing, or whatever.

One interesting corollary of the causal account is that it seems to provide a possible way of understanding, at least in the case of some psychological concepts, the puzzling relation between a criterion, in Wittgenstein's sense, and what it is a criterion for. The difficulty encountered in attempting to characterise this criterial relation has always been to specify a logical relation which is other than that of straight logical equivalence. In fact Armstrong draws attention in his book (*A Materialist Theory of the Mind* (1968) p. 92) to the striking fact that Wittgenstein's dictum, 'An "inner process" stands in need of outward criteria' could serve as the slogan of a causal analysis of mental concepts. Although on his theory the quotation marks could be removed from the words 'inner process'. Consider the most general characterisation of a mental state which Armstrong advances: it is, he says, 'a state of the person apt for producing certain ranges of behaviour' (p. 75, below). This characteristic behaviour would then become the criterion for the ascription of the relevant mental state.

Of course it will be tempting for a critic of the Identity Theory to complain that its suggested explanatory concepts are really little better than the notorious 'explanation' of the soporific power of opium in terms of a certain *virtus dormitiva* – it is due to a dormative principle. There does indeed appear to be something in this criticism. But it can in part be met if the alleged explanatory concept forms part of a theoretical framework whose overall explanatory power is capable of explaining and predicting further phenomena. Furthermore the position is strengthened by making reference to the second stage of the two-stage exposition of the Identity Theory as it is given by Smart and Armstrong. The first stage attempts to exhibit our mental concepts in such a way as to show their *compatibility* with a materialist metaphysic: this is seen as a task for purely philosophical analysis. The general form of Armstrong's stage-one account has already been indicated. The earlier account of Smart, which differed from that of Armstrong in stressing the causes rather than effects of mental states, was actually exclusively concerned with an analysis of sensation-reports, in what he described – in Ryle's phrase – as 'topic-neutral' language. To report, for instance, the occurrence of a yellowy-orange after-image amounted, to a first approximation, to reporting that 'something is going on in me which is like what goes on when I have my eyes open and there is an orange in front of me'.

Such schemata are not held actually to entail a materialist account of mental states in that the 'state of the person apt for . . .' or what 'is going on in me when . . .' could in fact turn out to be psychical, spiritual, mentalistic, in short, a non-physical occurrence. But then the claim of the second stage of the argument is that, as a matter of contingent fact, and on the basis of present scientific knowledge, it is most plausible to identify such occurrences with states of the central nervous system. This second stage is thus one not of philosophical analysis but of empirical fact.

A favoured model is the case of the scientific identification of the gene with the D.N.A. molecule. A gene is characterised in such a way as to be logically linked with its observable effects, the transmission of hereditary information. Exactly what the intrinsic nature was of the entities responsible for this transmission was at the time of their initial postulation unknown. But now, much later, the evidence for their identification with the D.N.A. molecule has become overwhelming. (Looked at in this light the assignment of a certain *virtus dormitiva* to opium might seem considerably less nugatory than would otherwise appear – it could be seen as the positing of some sort of structure or ingredient of opium, of a then unknown nature, possessing the observed soporific effects.) The general line of thought is that many of our ordinary explanatory concepts contain a sort of gap or lacuna which later empirical findings are able to plug.

IV. ALTERNATIVE FORMS OF THE IDENTITY THEORY

An indication can now be given of the various different forms of the Identity Theory which have been put forward and which are represented in this collection. On the one hand there are the various antipodean versions from what Feigl has called the 'United Front of Sophisticated Australian Materialists', notably Smart and Armstrong, though the precursor of this position was the exposition of U. T. Place (written while he was a member of Smart's department at Adelaide). Their outstanding characteristic is a tough-minded and uncompromising materialism: pains, thoughts and after-images exist – or at least the experience of having them does – but are in fact nothing but states of the central nervous system of the person who has them. As originally put forward by Place and Smart, the central-state materialist account was to apply only to that limited set of mental concepts considered resistant to a behaviourist treatment. But with the appearance of Armstrong's exposition it was extended to cover every one of our mental concepts, and Smart now goes along with Armstrong in this. This extension has, however, generated additional powerful objections.

Then there is the quite considerably different form of the theory put forward by Feigl. This is harder to classify. But it can still be seen as a different version of basically the same theory in that it, too, concerns a *contingent*, as opposed to a *logically necessary*, identification. Feigl was perhaps the first exponent of the theory to make explicit use of Frege's distinction between the sense of an expression and its reference, and of the utilisation of Frege's model of the empirically discovered identity of the Morning Star and Evening Star. In taking the common referents of phenomenal terms and certain neurophysiological terms (having, of course, logically independent senses) to be *raw feels*, Feigl might seem to be advancing a purely idealist version of the Identity Theory, as opposed to the Australian materialist version. But in point of fact Feigl sees himself as defending a *physicalist* position. (The term 'physicalist' has customarily been used for the view that every statement can be expressed in the language of physics.) This is so for Feigl because of his belief that 'the basic *laws* of the universe are the *physical* ones' (p. 40, below): all occurrences are related by and explainable in terms of the laws of the physical sciences (with the possible need to include 'emergent' laws in the case of biological phenomena). The term 'raw feels' was coined by the psychologist E. C. Tolman: by it is meant, roughly, the unconceptualised items of direct experience, sentience, the phenomenally given (e.g. sense-data or sensations). Feigl also appears to be following a suggestion of Tolman in construing such raw feels as the 'realities-in-themselves' which the neurophysiological terms denote.

Now there is, in addition to the above, a third form of the Identity Theory which has been dubbed by Richard Rorty the 'disappearance form', in contrast to the more familiar 'translation form', so called in virtue of the stage-one 'translation' of our ordinary mental concepts into topic-neutral language. It is this disappearance version which Rorty himself defends in the included article (Paper XX); and Professor P. K. Feyerabend's theory (see Paper XV) can also be classified as a 'disappearance' theory. The distinctive feature of this form is that no attempt is made to defend our ordinary thought and speech. On the contrary, the incompatibility of our ordinary mental concepts with scientific discoveries, and projected discoveries, is stressed: sensations and sensation-talk, for example, will simply disappear from a scientifically oriented language, much as demons and demon-talk have already disappeared. Their place might be taken by 'successor' concepts, which, nevertheless, would not stand in any simple relation to the present concepts. Not that it is necessarily suggested that this replacement would actually happen in practice, but in so far as it did not this would be largely because of evident inconvenience. We would, I suppose, for a while at least, be permitted, as

Berkeley allowed, to 'speak with the vulgar' so long as we were to 'think with the learned'.

Doubt has, as a matter fact, been raised (see James W. Cornman, 'On the Elimination of "Sensations" and Sensations', *Review of Metaphysics*, xxii (1968) pp. 15–35) whether the disappearance-theory is correctly termed an *identity* theory at all. But undoubtedly the general import is very similar and, moreover, as Rorty claims, the *is* of 'strict' identity can still perfectly properly be employed in statements of the form: 'What people now call "sensations" are (identical with) certain brain processes.' Significantly, in the face of various objections to his initial position, Smart confesses himself attracted to the disappearance or replacement theory of Feyerabend (see the final paragraph of 'Materialism', below) and Feigl, too, in his 1967 Postscript to 'The "Mental" and the "Physical"' shows some tendency to move in a similar direction.

V. IDENTITY STATEMENTS

The truth is that there has from the start been much difficulty in providing a coherent account of the proposed identity between mental states and neurophysiological states. Largely this arises because of the logical symmetry of *bona fide* identity statements: if A is identical with B, then equally B must be identical with A. Moreover if the identity is to be logically contingent, independent 'definitions' of the two terms must be provided. In Frege's example of the Morning and Evening Stars, the two terms on either side of the identity-sign possess equal status; there is no question of the Morning Star being *really* the Evening Star in any sense in which the Evening Star is not *really* the Morning Star. Worse still, on the translation Identity Theory mental states were to be *really* brain processes without brain processes being *really* mental states, but for all that the mental states were to remain unscathed! The following illustration is possibly instructive. Suppose for the sake of argument that the proposition 'Shakespeare is Bacon' is true; then someone might be inclined to remark that, in that case, there is no such person as Shakespeare (as commonly conceived) and so how can *he* be Bacon? Just such a point tends to arise for the Identity Theory; if mental states are, despite appearances, brain processes then there might seem to be no mental states to *be* brain processes. If the theory is true then it is false. To which a disappearance theorist can reply that that is precisely so; there are no mental states as commonly conceived. What people have misguidedly called 'mental states' are really brain processes, and what people have been calling 'Shakespeare' is in fact Bacon (in one of his roles, or wearing the particular 'hat' of the writer of the 'Shakespeare' plays). All the same this move needs to be treated with the greatest circumspection, for in some cases the results of applying it can be palpably absurd, as, for example, in the case of knowledge. Any argument along the lines 'what people now call "knowledge" is really x, y, z, therefore we should cease talking of knowledge, for there is something deficient about the concept' seems to me to possess no merit whatever. This may be because the term 'knowledge' carries little if any theoretical load and is, in any event, certainly not a straight referring expression.

Now the translation form of the Identity Theory would not suggest that the concept of knowledge might disappear, for there the suggestion was not that our ordinary psychological concepts are defective but that they are somehow unspecific. The topic-neutral analysis was in fact put forward in order to avoid the need to give an independent identity to one side of the alleged identity statements. In seeking models, proponents have characteristically turned to instances of contingent identities apparently found in the natural sciences. Such statements as 'Water is H_2O', 'Lightning is an electric discharge', 'Heat is mean kinetic energy', 'Solubility is the possession of such and such a structure', 'Genes are D.N.A. molecules' have been suggested. These certainly appear promising; for are they not genuine identity statements which, nevertheless, have an asymmetrical nature, being reductive in the sense that the right-hand side specifies the discovered nature of the left-hand side? The term 'theoretical identity' has sometimes been employed, for example by Feigl, and by Hilary Putnam (in 'Minds and Machines', *Dimensions of Mind*, ed. Sidney Hook (New York 1960) pp. 148–79). However the position is far from straightforward, because it can well be doubted both whether the scientific cases are indeed genuine identity statements, and whether they do really furnish viable models for the required theory of mind. The examples purport to give the physico-chemical or micro-structure of the things or properties in question, and it is possible to read them as providing *explanations* of familiar phenomena rather than as specifying what the things or properties *really are*. Thus it could be argued that reference to the mean kinetic energy of component molecules supplies an explanation of the familiar phenomena of heat and that heat itself should still be defined in terms of the boiling of kettles, the melting of wax, the burning of the skin, and so forth; or that the property of solubility should still be defined in terms of the fact that a substance which is soluble will dissolve when placed in water, this being explained by, rather than being, a certain physico-chemical structure.

It is doubtful if there is exactly any right or wrong thing to say in this dispute. But an interesting point is made by Putnam in a later article ('The Mental Life of Some Machines', *Intentionality, Minds, and Perception*, ed. Hector-Neri Castañeda (Detroit 1967) pp. 177–213). Putnam considers that it would only not be a 'wholly unmotivated extension of ordinary usage' to say that solubility *is* the possession of a particular physico-chemical composition if *that* particular composition is physically necessary to the property of solubility. Moreover Putnam argues that in the case of a psychological, or more broadly, a 'logical' or functionally defined state, like *preferring A to B*, it is known that 'we *cannot* discover laws by virtue of which it is physically necessary that an organism prefers A to B if and only if it is in a certain physical-chemical state' since it is known to be possible for the logical states of a system to be physically realised in an indefinite number of different ways. He further points out a paradoxical consequence of identifying such states with a certain structure. Suppose, to construct my own example, we found creatures on some other planet who were sufficiently like ourselves in appearance and behaviour for us to be ready to credit them with preferences, beliefs, and so on. But then suppose that we subsequently discovered that their 'central processes' were markedly different from our own. The consequences would be that on the Identity Theory we would be *forced* to withdraw the application of our own psychological vocabulary to them – or, absurdly, to endow it with a quite different meaning. If the identity of the Identity Theory is to be taken seriously, then what belief, say, *is* depends on the actual physical nature of the underlying state. This does not seem acceptable. There is good reason to say that we all know perfectly well what belief is, and what it is for a person to believe something, prior to scientific discoveries about brain mechanisms, and that such discoveries add not at all to our knowledge of the nature of belief. Instead such discoveries tell us only the changes in brain conditions which occur when people come to acquire beliefs. This knowledge may, of course, be to the highest degree useful from the practical point of view of manipulating people's beliefs, whether for therapeutic or less scrupulous reasons. But what really counts, as far as belief itself is concerned, is the functionally characterised state and not the physical structure which sustains or embodies it.

Something of this is apparent even in the case of the gene and the D.N.A. molecule; genes are D.N.A. molecules but not all D.N.A.

molecules are genes: only in respect of their function of transmitting hereditary information are certain D.N.A. molecules genes. However, in this case it must certainly be allowed that the discovery of the physical nature of genes really does add to our knowledge of what genes are. And I believe that the same may well be true in the case of those concepts which the Identity Theory was originally introduced to deal with, namely, the concepts of sensation, consciousness, mental imagery; and of course, of all other concepts just *in so far as* these too involve such concepts. This may be so, I suggest, because specific biological processes really are, as a matter of fact, physically necessary to consciousness. Feigl, for one, remarks that 'inductively it is plausible that sentience requires complex organic processes'; though I suspect one would be hard put to it to specify just what such inductive evidence consists of.

One further suggestion concerning the nature of the relation between mental and cerebral states should be mentioned. The suggestion has been made (see Max Deutscher, 'Mental and Physical Properties', *The Identity Theory of Mind*, ed. C. F. Presley (Brisbane 1967) pp. 65–83) that the appropriate notion that Identity Theorists are in fact operating with is not really that of identification *with* but rather of identification *as*. Thus the first step of the Smart–Armstrong exposition provides an account of mental states, as has been previously indicated, involving an unknown or unspecified element. Smart, for example, compared a sensation-report with the report 'Someone telephoned', where the someone turns out to be the doctor. Thus the someone is initially characterised only relationally, or known by description, as 'having telephoned' but is subsequently *identified as* the doctor (compare J. M. Hinton's 'the way of identification' p. 253, below). Analogously, mental states would be initially characterised purely relationally as states having specific causes and effects, and then subsequently scientifically identified as particular cerebral processes. This way of looking at the matter does at least help to ease the objection concerning the symmetry of identification *with* statements and the related need for providing independent identifications (as) of both terms. But it does not, of course, help to remove the objection that the physico-chemical aspect may not be the important thing in understanding mental states, nor of the need for the satisfaction of Leibniz's Law.

VI. LEIBNIZ'S LAW

Most of the traditional objections to an identity between mental and physical states have, in fact, hinged on this principle of Leibniz's Law, which governs the identity relation. The principle is that of the identity of indiscernibles, or rather the conjunction of this with its converse, the indiscernibility of identicals: if A is the very same item as B, then A and B must be indiscernible in the sense of possessing all their properties in common; and this for the very good reason that in such cases there is only one item in question, though one referred to by the different expressions 'A' and 'B'. However, stated in the form: 'A' can in any statement be substituted for 'B', and conversely, without changing the statement's truth-value, the principle is subject to numerous exceptions, as detailed presently; so that the Identity Theory is in no way threatened by a failure of substitutability which is of a kind that applies to *any* contingent identity statement.

In fact many of these traditional objections have been based on a failure to appreciate the possibility of contingent, as opposed to logical, identities. Once the contingent nature of the proposed identity is realised many of the traditional objections concerning the impossibility or absurdity of an identity between mental and physiological states or processes fail to hold up, though others still remain to be tackled. One group of objections which do disappear are those of an epistemological variety. For instance it has been customary to argue that mental states *could not* be physiological states because people had, and still have, knowledge of the former without possessing any knowledge of the latter. This argument, and others akin to it, no longer possesses any force. People were able to speak about genes before anything was known about D.N.A. molecules, but for all that genes *are* D.N.A. molecules. This point can be generalised to cover all of the so-called 'intensional predicates'; these include the whole range of what Russell called 'words for propositional attitudes', like 'believes that', 'hopes that', 'expects that', 'fears that'; and also modal predicates of the form 'is necessarily . . .' and 'is possibly . . .'. Such cases constitute exceptions to Leibniz's Law, if this is understood in terms of substitutability or if 'indiscernibility' is taken to include these alleged predicates, even although it remains true that if A=B, every property that A possesses B also possesses; for *ex hypothesi* A *is* B. That is, it can simply be denied that the so-called 'intensional properties' are really genuine properties, characteristics, or attributes of the thing in question at all. It may be true, for example, that Tom believes (or fears, etc.) that the Morning Star is likely to explode, without its also being true that Tom believes (or fears, etc.) that the Evening Star is likely to explode, even although, unknown to Tom, the Morning Star *is* the Evening Star. Again it is necessarily true that the Morning Star is visible in the morning, yet not necessarily true that the Evening Star is visible in the morning, though both are the planet Venus. But this is surely because such expressions as 'being believed by Tom to be likely to explode' and 'being necessarily visible in the morning' do not specify genuine properties, not even relational properties, of Venus, or whatever object is in question. Be this as it may, the really important point is that since these apparent exceptions to Leibniz's Law apply to undisputed cases of identity, it is no ground for objection to the mind–brain identity proposal that they crop up over this.

Prima facie objections still remain, however, in the case of non-intensional properties. Thus it may be objected that beliefs are true, false, well-founded or absurd; after-images are yellow or green or hazy; but that no brain process could intelligibly be said to be any of these things. Conversely that brain processes are located within the skull, are fast or slow, of such-and-such an electro-chemical nature; but that mental states could not be described in these terms. Replies by advocates of the Identity Theory often turn on two important moves: either just insisting that such objections simply beg the question against the theory, sometimes coupled with the suggestion that additional rules could be adopted which would render descriptions not now applicable legitimate (see Smart, p. 62, below; Shaffer p. 116, below); or of so choosing the exact nature of the terms between which the identity is to hold that the objections simply fail to arise. These points are of particular importance, in the case of what is probably the most refractory objection of this type, namely, that concerning spatial location. This matter of location is crucial; both because, as proponents of the theory agree, same spatial location enters into the very meaning of the identity, and because, as previously mentioned, the mental has traditionally been regarded as essentially non-spatial – though still temporally located, unlike the case of abstract objects. A further move made in attempted solution has been to invoke the idea of what has been called 'partial location'. The suggestion here is that a person's pains, images or thoughts occur wherever he happens to be, so that if I experience a pain whilst in the reading room of the Library then that is where the experience occurs. So if, following a suggestion of Thomas Nagel (see p. 218, below), the two terms between which the identity is to hold are taken to be, on the one hand, my having a sensation, and on the other, my body's being in a certain physical state, then both will be located to the same degree; namely again, wherever I happen to be. Difficulties arise, however, when considering just how far this partial location can be narrowed down. Does the having of the pain occur in one part of the room rather than another? Does it 'move' when I shift my position on the chair? It is, to be sure, perfectly natural to say that I experience a pain, or that a thought occurs to me, when I am at such and such a place. But whether this can be utilised in such a way as to remove objections concerning locatability is still a matter of dispute.

Another basic objection raised against the brain-process theory concerns the alleged incorrigibility of introspective or first-person reports of, at any rate, sensations, thoughts, images and intentions. The significance of this point is not perhaps primarily in regard to the satisfaction of Leibniz's Law, so much as the correlation between mental and cerebral states on which, at least on most versions, the Identity Theory is founded. If then I 'incorrigibly' report the occurrence of a severe pain in my left arm, but the brain scientist fails to detect the occurrence of the usual cerebral correlate, what is to be said? Smart's initial reply (see Paper IX) to Professor Baier, who raised this point (Paper VIII), was to the effect that since the identity he proposed was purely contingent, he simply believed that this would never in fact happen, but that if it did then this would refute his theory. However, towards the end of his reply Smart introduced another suggestion, namely, that first-person reports are never in fact incorrigible at all, on the ground that the report and what is reported constitute distinct occurrences so that, logically, it is always possible for one to occur without the other. (This line of thought is carried to extraordinary lengths in Armstrong's *A Materialist Theory of the Mind* where it is asserted, for example, that there can be *felt* pains of which one is unaware (see p. 312 of that book); this at least will surely not do.)

There are two immediate objections to this. In the first place, it seems extremely doubtful whether a sincere first-person report of an intense pain could ever become corrigible without a radical change in our concept of pain; as Baier remarks, it makes no sense to say 'I have a pain unless I am mistaken': there are no pain hallucinations. Equally it would seem bizarre to suggest that a man might be informed (as opposed to taught) that he was in pain. In the second place, if the incorrigibility of such reports is called in question it is somewhat difficult to see how the required psycho-physical correlations could ever be set up at all. So perhaps with this suggestion Smart is unwittingly sawing off the branch on which he is sitting.

VII. THE STATUS OF THE IDENTITY THEORY

Little has so far been said about the empirical side of the Identity Theory. Its proponents normally wish to maintain not only that it is free from logical objections but also that it is a reasonable and plausible hypothesis. This they aim to do in the light of current scientific knowledge, notably of supposed psycho-neurophysiological correlations (though if the theory is correct it would be more appropriate to speak of correlations between descriptions or observations). The subsistence of such correlations is, of course, accepted by other theories of mind. By, for example, the notorious doctrine of Epiphenomenalism, which asserts that while mental phenomena are caused by correlated brain events, they themselves are without causal influence either on any physical events or on other mental phenomena.

The contention then would be that these correlations are best interpreted in terms of identity and not in terms of relations between distinct occurrences, whether causally related or not. The recommendation is made primarily on grounds of simplicity and economy, of Occam's razor. Not only are superfluous entities disposed of but the subsistence of the correlations becomes explicable. Without this, these correlations would have to be just accepted as brute and inexplicable facts which, moreover, could not be fitted into the general scientific framework. Correlation 'laws' relating the inter-subjectively confirmable with the non-intersubjectively confirmable would be, as Feigl expresses it, 'nomological danglers'.

However I doubt whether the choice between the Identity Theory and the rival theories of Epiphenomenalism and Psycho-physical Parallelism can correctly be regarded as an ordinary scientific issue. The crux, is, as would be generally acknowledged, that it is in principle impossible for any experimental test to resolve the dispute. The case is possibly different where the choice is between any of these theories and a theory of mind–brain interactionism. For in this case it is plausible to argue that the breaks in the chain of physical causation should be, in principle, empirically detectable. The hope would be that if this issue could be experimentally decided against Interactionism, then Epiphenomenalism and Psycho-physical Parallelism could be rejected on other grounds. This does not seem an unreasonable hope. For these doctrines involve the truly incredible view that none of our mental states can be causally effective: no thoughts, decisions, pains, or acts of attention would themselves have any causal result on behaviour. Moreover, the very existence and the distribution of these states becomes totally inexplicable, both from a biological point of view and in terms of the above-mentioned framework of the natural sciences. The great strength of the Identity Theory is that it allows causal efficacy to mental occurrences: itches really do cause one to scratch, decisions result in appropriate action, attending to a task produces more efficient performance; and so on.

However, the case for the Identity Theory has not yet been convincingly made out. Some of the logical objections remain inadequately answered; the very intelligibility of the position is still in dispute; and, of course, its final acceptability must partly await further scientific research, including psychical research, the claims of which Armstrong describes as 'the small black cloud on the horizon of a Materialist theory of mind' (*A Materialist Theory of the Mind*, p. 364). The extension of the theory to cover all of our mental concepts is, to my mind, not at all plausible. It appears to depend on too primitive a conception of these concepts, roughly that all refer to specific states: almost a *unum nomen–unum nominatum* view. But, as a great deal of recent philosophising has shown, such a view is quite untenable. Consider, for example, the notion of promising. Many philosophers would contend that arguments, notably those of J. L. Austin, had established that this notion is primarily performative: to promise is to perform a socially institutionalised act. A person who promises is not reporting the existence of a state within himself which normally has the causal result of ensuring that the promised act is done. The very uttering of the words 'I promise' in appropriate circumstances is actually to make the promise; a person thereby *commits* himself to doing the act in question, he is not describing or reporting anything. Possibly he forgets about his promise until, at a later date, he is reminded of it, and, being a man of his word, keeps it. (There clearly need be no direct causal connection.) It may indeed be the case that such points can be accommodated within the Identity Theory, but if so, this has yet to be shown. Certainly no crude application of it to every psychological concept is likely to succeed.

What has, however, been established, is that the Identity Theory as such can no longer be lightly dismissed. Whether it ultimately manages to survive or not, what can at least be confidently claimed is that, at the present time, it provides one very fruitful focus of interest for discussions of problems in the philosophy of mind.

PART ONE

Statements of the Theory

I Mind–body, *not* a pseudo-problem

Herbert Feigl

Any serious effort toward a consistent, coherent, and synoptic account of the place of mind in nature is fraught with embarrassing perplexities. Philosophical temperaments notoriously differ in how they react to these perplexities. Some thinkers apparently like to wallow in them and finally declare the mind–body problem unsolvable: '*Ignoramus et ignorabimus.*' Perhaps this is an expression of intellectual masochism, or a rationalisation of intellectual impotence. It may of course also be an expression of genuine humility. Others, imbued with greater confidence in the powers of philosophical insight or in the promises of scientific progress, offer dogmatic solutions of the old puzzle. And still others, recognising the speculative and precarious character of metaphysical solutions, and deeply irritated by the many bafflements, try to undercut the whole issue and declare it an imaginary problem. But the perplexities persist and provoke further efforts – often only minor variants of older ones – toward removing this perennial bone of contention from the disputes of philosophers and scientists. Wittgenstein, who tried to 'dissolve' the problem, admitted candidly. (*Philosophical Investigations*, section 412): 'The feeling of an unbridgeable gulf between consciousness and brain-process. ... This idea of a difference in kind is accompanied by slight giddiness', but he added quickly 'which occurs when we are performing a piece of logical sleight-of-hand'.

As I see it, Wittgenstein's casuistic treatment of the problem is merely one of the more recent in a long line of positivistic (ametaphysical, if not anti-metaphysical) attempts to show that the mind–body problem arises out of conceptual confusions, and that proper attention to the way in which we use mental and physical terms in ordinary language will relieve us of the vexatious problem. Gilbert Ryle, B. F. Skinner, and, anticipating all of them, R. Carnap, have tried to obviate the problem in a similar way. The use of mental or 'subjective' terms is acquired by learning the language we all speak in everyday life; this language, serving as a medium of

communication among human beings, is by its very nature *intersubjective*; it is on the basis of publicly accessible cues that, for
example, the mother tells the child 'you feel tired', 'now you are
glad', 'you have a headache', etc., and that the child learns to use
such phrases as 'feeling tired', 'being glad', 'having a headache' as
applied not only to others, but also to himself when he is in the sort
of condition which originally manifested itself in the cues (symptoms,
behaviour situations and sequences, test conditions and results, etc.)
observable by others. But here is the rub. Even if we *learn* the use
of subjective terms in the way indicated, once we have them in
our vocabulary we *apply* them to states or conditions to which we,
as individual subjects, have a 'privileged access'. If I report moods,
feelings, emotions, sentiments, thoughts, images, dreams, etc., that
I experience, I am *not referring* to my *behaviour*, be it actually
occurring or likely to occur under specified conditions. I am referring
to those states or processes of my direct experience which I live
through (enjoy or suffer), to the 'raw feels' of my awareness. These
'raw feels' are accessible to other persons only indirectly by inference
– but it is *myself* who *has* them.

I do not wish to deny that ordinary language serves many purposes
quite adequately. As I see it, ordinary language unhesitatingly com-
bines mental (phenomenal) and physical (behavioural) terms in many
descriptions and explanations of human and animal conduct or
behaviour. 'Eagerness was written all over his face'; 'He was trem-
bling with anxiety'; 'No doubt his gastric ulcer is due to his suppressed hostility'; 'An attack of the flu left him in a discouraged
and depressed mood for several days'; 'A resolute decision finally
enabled him to overcome his addiction.' As these few illustrations
indicate, ordinary language clearly reflects an interactionistic view
of the relations of the mental and the physical. As long as we are
not too particular about squaring our accounts with the facts
established, or at least strongly suggested, by the advances of
psycho-physiology, we can manage to keep out of logical troubles.
Some philosophers, such as Ryle, Strawson, Hampshire, and other
practitioners of the ordinary-language approach, have most persuasively shown that we can talk about the mental life of '*persons*',
i.e. about episodes, dispositions, actions, intentions, motives, purposes,
skills, and traits, without getting bogged down in the mind-body
puzzles. But, notoriously, there is in this approach scarcely any
reference to the facts and regularities of neurophysiology. Moreover,
not all is well logically with these neobehaviouristic analyses.
'Persons' remains a term insufficiently explicated, and what I could

glean from Strawson's analysis[1] is that he defines 'person' as a sort of synthetically glued-together unity of a living body and its mental states. Strawson accounts for introspection in terms of 'self-ascription'. While this is helpful, it cannot be the whole story about mental states: infants, idiots, and at least some of the higher animals undoubtedly have 'raw feels', but are not 'self-ascribers'. If highly learned men nowadays express (philosophical) doubts about *other minds*, and debate seriously as to whether or not very complex robots have direct experiences, then obviously a better philosophical clarification of the relations of the mental to the physical is urgently needed.

The crucial and central puzzle of the mind–body problem, at least since Descartes, has consisted in the challenge to render an adequate account of the relation of the 'raw feels', as well as of other mental facts (intentions, thoughts, volitions, desires, etc.) to the corresponding neurophysiological processes. The problems may fairly clearly be divided into scientific and philosophical components. The scientific task is pursued by psycho-physiology, i.e. an exploration of the empirically ascertainable correlations of 'raw feels', phenomenal patterns, etc., with the events and processes in the organism, especially in its central nervous system (if not in the cerebral cortex alone). The philosophical task consists in a logical and epistemological clarification of the concepts by means of which we may formulate and/or interpret those correlations.

Scientifically, the most plausible view to date is that of a one–one (or at least a one–many) correspondence of mental states to neurophysiological process-patterns. The investigations of Wolfgang Köhler, E. D. Adrian, W. Penfield, D. O. Hebb, W. S. McCulloch, *et al.*, strongly confirm such a correspondence in the form of an isomorphism of the patterns in the phenomenal fields with the simultaneous patterns of neural processes in various areas of the brain. The philosopher must of course regard this isomorphism as empirically establishable or refutable, and hence as logically contingent. It is conceivable that further empirical evidence may lead the psycho-physiologists to abandon or to modify this view, which on the whole has served so well at least as a fruitful working hypothesis. It is conceivable that some of the as yet more obscure psychosomatic phenomena or possibly the still extremely problematic and

[1] P. F. Strawson, 'Persons', *Minnesota Studies in the Philosophy of Science*, II, ed. H. Feigl, G. Maxwell, M. Scriven (Minneapolis 1958) pp. 330–53; reprinted (with some alterations) in P. F. Strawson, *Individuals, an Essay in Descriptive Metaphysics* (1959).

controversial 'facts' of parapsychology will require emergentist or even interactionistic explanations. (As an empiricist I must at least go through the motions of an 'open mind' in these regards!) But tentatively assuming isomorphism of some sort, a hypothesis which is favoured by many 'naturalistic' philosophers, are we then to interpret it philosophically along the lines of traditional epiphenomenalism? Although Professor Köhler[2] does not commit himself explicitly to this view, I am practically certain that this is the general outlook within which he operates. If the basic physical laws of the universe should be sufficient for the derivation of biological and neurophysiological regularities, if the occurrence of neural patterns (physical *Gestalten*) is not a case of genuine emergent novelty but a matter of the combination of more elementary physical configurations, and if, finally, the experimential patterns correspond in some way isomorphically to neural process patterns, then this *is* epiphenomenalism in modern dress.

It will be best here not to use the somewhat ambiguous label 'parallelism'. Psycho-physiological parallelism, as held by some thinkers in an earlier period, allowed for a 'mental causality' to correspond to 'physical (i.e. neurophysiological) causality'. Sometimes it even connoted an all-pervasive correspondence of mental and physical attributes (in the manner of Spinoza), and thus amounted to a form of panpsychism. But the favoured outlook of modern psycho-physiology amounts to postulating causal relations, i.e. dynamic functional dependencies only on the physical side, and then to connect the neural process patterns merely by laws of (simultaneous) coexistence or co-occurrence with the corresponding mental states. Only a small subset of neural processes is thus accompanied by mental processes.

Traditionally the most prominent objection to epiphenomenalism has been the argument from the 'efficacy of consciousness'. We seem to know from our direct experience that moods, pleasure, displeasure, pain, attention, vigilance, intention, deliberation, choice, etc., make a difference in the ensuing behaviour. But, of course, this subjective impression of the causal relevance and efficacy of mental states can easily be explained by the epiphenomenalist: Since, *ex hypothesi*, some dynamically relevant physical conditions are invariably accompanied by mental states, there is, then, also a regular occurrence of certain types of behaviour (or of intra-organismic events) consequent upon mental states. For empiricists holding an essentially Humean

[2] Wolfgang Köhler (co-author), *The Place of Values in a World of Facts* (New York 1938).

conception of causality, it is then quite permissible in this sense
to speak of the causal efficacy of mental states. There are, it should
be noted, countless highly 'teleological' processes that occur in our
organism evidently without the benefit of any mental influence,
guidance, or instigation. For example, the kinds of regenerations
and restitutions that are involved in recoveries from many types of
physical injury or disease appear as if they were most cleverly
'designed', yet for many of these phenomena purely physiological
(and perhaps ultimately physico-chemical) explanations are available. Yet according to the epiphenomenalistic doctrine such explanations are sufficient also for behaviour which we ordinarily consider
instigated, regulated, or modulated by mental factors. If an effort
of concentration facilitates learning algebra, piano-playing, or the
like, then consciousness cannot be regarded as a causally irrelevant
or superfluous 'luxury'. I don't think we need to apologise for arguments of this sort. It is true radical Materialists and Behaviourists
reject such arguments as 'tender-minded', but then radical Materialism or Behaviourism typically *repress* or *evade* the mind–body
problem. They do not offer a genuine solution. Epiphenomenalism,
while not evading the problem, offers a very queer solution. It
accepts two fundamentally different sorts of laws – the usual causal
laws and laws of psycho-physiological correspondence. The physical
(causal) laws connect the events in the physical world in the manner
of a complex network, while the correspondence laws involve relations of physical events with purely mental 'danglers'. These correspondence laws are peculiar in that they may be said to postulate
'effects' (mental states as dependent variables) which by themselves
do not function, or at least do not seem to be needed, as 'causes'
(independent variables) for any observable behaviour.

Laws of concomitance in the physical world could usually be
accounted for in terms of underlying *identical* structures. Thus,
for example, the correspondence of certain optical, electrical, and
magnetic properties of various substances, as expressed in simple
functional relations between the refraction index, the dielectric
constant, and the magnetic permeability, is explainable on the basis
of the atomic structure of those substances. Or, to take a slightly
different example, it is in terms of a theory of *one* (unitary) electric
current that we explain the thermal, chemical, magnetic, and optical
effects which may severally or jointly be used in an 'operational
definition' of the intensity of the current. Similarly, it is at least a
partially successful working programme of psycho-physiology to
reduce certain correlated macro-behavioural features to underlying

identical neurophysiological structures and processes. It should be emphasised, however, that a further step is needed if we are to overcome the dualism in the epiphenomenalist interpretation of the correlation of subjective mental states with brain states.

The classical attempts in the direction of such unification or of a monistic solution are well known: double-aspect, double-knowledge, twofold-access, or double-language doctrines have been proposed in various forms. The trouble with most of these is that they rely on vague metaphors or analogies and that it is extremely difficult to translate them into straightforward language. I can here only briefly indicate the lines along which I think the 'world knot' – to use Schopenhauer's striking designation for the mind–body puzzles – may be disentangled. The indispensable step consists in a critical reflection upon the meanings of the terms 'mental' and 'physical', and along with this a thorough clarification of such traditional philosophical terms as 'private' and 'public', 'subjective' and 'objective', 'psychological space(s)' and 'physical space', 'intentionality', 'purposiveness', etc. The solution that appears most plausible to me, and that is entirely consistent with a thoroughgoing naturalism, is an *identity theory* of the mental and the physical, as follows: Certain neurophysiological terms denote (refer to) the very same events that are also denoted (referred to) by certain phenomenal terms. The identification of the objects of this twofold reference is of course logically contingent, although it constitutes a very fundamental feature of our world as we have come to conceive it in the modern scientific outlook. Utilising Frege's distinction between *Sinn* ('meaning', 'sense', 'intension') and *Bedeutung* ('referent', '*denotatum*', 'extension'), we may say that neurophysiological terms and the corresponding phenomenal terms, though widely differing in *sense*, and hence in the modes of confirmation of statements containing them, do have identical *referents*. I take these referents to be the immediately experienced qualities, or their configurations in the various phenomenal fields.

Well-intentioned critics have tried to tell me that this is essentially the metaphysics of panpsychism. To this I can only reply: (1) If this be metaphysics, make the least of it! (2) It is not panpsychism at all – either the 'pan' or the 'psyche' has to be deleted in the formulation. By way of very brief and unavoidably crude and sketchy comments let me explain my view a little further. The transition from the Logical Positivism of the Vienna Circle to the currently prevalent form of Logical Empiricism, as I interpret it, involved a complete emancipation from radical phenomenalism, behaviourism, operationalism and their all-too-restrictive criteria of factual meaning-fulness. Parallel with the critique of philosophical doubt by the Neo-Wittgensteinians, Logical Empiricists nowadays have no patience with sceptical questions regarding the existence of physical objects or of other minds. 'Sceptical doubts' of these sorts are illegitimate not because the beliefs in question are incapable of confirmation or disconfirmation, but because doubts of this pervasive character would call into question the very principles of confirmation and disconfirmation that underlie all empirical inquiry – both on the level of commonsense and on that of science. There can be no question that assertions of the existence of stars and atoms, or of the occurrence of conscious and unconscious mental processes, are subject to the normal procedures of inductive, analogical, or hypothetico-deductive confirmation or disconfirmation. It is pre-posterous (not to say philosophically perverse or naughty) to deny that we have well-confirmed knowledge concerning imperceptible physical objects or concerning the mental states of other human beings. A mature epistemology can make explicit the principles of such, often highly indirect, confirmations or disconfirmations. And along with this a liberalised meaning-criterion can be formulated, broad enough to include whatever is needed by way of common-sense or scientific hypotheses, and yet sufficiently restrictive to ex-clude transcendent metaphysical (pseudo–) beliefs. Freed from the torments of philosophical doubt and from the associated reductive tendencies and fallacies of phenomenalism as well as of radical behaviourism, we can now with a good intellectual conscience embrace a genuinely critical and empirical realism.

Once this position is attained, a mind–body identity theory of the kind sketched above appears as the most adequate interpretation of all the relevant facts and considerations. This is not panpsychism for the simple reason that nothing in the least like a psyche is ascribed to lifeless matter, and certainly at most something very much less than a psyche is ascribed to plants or lower animals. The panpsychists claimed to reason by analogy, but this is precisely what they did not do in fact. The difference between the nervous system of, say, an earthworm and of a human being is so tremendous that we should in all consistency assume a correspondingly large difference in their respective mental states. And even on the human level there is no need whatever for the assumption of a psyche in the traditional sense of a soul that could act upon the brain, let alone be separable from it. One may, of course, doubt whether a purely Humean conception of the *self* (as a bundle and succession of direct data) will be sufficient for an adequate psychology. Nevertheless no substantial entity is required. Events, processes, and their properly defined organisation and integration, should be perfectly sufficient. Professor Stephen C. Pepper suggested to me in conversation that my view might be labelled 'pan-quality-ism'. While this locution is not pleasant to the ear, it does come much closer to a correct characterisation than 'panpsychism'. But since Paul E. Meehl,[a] who understands my view at least as thoroughly as does Professor Pepper, has designated me a 'materialist', perhaps one last word of elucidation may be in order.

I am indeed in agreement with one main line of traditional materialism in that I assume, as does Professor Köhler, that the basic *laws* of the universe are the *physical* ones. But (and this is so brief and crude a formulation that I fear I shall be misunderstood again) this does not commit me in the least as to the nature of the *reality* whose regularities are formulated in the physical laws. This reality is known to us by acquaintance only in the case of our direct experience which, according to my view, is the referent also of certain neurophysiological concepts. And if we are realists in regard to the physical world, we must assume that the concepts of theoretical physics, to the extent that they are instantialised in particulars, are not merely calculational devices for the prediction of observational data, but that they denote realities which are unknown by acquaintance, but which may in some way nevertheless be not entirely discontinuous with the qualities of direct experience. But – 'whereof we cannot speak, thereof we must be silent'. If this is metaphysics, it seems to me entirely innocuous. I have little sympathy with the mysticism of Eddington or the psychovitalism of Bergson. I reject the former because there is literally nothing that can be responsibly said in a phenomenal language about qualities that do not fall within the scope of acquaintance. Extrapolation will carry us at most to the concepts of unconscious wishes, urges or conflicts as postulated by such 'depth-psychologies' as psychoanalysis. And even here, future scientific developments may be expected to couch these concepts much more fruitfully in the language of neurophysiology and endocrinology. And I reject psychovitalism because it involves dualistic interaction. At the very best 'intuition' (empathetic imagination) may be heuristically helpful in that it can suggest scientific hypotheses in psychology (possibly even in biology), but these suggestions are extremely precarious, and hence must

[a] Paul F. Meehl (co-author), *What, Then, is Man?*, Graduate Study No. III (St Louis 1958).

always be relentlessly scrutinised in the light of objective evidence.[4]

Does the identity theory simplify our conception of the world? I think it does. Instead of conceiving of two realms or two concomitant types of events, we have only one reality which is represented in two different conceptual systems – on the one hand, that of physics and on the other hand, where applicable (in my opinion only to an extremely small part of the world) that of phenomenological psychology. I realise fully that the simplification thus achieved is a matter of *philosophical interpretation*. For a synoptic, coherent account of the relevant facts of perception, introspection, and psychosomatics, and of the logic of theory-construction in the physical sciences, I think that the identity view is preferable to any other proposed solution of the mind–body problem. Call my view metaphysical if you must; I would rather call it *metascientific*, in the sense that it is the result of a comprehensive reflection on the *results* of science as well as on the logic and epistemology of scientific *method*. But I admit that for the ordinary purposes of psychology, psycho-physiology, and psychiatry an epiphenomenalist position is entirely adequate, if only the traditional, picturesque but highly misleading locutions (e.g. 'substantial material reality and its shadowy mental accompaniments') are carefully avoided.

I conclude that the mind–body problem is not a pseudo-problem. There are, first, a great many genuine but unanswered questions in psycho-physiology. And, secondly, there is plenty of work left for philosophers in the logical analysis of the intricate relations between phenomenal and physical terms. Problems of this complexity cannot be relegated to the limbo of nonsensical questions. I doubt quite generally whether many issues in modern epistemology can be simply 'dissolved' in the manner in which some artificially concocted pseudo-problems can be disposed of by a minimum of reflection on the proper use of terms. Questions like 'How fast does Time flow?', 'Do we really see physical objects?', 'Why is there anything at all rather than nothing?', 'Why is the world the way it is?', etc., can indeed be very quickly shown to rest on elementary conceptual confusions. But the issues of perception, of reality, and of the mental and the physical require circumspect, perspicacious and painstaking analyses.

[4] Feigl, 'Critique of Intuition from the Point of View of Scientific Empiricism', *Philosophy East and West*, 8 (1958) pp. 1–16.

II Is consciousness a brain process?

U. T. Place

The thesis that consciousness is a process in the brain is put forward as a reasonable scientific hypothesis, not to be dismissed on logical grounds alone. The conditions under which two sets of observations are treated as observations of the same process, rather than as observations of two independent correlated processes, are discussed. It is suggested that we can identify consciousness with a given pattern of brain activity, if we can explain the subject's introspective observations by reference to the brain processes with which they are correlated. It is argued that the problem of providing a physiological explanation of introspective observations is made to seem more difficult than it really is by the 'phenomenological fallacy', the mistaken idea that descriptions of the appearances of things are descriptions of the actual state of affairs in a mysterious internal environment.

I. INTRODUCTION

The view that there exists a separate class of events, mental events, which cannot be described in terms of the concepts employed by the physical sciences no longer commands the universal and unquestioning acceptance among philosophers and psychologists which it once did. Modern physicalism, however, unlike the materialism of the seventeenth and eighteenth centuries, is behaviouristic. Consciousness on this view is either a special type of behaviour, 'sampling' or 'running-back-and-forth' behaviour as Tolman has it[1] or a disposition to behave in a certain way, an itch, for example, being a temporary propensity to scratch. In the case of cognitive concepts like 'knowing', 'believing', 'understanding', 'remembering', and volitional concepts like 'wanting' and 'intending', there can be little

[1] E. C. Tolman, *Purposive Behaviour in Animals and Men* (Berkeley 1932).

doubt, I think, that an analysis in terms of dispositions to behave is fundamentally sound.[2] On the other hand, there would seem to be an intractable residue of concepts clustering around the notions of consciousness, experience, sensation, and mental imagery, where some sort of inner process story is unavoidable.[3] It is possible, of course, that a satisfactory behaviouristic account of this conceptual residuum will ultimately be found. For our present purposes, however, I shall assume that this cannot be done and that statements about pains and twinges, about how things look, sound, and feel, about things dreamed of or pictured in the mind's eye, are statements referring to events and processes which are in some sense private or internal to the individual of whom they are predicated. The question I wish to raise is whether in making this assumption we are inevitably committed to a dualist position in which sensations and mental images form a separate category of processes over and above the physical and physiological processes with which they are known to be correlated. I shall argue that an acceptance of inner processes does not entail dualism and that the thesis that consciousness is a process in the brain cannot be dismissed on logical grounds.

II. The 'Is' of Definition and the 'Is' of Composition

I want to stress from the outset that in defending the thesis that consciousness is a process in the brain, I am not trying to argue that when we describe our dreams, fantasies, and sensations we are talking about processes in our brains. That is, I am not claiming that statements about sensations and mental images are reducible to or analysable into statements about brain processes, in the way in which 'cognition statements' are analysable into statements about behaviour. To say that statements about consciousness are statements about brain processes is manifestly false. This is shown (a) by the fact that you can describe your sensations and mental imagery without knowing anything about your brain processes or even that such things exist, (b) by the fact that statements about one's consciousness and statements about one's brain processes are verified in entirely different ways, and (c) by the fact that there is nothing self-contradictory about the statement 'X has a pain but there is nothing going on in his brain'. What I do want to assert, however, is that the statement

[2] L. Wittgenstein, *Philosophical Investigations* (Oxford 1953); G. Ryle, *The Concept of Mind* (1949).

[3] Place, 'The Concept of Heed', *British Journal of Psychology*, XLV (1954), 243–55.

'Consciousness is a process in the brain', although not necessarily true, is not necessarily false. 'Consciousness is a process in the brain' in my view is neither self-contradictory nor self-evident; it is a reasonable scientific hypothesis, in the way that the statement 'Lightning is a motion of electric charges' is a reasonable scientific hypothesis.

The ail but universally accepted view that an assertion of identity between consciousness and brain processes can be ruled out on logical grounds alone derives, I suspect, from a failure to distinguish between what we may call the 'is' of definition and the 'is' of composition. The distinction I have in mind here is the difference between the function of the word 'is' in statements like 'A square is an equilateral rectangle', 'Red is a colour', 'To understand an instruction is to be able to act appropriately under the appropriate circumstances', and its function in statements like 'His table is an old packing-case', 'Her hat is a bundle of straw tied together with string', 'A cloud is a mass of water droplets or other particles in suspension.' These two types of 'is' statements have one thing in common. In both cases it makes sense to add the qualification 'and nothing else'. In this they differ from those statements in which the 'is' is an 'is' of predication; the statements 'Toby is eighty years old and nothing else', 'Her hat is red and nothing else' or 'Giraffes are tall and nothing else', for example, are nonsense. This logical feature may be described by saying that in both cases both the grammatical subject and the grammatical predicate are expressions which provide an adequate characterisation of the state of affairs to which they both refer.

In another respect, however, the two groups of statements are strikingly different. Statements like 'A square is an equilateral rectangle' are necessary statements which are true by definition. Statements like 'His table is an old packing-case', on the other hand, are contingent statements which have to be verified by observation. In the case of statements like 'A square is an equilateral rectangle' or 'Red is a colour', there is a relationship between the meaning of the expression forming the grammatical predicate and the meaning of the expression forming the grammatical subject, such that whenever the subject expression is applicable the predicate must also be applicable. If you can describe something as red then you must also be able to describe it as coloured. In the case of statements like 'His table is an old packing-case', on the other hand, there is no such relationship between the meanings of the expressions 'his table' and 'old packing-case'; it merely so happens that in this case both expressions are applicable to and at the same time provide an adequate characterisation of the same object. Those who contend that the statement 'Consciousness is a brain process' is logically untenable, base their claim, I suspect, on the mistaken assumption that if the meanings of two statements or expressions are quite un-connected, they cannot both provide an adequate characterisation of the same object or state of affairs: if something is a state of consciousness, it cannot be a brain process, since there is nothing self-contradictory in supposing that someone feels a pain when there is nothing happening inside his skull. By the same token we might be led to conclude that a table cannot be an old packing-case, since there is nothing self-contradictory in supposing that someone has a table, but is not in possession of an old packing-case.

III. THE LOGICAL INDEPENDENCE OF EXPRESSIONS AND THE ONTOLOGICAL INDEPENDENCE OF ENTITIES

There is, of course, an important difference between the table/packing-case and the consciousness/brain process case in that the statement 'His table is an old packing-case'.is a particular proposition which refers only to one particular case, whereas the statement 'Consciousness is a process in the brain' is a general or universal proposition applying to all states of consciousness whatever. It is fairly clear, I think, that if we lived in a world in which all tables without exception were packing-cases, the concepts of 'table' and 'packing-case' in our language would not have their present logically independent status. In such a world a table would be a species of packing-case in much the same way that red is a species of colour. It seems to be a rule of language that whenever a given variety of object or state of affairs has two characteristics or sets of characteristics, one of which is unique to the variety of object or state of affairs in question, the expression used to refer to the characteristic or set of characteristics which defines the variety of object or state of affairs in question will always entail the expression used to refer to the other characteristic or set of characteristics. If this rule admitted of no exception it would follow that any expression which is logically independent of another expression which uniquely char-acterises a given variety of object or state of affairs must refer to a characteristic or set of characteristics which is not normally or necessarily associated with the object or state of affairs in question. It is because this rule applies almost universally, I suggest, that we are normally justified in arguing from the logical independence of two expressions to the ontological independence of the states of affairs to which they refer. This would explain both the undoubted force of the argument that consciousness and brain processes must be independent entities because the expressions used to refer to them are logically independent and, in general, the curious phenomenon whereby questions about the furniture of the universe are often fought and not infrequently decided merely on a point of logic.

The argument from the logical independence of two expressions to the ontological independence of the entities to which they refer breaks down in the case of brain processes and consciousness, I believe, because this is one of a relatively small number of cases where the rule stated above does not apply. These exceptions are to be found, I suggest, in those cases where the operations which have to be performed in order to verify the presence of the two sets of characteristics inhering in the object or state of affairs in question can seldom if ever be performed simultaneously. A good example here is the case of the cloud and the mass of droplets or other particles in suspension. A cloud is a large semi-transparent mass with a fleecy texture suspended in the atmosphere whose shape is subject to continual and kaleidoscopic change. When observed at close quarters, however, it is found to consist of a mass of tiny particles, usually water droplets, in continuous motion. On the basis of this second observation we conclude that a cloud is a mass of tiny particles and nothing else. But there is no logical connection in our language between a cloud and a mass of tiny particles; there is nothing self-contradictory in talking about a cloud which is not composed of tiny particles in suspension. There is no contradiction involved in supposing that clouds consist of a dense mass of fibrous tissue; indeed, such a consistency seems to be implied by many of the functions performed by clouds in fairy stories and mythology. It is clear from this that the terms 'cloud' and 'mass of tiny particles in suspension' mean quite different things. Yet we do not conclude from this that there must be two things, the mass of particles in suspension and the cloud. The reason for this, I suggest, is that although the characteristics of being a cloud and being a mass of tiny particles in suspension are invariably associated, we never make the observations necessary to verify the statement 'That is a cloud' and those necessary to verify the statement 'This is a mass of tiny particles in suspension' at one and the same time. We can observe the micro-structure of a cloud only when we are enveloped by it, a condition which effectively prevents us from observing those characteristics which from a distance lead us to describe it as a cloud. Indeed, so disparate are these two experiences that we use different words to describe them. That which is a cloud when we observe it from a distance becomes a fog or mist when we are enveloped by it.

IV. WHEN ARE TWO SETS OF OBSERVATIONS OBSERVATIONS OF THE SAME EVENT?

The example of the cloud and the mass of tiny particles in suspension was chosen because it is one of the few cases of a general proposition involving what I have called the 'is' of composition which does not involve us in scientific technicalities. It is useful because it brings out the connection between the ordinary everyday cases of the 'is' of composition like the table/packing-case example and the more technical cases like 'Lightning is a motion of electric charges' where the analogy with the consciousness/brain process case is most marked. The limitation of the cloud/tiny particles in suspension case is that it does not bring out sufficiently clearly the crucial problems of how the identity of the states of affairs referred to by the two expressions is established. In the cloud case the fact that something is a cloud and the fact that something is a mass of tiny particles in suspension are both verified by the normal processes of visual observation. It is arguable, moreover, that the identity of the entities referred to by the two expressions is established by the continuity between the two sets of observations as the observer moves towards or away from the cloud. In the case of brain processes and consciousness there is no such continuity between the two sets of observations involved. A closer introspective scrutiny will never reveal the passage of nerve impulses over a thousand synapses in the way that a closer scrutiny of a cloud will reveal a mass of tiny particles in suspension. The operations required to verify statements about consciousness and statements about brain processes are fundamentally different.

To find a parallel for this feature we must examine other cases where an identity is asserted between something whose occurrence is verified by the ordinary processes of observation and something whose occurrence is established by special procedures. For this purpose I have chosen the case where we say that lightning is a motion of electric charges. As in the case of consciousness, however closely we scrutinise the lightning we shall never be able to observe the electric charges, and just as the operations for determining the nature of one's state of consciousness are radically different from those involved in determining the nature of one's brain processes, so the operations for determining the occurrence of lightning are radically

different from those involved in determining the occurrence of a
motion of electric charges. What is it, therefore, that leads us to say
that the two sets of observations are observations of the same event?
It cannot be merely the fact that the two sets of observations are
systematically correlated such that whenever there is lightning there
is always a motion of electric charges. There are innumerable cases
of such correlations where we have no temptation to say that the
two sets of observations are observations of the same event. There is
a systematic correlation, for example, between the movement of the
tides and the stages of the moon, but this does not lead us to say
that records of tidal levels are records of the moon's stages or vice
versa. We speak rather of a causal connection between two independent events or processes.

The answer here seems to be that we treat the two sets of observations as observations of the same event in those cases where the
technical scientific observations set in the context of the appropriate
body of scientific theory provide an immediate explanation of the
observations made by the man in the street. Thus we conclude that
lightning is nothing more than a motion of electric charges, because
we know that a motion of electric charges through the atmosphere,
such as occurs when lightning is reported, gives rise to the type of
visual stimulation which would lead an observer to report a flash of
lightning. In the moon/tide case, on the other hand, there is no
such direct causal connection between the stages of the moon and
the observations made by the man who measures the height of the
tide. The causal connection is between the moon and the tides, not
between the moon and the measurement of the tides.

V. The Physiological Explanation of Introspection and the Phenomenological Fallacy

If this account is correct, it should follow that in order to establish
the identity of consciousness and certain processes in the brain, it
would be necessary to show that the introspective observations reported by the subject can be accounted for in terms of processes
which are known to have occurred in his brain. In the light of this
suggestion it is extremely interesting to find that when a physiologist,
as distinct from a philosopher, finds it difficult to see how consciousness could be a process in the brain, what worries him is not any
supposed self-contradiction involved in such an assumption, but the
apparent impossibility of accounting for the reports given by the
subject of his conscious processes in terms of the known properties

of the central nervous system. Sir Charles Sherrington has posed
the problem as follows:

> The chain of events stretching from the sun's radiation entering
> the eye to, on the one hand, the contraction of the pupillary
> muscles, and on the other, to the electrical disturbances in the
> brain-cortex are all straightforward steps in a sequence of physical
> 'causation', such as, thanks to science, are intelligible. But in the
> second serial chain there follows on, or attends, the stage of brain-
> cortex reaction an event or set of events quite inexplicable to us,
> which both as to themselves and as to the causal tie between them
> and what preceded them science does not help us; a set of events
> seemingly incommensurable with any of the events leading up to
> it. The self 'sees' the sun; it senses a two-dimensional disc of
> brightness, located in the 'sky', this last a field of lesser brightness,
> and overhead shaped as a rather flattened dome, coping the self
> and a hundred other visual things as well. Of hint that this is
> within the head there is none. Vision is saturated with this strange
> property called 'projection', the unargued inference that what it
> sees is at a 'distance' from the seeing 'self'. Enough has been said
> to stress that in the sequence of events a step is reached where a
> physical situation in the brain leads to a psychical, which however
> contains no hint of the brain or any other bodily part.... The
> supposition has to be, it would seem, two continuous series of
> events, one physico-chemical, the other psychical, and at times
> interaction between them.[4]

Just as the physiologist is not likely to be impressed by the
philosopher's contention that there is some self-contradiction involved in supposing consciousness to be a brain process, so the
philosopher is unlikely to be impressed by the considerations which
lead Sherrington to conclude that there are two sets of events, one
physico-chemical, the other psychical. Sherrington's argument, for
all its emotional appeal, depends on a fairly simply logical mistake,
which is unfortunately all too frequently made by psychologists and
physiologists and not infrequently in the past by the philosophers
themselves. This logical mistake, which I shall refer to as the
'phenomenological fallacy', is the mistake of supposing that when
the subject describes his experience, when he describes how things
look, sound, smell, taste, or feel to him, he is describing the literal
properties of objects and events on a peculiar sort of internal cinema
or television screen, usually referred to in the modern psychological
literature as the 'phenomenal field'. If we assume, for example,
that when a subject reports a green after-image he is asserting the

[4] Sir Charles Sherrington, *The Integrative Action of the Nervous System*
(Cambridge 1947) pp. xx–xxi.

occurrence inside himself of an object which is literally green, it is clear that we have on our hands an entity for which there is no place in the world of physics. In the case of the green after-image there is no green object in the subject's environment corresponding to the description that he gives. Nor is there anything green in his brain; certainly there is nothing which could have emerged when he reported the appearance of the green after-image. Brain processes are not the sort of things to which colour concepts can be properly applied.

The phenomenological fallacy on which this argument is based depends on the mistaken assumption that because our ability to describe things in our environment depends on our consciousness of them, our descriptions of things are primarily descriptions of our conscious experience and only secondarily, indirectly, and inferentially descriptions of the objects and events in our environments. It is assumed that because we recognise things in our environment by their look, sound, smell, taste, and feel, we begin by describing their phenomenal properties, i.e. the properties of the looks, sounds, smells, tastes, and feels which they produce in us, and infer their real properties from their phenomenal properties. In fact, the reverse is the case. We begin by learning to recognise the real properties of things in our environment. We learn to recognise them, of course, by their look, sound, smell, taste, and feel; but this does not mean that we have to learn to describe the look, sound, smell, taste, and feel of things before we can describe the things themselves. Indeed, it is only after we have learned to describe the things in our environment that we learn to describe our consciousness of them. We describe our conscious experience not in terms of the mythological 'phenomenal properties' which are supposed to inhere in the mythological 'objects' in the mythological 'phenomenal field', but by reference to the actual physical properties of the concrete physical objects, events, and processes which normally, though not perhaps in the present instance, give rise to the sort of conscious experience which we are trying to describe. In other words when we describe the after-image as green, we are not saying that there is something, the after-image, which is green; we are saying that we are having the sort of experience which we normally have when, and which we have learned to describe as, looking at a green patch of light.

Once we rid ourselves of the phenomenological fallacy we realise that the problem of explaining introspective observations in terms of brain processes is far from insuperable. We realise that there is nothing that the introspecting subject says about his conscious experiences which is inconsistent with anything the physiologist might want to say about the brain processes which cause him to describe the environment and his consciousness of that environment in the way he does. When the subject describes his experience by saying that a light which is in fact stationary appears to move, all the physiologist or physiological psychologist has to do in order to explain the subject's introspective observations is to show that the brain process which is causing the subject to describe his experience in this way is the sort of process which normally occurs when he is observing an actual moving object and which therefore normally causes him to report the movement of an object in his environment. Once the mechanism whereby the individual describes what is going on in his environment has been worked out, all that is required to explain the individual's capacity to make introspective observations is an explanation of his ability to discriminate between those cases where his normal habits of verbal descriptions are appropriate to the stimulus situation and those cases where they are not, and an explanation of how and why, in those cases where the appropriateness of his normal descriptive habits is in doubt, he learns to issue his ordinary descriptive protocols preceded by a qualificatory phrase like 'it appears', 'seems', 'looks', 'feels', etc.[5]

[5] I am greatly indebted to my fellow-participants in a series of informal discussions on this topic which took place in the Department of Philosophy, University of Adelaide, in particular to Mr C. B. Martin for his persistent and searching criticism of my earlier attempts to defend the thesis that consciousness is a brain process, to Professor D. A. T. Gasking, of the University of Melbourne, for clarifying many of the logical issues involved, and to Professor J. J. C. Smart for moral support and encouragement in what often seemed a lost cause.

III Sensations and brain processes

J. J. C. Smart

This paper[1] takes its departure from arguments to be found in U. T. Place's 'Is consciousness a brain process?'[2] I have had the benefit of discussing Place's thesis in a good many universities in the United States and Australia, and I hope that the present paper answers objections to his thesis which Place has not considered and that it presents his thesis in a more nearly unobjectionable form. This paper is meant also to supplement the paper 'The "Mental" and the "Physical"' by H. Feigl,[3] which in part argues for a similar thesis to Place's.

Suppose that I report that I have at this moment a roundish, blurry-edged after-image which is yellowish towards its edge and is orange towards its centre. What is it that I am reporting? One answer to this question might be that I am not reporting anything, that when I say that it looks to me as though there is a roundish yellowy-orange patch of light on the wall I am expressing some sort of *temptation*, the temptation to say that there is a roundish yellowy-orange patch on the wall (though I may know that there is not such a patch on the wall). This is perhaps Wittgenstein's view in the *Philosophical Investigations* (see sections 367, 370). Similarly, when I 'report' a pain, I am not really reporting anything (or, if you like, I am reporting in a queer sense of 'reporting'), but am doing

---

[1] This is a very slightly revised version (which first appeared in *The Philosophy of Mind*, ed. V. G. Chappell (Englewood Cliffs, N.J. 1962)) of a paper which was first published in the *Philosophical Review*, LXVIII (1959) pp. 141–56. Since that date there have been criticisms of my paper by J. T. Stevenson (see Paper VI), to which I have replied in Paper VII, and by G. Pitcher and by W. D. Joske, *Australasian Journal of Philosophy*, XXXVIII (1960) pp. 150–60, to which I have replied in the same volume of that journal, pp. 252–4.

[2] *British Journal of Psychology*, XLVII (1956) pp. 44–50; reprinted in this volume as Paper II. (Page references are to the reprint in this volume).

[3] *Minnesota Studies in the Philosophy of Science*, II, pp. 370–497.

a sophisticated sort of wince. (See section 244: 'The verbal expression of pain replaces crying and does not describe it.' Nor does it describe anything else?)[4] I prefer most of the time to discuss an after-image rather than a pain, because the word 'pain' brings in something which is irrelevant to my purpose: the notion of 'distress'. I think that 'he is in pain' entails 'he is in distress', that is, that he is in a certain agitation-condition.[5] Similarly, to say 'I am in pain' may be to do more than 'replace pain behaviour': it may be partly to report something, though this something is quite non-mysterious, being an agitation-condition, and so susceptible of behaviouristic analysis. The suggestion I wish if possible to avoid is a different one, namely that 'I am in pain' is a genuine report, and that what it reports is an irreducibly psychical something. And similarly the suggestion I wish to resist is also that to say 'I have a yellowish-orange after-image' is to report something irreducibly psychical.

Why do I wish to resist this suggestion? Mainly because of Occam's razor. It seems to me that science is increasingly giving us a viewpoint whereby organisms are able to be seen as physico-chemical mechanisms:[6] it seems that even the behaviour of man himself will one day be explicable in mechanistic terms. There does seem to be, so far as science is concerned, nothing in the world but increasingly complex arrangements of physical constituents. All except for one place: in consciousness. That is, for a full description of what is going on in a man you would have to mention not only the physical processes in his tissues, glands, nervous system, and so forth, but also his states of consciousness: his visual, auditory, and tactual sensations, his aches and pains. That these should be *correlated* with brain processes does not help, for to say that they are *correlated* is to say that they are something 'over and above'. You cannot correlate something with itself. You correlate footprints with burglars, but not Bill Sikes the burglar with Bill Sikes the burglar. So sensations, states of consciousness, do seem to be the

---

[4] Some philosophers of my acquaintance, who have the advantage over me in having known Wittgenstein, would say that this interpretation of him is too behaviouristic. However, it seems to me a very natural interpretation of his printed words, and whether or not it is Wittgenstein's real view it is certainly an interesting and important one. I wish to consider it here as a possible rival both to the 'brain-process' thesis and to straight-out old-fashioned dualism.

[5] See Ryle, *The Concept of Mind*, p. 93.

[6] On this point, see Paul Oppenheim and Hilary Putnam. 'Unity of Science as a Working Hypothesis', in *Minnesota Studies in the Philosophy of Science*, II pp. 3–36.

one sort of thing left outside the physicalist picture, and for various reasons I just cannot believe that this can be so. That everything should be explicable in terms of physics (together of course with descriptions of the ways in which the parts are put together – roughly, biology is to physics as radio-engineering is to electromagnetism) except the occurrence of sensations seems to me to be frankly un-believable. Such sensations would be 'nomological danglers', to use Feigl's expression.[7] It is not often realised how odd would be the laws whereby these nomological danglers would dangle. It is some-times asked, 'Why can't there be psycho-physical laws which are of a novel sort, just as the laws of electricity and magnetism were novelties from the standpoint of Newtonian mechanics?' Certainly we are pretty sure in the future to come across new ultimate laws of a novel type, but I expect them to relate simple constituents: for example, whatever ultimate particles are then in vogue. I cannot believe that ultimate laws of nature could relate simple constituents to configurations consisting of perhaps billions of neurons (and goodness knows how many billion billions of ultimate particles) all put together for all the world as though their main purpose in life was to be a negative feedback mechanism of a complicated sort. Such ultimate laws would be like nothing so far known in science. They have a queer 'smell' to them. I am just unable to believe in the nomological danglers themselves, or in the laws whereby they would dangle. If any philosophical arguments seemed to compel us to believe in such things, I would suspect a catch in the argument. In any case it is the object of this paper to show that there are no philosophical arguments which compel us to be dualists.

The above is largely a confession of faith, but it explains why I find Wittgenstein's position (as I construe it) so congenial. For on this view there are, in a sense, no sensations. A man is a vast arrange-ment of physical particles, but there are not, over and above this, sensations or states of consciousness. There are just behavioural facts about this vast mechanism, such as that it expresses a temptation (behaviour disposition) to say 'there is a yellowish-red patch on the wall' or that it goes through a sophisticated sort of wince, that is, says 'I am in pain.' Admittedly Wittgenstein says that though the sensation 'is not a something', it is nevertheless 'not a nothing either' (section 304), but this need only mean that the word 'ache' has a use. An ache is a thing, but only in the innocuous sense in which

---

[7] Feigl, ibid., p. 428. Feigl uses the expression 'nomological danglers' for the laws whereby the entities dangle: I have used the expression to refer to the dangling entities themselves.

the plain man, in the first paragraph of Frege's *Foundations of Arithmetic*, answers the question 'What is the number one?' by 'A thing.' It should be noted that when I assert that to say 'I have a yellowish-orange after-image' is to express a temptation to assert the physical-object statement 'There is a yellowish-orange patch on the wall', I mean that saying 'I have a yellowish-orange after-image' is (partly) the exercise of the disposition[8] which is the temptation. It is not to *report* that I have the temptation, any more than is 'I love you' normally a report that I love someone. Saying 'I love you' is just part of the behaviour which is the exercise of the disposition of loving someone.

Though for the reasons given above I am very receptive to the above 'expressive' account of sensation statements, I do not feel that it will quite do the trick. Maybe this is because I have not thought it out sufficiently, but it does seem to me as though, when a person says 'I have an after-image', he *is* making a genuine report, and that when he says 'I have a pain', he *is* doing more than 'replace pain-behaviour', and that this 'more' is not just to say that he is in distress. I am not so sure, however, that to admit this is to admit that there are non-physical correlates of brain processes. Why should not sensations just be brain processes of a certain sort? There are, of course, well-known (as well as lesser-known) philosophical objections to the view that reports of sensations are reports of brain processes, but I shall try to argue that these arguments are by no means as cogent as is commonly thought to be the case.

Let me first try to state more accurately the thesis that sensations are brain processes. It is not the thesis that, for example, 'after-image' or 'ache' means the same as 'brain process of sort X' (where 'X' is replaced by a description of a certain sort of brain process). It is that in so far as 'after-image' or 'ache' is a report of a process, it is a report of a process that *happens to be* a brain process. It follows that the thesis does not claim that sensation statements can be *translated* into statements about brain processes.[9] Nor does it claim

---

[8] Wittgenstein did not like the word 'disposition'. I am using it to put in a nutshell (and perhaps inaccurately) the view which I am attributing to Wittgenstein. I should like to repeat that I do not wish to claim that my interpretation of Wittgenstein is correct. Some of those who knew him do not interpret him in this way. It is merely a view which I find myself extracting from his printed words and which I think is important and worth discussing for its own sake.

[9] See Place, p. 43, above; and Feigl, in *Minnesota Studies in the Philosophy of Science*, II, p. 390.

that the logic of a sensation statement is the same as that of a brain-process statement. All it claims is that in so far as a sensation statement is a report of something, that something is in fact a brain process. Sensations are nothing over and above brain processes. Nations are nothing 'over and above' citizens, but this does not prevent the logic of nation statements being very different from the logic of citizen statements, nor does it ensure the translatability of nation statements into citizen statements. (I do not, however, wish to assert that the relation of sensation statements to brain-process statements is very like that of nation statements to citizen statements. Nations do not just *happen to be* nothing over and above citizens, for example. I bring in the 'nations' example merely to make a negative point: that the fact that the logic of A-statements is different from that of B-statements does not ensure that A's are anything over and above B's.)

REMARKS ON IDENTITY

When I say that a sensation is a brain process or that lightning is an electric discharge, I am using 'is' in the sense of strict identity. (Just as in the – in this case necessary – proposition '7 is identical with the smallest prime number greater than 5'.) When I say that a sensation is a brain process or that lightning is an electric discharge I do not mean just that the sensation is somehow spatially or temporally continuous with the brain process or that the lightning is just spatially or temporally continuous with the discharge. When on the other hand I say that the successful general is the same person as the small boy who stole the apples I mean only that the successful general I see before me is a time slice[10] of the same four-dimensional object of which the small boy stealing apples is an earlier time slice. However, the four-dimensional object which has the general-I-see-before-me for its late time slice is identical in the strict sense with the four-dimensional object which has the small-boy-stealing-apples for an early time slice. I distinguish these two senses of 'is identical with' because I wish to make it clear that the brain-process doctrine asserts identity in the *strict* sense.

I shall now discuss various possible objections to the view that

[10] See J. H. Woodger, *Theory Construction,* International Encyclopedia of Unified Science, II, No. 5 (Chicago, 1939) p. 38. I here permit myself to speak loosely. For warnings against possible ways of going wrong with this sort of talk, see my note 'Spatialising Time', *Mind,* LXIV (1955) pp. 239–41.

the processes reported in sensation statements are in fact processes in the brain. Most of us have met some of these objections in our first year as philosophy students. All the more reason to take a good look at them. Others of the objections will be more recondite and subtle.

Objection 1.

Any illiterate peasant can talk perfectly well about his after-images, or how things look or feel to him, or about his aches and pains, and yet he may know nothing whatever about neurophysiology. A man may, like Aristotle, believe that the brain is an organ for cooling the body without any impairment of his ability to make true statements about his sensations. Hence the things we are talking about when we describe our sensations cannot be processes in the brain.

Reply.

You might as well say that a nation of slugabeds, who never saw the Morning Star or knew of its existence, or who had never thought of the expression 'the Morning Star', but who used the expression 'the Evening Star' perfectly well, could not use this expression to refer to the same entity as we refer to (and describe as) 'the Morning Star'.[11]

You may object that the Morning Star is in a sense not the very same thing as the Evening Star, but only something spatio-temporally continuous with it. That is, you may say that the Morning Star is not the Evening Star in the strict sense of 'identity' that I distinguished earlier.

There is however, a more plausible example. Consider lightning.[12] Modern physical science tells us that lightning is a certain kind of electrical discharge due to ionisation of clouds of water vapour in the atmosphere. This, it is now believed, is what the true nature of lightning is. Note that there are not two things: a flash of lightning and an electrical discharge. There is one thing, a flash of lightning, which is described scientifically as an electrical discharge to the earth from a cloud of ionised water molecules. The case is not at all like that of explaining a footprint by reference to a burglar. We say that what lightning really is, what its true nature as revealed by science is, is an electrical discharge. (It is not the true nature of a footprint to be a burglar.)

To forestall irrelevant objections, I should like to make it clear

[11] Cf. Feigl in *Minnesota Studies in the Philosophy of Science*, II, p. 439.
[12] See Place, p. 47, above; also Feigl in *Minnesota Studies in the Philosophy of Science*, II, p. 438.

that by 'lightning' I mean the publicly observable physical object lightning, not a visual sense-datum of lightning. I say that the publicly observable physical object lightning is in fact the electrical discharge, not just a correlate of it. The sense-datum, or rather the having of the sense-datum, the 'look' of lightning, may well in my view be a correlate of the electrical discharge. For in my view it is a brain state *caused* by the lightning. But we should no more confuse sensations of lightning with lightning than we confuse sensations of a table with the table.

In short, the reply to Objection 1 is that there can be contingent statements of the form 'A is identical with B', and a person may well know that something is an A without knowing that it is a B. An illiterate peasant might well be able to talk about his sensations without knowing about his brain processes, just as he can talk about lightning though he knows nothing of electricity.

Objection 2.

It is only a contingent fact (if it is a fact) that when we have a certain kind of sensation there is a certain kind of process in our brain. Indeed it is possible, though perhaps in the highest degree unlikely, that our present physiological theories will be as out of date as the ancient theory connecting mental processes with goings on in the heart. It follows that when we report a sensation we are not reporting a brain process.

Reply.

The objection certainly proves that when we say 'I have an after-image' we cannot *mean* something of the form 'I have such and such a brain process.' But this does not show that what we report (having an after-image) is not *in fact* a brain process. 'I see lightning' does not *mean* 'I see an electrical discharge.' Indeed, it is logically possible (though highly unlikely) that the electrical discharge account of lightning might one day be given up. Again, 'I see the Evening Star' does not *mean* the same as 'I see the Morning Star', and yet 'The Evening Star and the Morning Star are one and the same thing' is a contingent proposition. Possibly Objection 2 derives some of its apparent strength from a 'Fido' – Fido theory of meaning. If the meaning of an expression were what the expression named, then of course it *would* follow from the fact that 'sensation' and 'brain process' have different meanings, that they cannot name one and the same thing.

Objection 3.[18]

Even if Objections 1 and 2 do not prove that sensations are something over and above brain processes, they do prove that the qualities of sensations are something over and above the qualities of brain processes. That is, it may be possible to get out of asserting the existence of irreducibly psychic processes, but not out of asserting the existence of irreducibly psychic *properties*. For suppose we identify the Morning Star with the Evening Star. Then there must be some properties which logically imply that of being the Morning Star, and quite distinct properties which entail that of being the Evening Star. Again, there must be some properties (for example, that of being a yellow flash) which are logically distinct from those in the physicalist story.

Indeed, it might be thought that the objection succeeds at one jump. For consider the property of 'being a yellow flash'. It might seem that this property lies inevitably outside the physicalist framework within which I am trying to work (either by 'yellow' being an objective emergent property of physical objects, or else by being a power to produce yellow sense-data, where 'yellow' in this second instantiation of the word, refers to a purely phenomenal or introspectible quality). I must therefore digress for a moment and indicate how I deal with secondary qualities. I shall concentrate on colour.

First of all, let me introduce the concept of a normal percipient. One person is more a normal percipient than another if he can make colour discriminations that the other cannot. For example, if A can pick a lettuce leaf out of a heap of cabbage leaves, whereas B cannot though he can pick a lettuce leaf out of a heap of beetroot leaves, then A is more normal than B. (I am assuming that A and B are not given time to distinguish the leaves by their slight difference in shape, and so forth.) From the concept of 'more normal than' it is easy to see how we can introduce the concept of 'normal'. Of course, Eskimos may make the finest discriminations at the blue end of the spectrum, Hottentots at the red end. In this case the concept of a normal percipient is a slightly idealised one, rather like that of 'the mean sun' in astronomical chronology. There is no need to go into such subtleties now. I say that 'This is red' means something roughly like 'A normal percipient would not easily pick this out of a clump of geranium petals though he would pick it out of a clump of lettuce leaves.' Of course it does not exactly mean this: a person might know

[18] I think this objection was first put to me by Professor Max Black. I think it is the most subtle of any of those I have considered, and the one which I am least confident of having satisfactorily met.

the meaning of 'red' without knowing anything about geraniums, or even about normal percipients. But the point is that a person can be *trained* to say 'This is red' of objects which would not easily be picked out of geranium petals by a normal percipient, and so on. (Note that even a colour-blind person can reasonably assert that something is red, though of course he needs to use another human being, not just himself, as his 'colour meter'. This account of secondary qualities explains their unimportance in physics. For obviously the discriminations and lack of discriminations made by a very complex neurophysiological mechanism are hardly likely to correspond to simple and non-arbitrary distinctions in nature.

I therefore elucidate colours as powers, in Locke's sense, to evoke certain sorts of discriminatory responses in human beings. They are also, of course, powers to cause sensations in human beings (an account still nearer Locke's). But these sensations, I am arguing, are identifiable with brain processes.

Now how do I get over the objection that a sensation can be identified with a brain process only if it has some phenomenal property, not possessed by brain processes, whereby one half of the identification may be, so to speak, pinned down?

Reply.
My suggestion is as follows. When a person says, 'I see a yellowish-orange after-image', he is saying something like this: '*There is something going on which is like what is going on when* I have my eyes open, am awake, and am an orange illuminated in good light in front of me, that is, when I really see an orange.' (And there is no reason why a person should not say the same thing when he is having a veridical sense-datum, so long as we construe 'like' in the last sentence in such a sense that something can be like itself.) Notice that the italicised words, namely 'there is something going on which is like what is going on when', are all quasi-logical or topic-neutral words. This explains why the ancient Greek peasant's reports about his sensations can be neutral between dualistic metaphysics or my materialistic metaphysics. It explains how sensations can be brain processes and yet how a man who reports them need know nothing about brain processes. For he reports them only very abstractly as 'something going on which is like what is going on when....' Similarly, a person may say 'someone is in the room', thus reporting truly that the doctor is in the room, even though he has never heard of doctors. (There are not two people in the room 'someone' *and* the doctor.) This account of sensation statements also explains the

singular elusiveness of 'raw feels' – why no one seems to be able to pin any properties on them.[14] Raw feels, in my view, are colourless for the very same reason that *something* is colourless. This does not mean that sensations do not have plenty of properties, for if they are brain processes they certainly have lots of neurological properties. It only means that in speaking of them as being like or unlike one another we need not know or mention these properties.

This, then, is how I would reply to Objection 3. The strength of my reply depends on the possibility of our being able to report that one thing is like another without being able to state the respect in which it is like. I do not see why this should not be so. If we think cybernetically about the nervous system we can envisage it as able to respond to certain likenesses of its internal processes without being able to do more. It would be easier to build a machine which would tell us, say on a punched tape, whether or not two objects were similar, than it would be to build a machine which would report wherein the similarities consisted.

Objection 4.
The after-image is not in physical space. The brain process is. So the after-image is not a brain process.

Reply.
This is an *ignoratio elenchi*. I am not arguing that the after-image is a brain process, but that the experience of having an after-image is a brain process. It is the *experience* which is reported in the introspective report. Similarly, if it is objected that the after-image is yellowy-orange, my reply is that it is the experience of seeing yellowy-orange that is being described, and this experience is not a yellowy-orange something. So to say that a brain process cannot be yellowy-orange is not to say that a brain process cannot in fact be the experience of having a yellowy-orange after-image. There is, in a sense, no such thing as an after-image or a sense-datum, though there is such a thing as the experience of having an image, and this experience is described indirectly in material object language, not in phenomenal language, for there is no such thing.[15] We describe

[14] See B. A. Farrell, 'Experience', *Mind*, LIX (1950) 170–98, especially p. 174
[15] Dr J. R. Smythies claims that a sense-datum language could be taught independently of the material object language ('A Note on the Fallacy of "Phenomenological Fallacy" ', *British Journal of Psychology*, XLVIII (1957) pp. 141–4). I am not so sure of this: there must be some public criteria for

the experience by saying, in effect, that it is like the experience we have when, for example, we really see a yellowy-orange patch on the wall. Trees and wallpaper can be green, but not the experience of seeing or imagining a tree or wallpaper. (Or if they are described as green or yellow this can only be in a derived sense.)

Objection 5.

It would make sense to say of a molecular movement in the brain that it is swift or slow, straight or circular, but it makes no sense to say this of the experience of seeing something yellow.

Reply.

So far we have not given sense to talk of experiences as swift or slow, straight or circular. But I am not claiming that 'experience' and 'brain process' mean the same or even that they have the same logic. 'Somebody' and 'the doctor' do not have the same logic, but this does not lead us to suppose that talking about somebody telephoning is talking about someone over and above, say, the doctor. The ordinary man when he reports an experience is reporting that something is going on, but he leaves it open as to what sort of thing is going on, whether in a material solid medium or perhaps in some sort of gaseous medium, or even perhaps in some sort of non-spatial medium (if this makes sense). All that I am saying is that 'experience' and 'brain process' may in fact refer to the same thing, and if so we may easily adopt a convention (which is not a change in our present rules for the use of experience words but an addition to them) whereby it would make sense to talk of an experience in terms appropriate to physical processes.

Objection 6.

Sensations are private, brain processes are *public*. If I sincerely say 'I see a yellowish-orange after-image', and I am not making a verbal mistake, then I cannot be wrong. But I can be wrong about a brain process. The scientist looking into my brain might be having an illusion. Moreover, it makes sense to say that two or more people are observing the same brain process but not that two or more people are reporting the same inner experience.

---

a person having got a rule wrong before we can teach him the rule. I suppose someone might *accidentally* learn colour words by Dr Smythies' procedure. I am not, of course, denying that we can learn a sense-datum language in the sense that we can learn to report our experience. Nor would Place deny it.

Reply.
This shows that the language of introspective reports has a different logic from the language of material processes. It is obvious that until the brain-process theory is much improved and widely accepted there will be no *criteria* for saying 'Smith has an experience of such-and-such a sort' *except* Smith's introspective reports. So we have adopted a rule of language that (normally) what Smith says goes.

Objection 7.
I can imagine myself turned to stone and yet having images, aches, pains, and so on.

Reply.
I can imagine that the electrical theory of lightning is false, that lightning is some sort of purely optical phenomenon. I can imagine that lightning is not an electrical discharge. I can imagine that the Evening Star is not the Morning Star. But it is. All the objection shows is that 'experience' and 'brain process' do not have the same meaning. It does not show that an experience is not in fact a brain process.

This objection is perhaps much the same as one which can be summed up by the slogan: 'What can be composed of nothing cannot be composed of anything.'[16] The argument goes as follows: on the brain-process thesis the identity between the brain process and the experience is a contingent one. So it is logically possible that there should be no brain process, and no process of any other sort either (no heart process, no kidney process, no liver process). There would be the experience but no 'corresponding' physiological process with which we might be able to identify it empirically.

· I suspect that the objector is thinking of the experience as a ghostly entity. So it is composed of something, not of nothing, after all. On his view it is composed of ghost stuff, and on mine it is composed of brain stuff. Perhaps the counter-reply will be[17] that the experience is simple and uncompounded, and so it is not composed of anything after all. This seems to be a quibble, for, if it were taken seriously, the remark 'What can be composed of nothing cannot be composed of anything' could be recast as an *a priori* argument against Democritus and atomism and for Descartes and infinite divisibility. And it seems odd that a question of this sort could be

---

[16] I owe this objection to Dr C. B. Martin. I gather that he no longer wishes to maintain this objection, at any rate in its present form.

[17] Martin did not make this reply, but one of his students did.

settled *a priori*. We must therefore construe the word 'composed' in a very weak sense, which would allow us to say that even an indivisible atom is·composed of something (namely, itself). The dualist cannot really say that an experience can be composed of nothing. For he holds that experiences are something over and above material processes, that is, that they are a sort of ghost stuff. (Or perhaps ripples in an underlying ghost stuff.) I say that the dualist's hypothesis is a perfectly intelligible one. But I say that experiences are not to be identified with ghost stuff but with brain stuff. This is another hypothesis, and in my view a very plausible one. The present argument cannot knock it down *a priori*.

Objection 8.

The 'beetle in the box' objection (see Wittgenstein, *Philosophical nvestigations*, section 293). How could descriptions of experiences, if these are genuine reports, get a foothold in language? For any rule of language must have public criteria for its correct application.

Reply.

The change from describing how things are to describing how we feel is just a change from uninhibitedly saying 'this is so' to saying 'this looks so.' That is, when the naïve person might be tempted to say 'There is a patch of light on the wall which moves whenever I move my eyes' or 'A pin is being stuck into me', we have learned how to resist this temptation and say 'It *looks as though* there is a patch of light on the wallpaper' or 'It *feels as though* someone were sticking a pin into me.' The introspective account tells us about the individual's state of consciousness in the same way as does 'I see a patch of light' or 'I feel a pin being stuck into me': it differs from the corresponding perception statement in so far as it withdraws any claim about what is actually going on in the external world. From the point of view of the psychologist, the change from talking about the environment to talking about one's perceptual sensations is simply a matter of disinhibiting certain reactions. These are reactions which one normally suppresses because one has learned that in the prevailing circumstances they are unlikely to provide a good indication of the state of the environment.[18] To say that something looks green to me is simply to say that my experience is like the experience I get when I see something that really is green. In my reply to Objection 3, I pointed out the extreme openness or generality of statements which report experiences. This explains why

[18] I owe this point to Place, in correspondence.

there is no language of private qualities. (Just as 'someone', unlike 'the doctor', is a colourless word.)[19]

If it is asked what is the difference between those brain processes which, in my view, are experiences and those brain processes which are not, I can only reply that it is at present unknown. I have been tempted to conjecture that the difference may in part be that between perception and reception (in D. M. MacKay's terminology) and that the type of brain process which is an experience might be identifiable with MacKay's active 'matching response'.[20] This, however, cannot be the whole story, because sometimes I can perceive something unconsciously, as when I take a handkerchief out of a drawer without being aware that I am doing so. But at the very least we can classify the brain processes which are experiences as those brain processes which are, or might have been, causal conditions of those pieces of verbal behaviour which we call reports of immediate experience.

I have considered a number of objections to the brain-process thesis. I wish now to conclude with some remarks on the logical status of the thesis itself. U. T. Place seems to hold that it is a straight-out scientific hypothesis.[21] If so, he is partly right and partly wrong. If the issue is between (say) a brain-process thesis and a heart thesis, or a liver thesis, or a kidney thesis, then the issue is a purely empirical one, and the verdict is overwhelmingly in favour of the brain. The right sorts of things don't go on in the heart, liver, or kidney, nor do these organs possess the right sort of complexity of structure. On the other hand, if the issue is between a brain-or-liver-or-kidney thesis (that is, some form of materialism) on the one hand and epiphenomenalism on the other hand, then the issue is not an empirical one. For there is no conceivable experiment which could decide between materialism and epiphenomenalism. This

[19] The 'beetle in the box' objection is, *if it is sound*, an objection to *any* view, and in particular the Cartesian one, that introspective reports are genuine reports. So it is no objection to a weaker thesis that I would be concerned to uphold, namely, that if introspective reports 'experiences' are genuinely reports, then the things they are reports of are in fact brain-processes.

[20] See his article 'Towards an Information-Flow Model of Human Behaviour', *British Journal of Psychology*, XLVII (1956) pp. 30–43.

[21] Paper II. For a further discussion of this, in reply to the original version of the present paper, see Paper V.

latter issue is not like the average straight-out empirical issue in science, but like the issue between the nineteenth-century English naturalist Philip Gosse[22] and the orthodox geologists and palaeontologists of his day. According to Gosse, the earth was created about 4000 B.C. exactly as described in *Genesis*, with twisted rock strata, 'evidence' of erosion, and so forth, and all sorts of fossils, all in their appropriate strata, just as if the usual evolutionist story had been true. Clearly this theory is in a sense irrefutable: no evidence can possibly tell against it. Let us ignore the theological setting in which Philip Gosse's hypothesis had been placed, thus ruling out objections of a theological kind, such as 'what a queer God who would go to such elaborate lengths to deceive us'. Let us suppose that it is held that the universe just *began* in 4004 B.C. with the initial conditions just everywhere as they were in 4004 B.C., and in particular that our own planet began with sediment in the rivers, eroded cliffs, fossils in the rocks, and so on. No scientist would ever entertain this as a serious hypothesis, consistent though it is with all possible evidence. The hypothesis offends against the principles of parsimony and simplicity. There would be far too many brute and inexplicable facts. Why are pterodactyl bones just as they are? No explanation in terms of the evolution of pterodactyls from earlier forms of life would any longer be possible. We would have millions of facts about the world as it was in 4004 B.C. that just have to be *accepted*.

The issue between the brain-process theory and epiphenomenalism seems to be of the above sort. (Assuming that a behaviouristic reduction of introspective reports is not possible.) If it be agreed that there are no cogent philosophical arguments which force us into accepting dualism, and if the brain-process theory and dualism are equally consistent with the facts, then the principles of parsimony and simplicity seem to me to decide overwhelmingly in favour of the brain-process theory. As I pointed out earlier, dualism involves a large number of irreducible psycho-physical laws (whereby the 'nomological danglers' dangle) of a queer sort, that just have to be taken on trust, and are just as difficult to swallow as the irreducible facts about the palaeontology of the earth with which we are faced on Philip Gosse's theory.

[22] See the entertaining account of Gosse's book *Omphalos* by Martin Gardner in *Fads and Fallacies in the Name of Science*, 2nd ed. (New York 1957) pp. 124–7.

IV The nature of mind[1]

D. M. Armstrong

Men have minds, that is to say, they perceive, they have sensations, emotions, beliefs, thoughts, purposes, and desires. What is it to have a mind? What is it to perceive, to feel emotion, to hold a belief, or to have a purpose? In common with many other modern philosophers, I think that the best clue we have to the nature of mind is furnished by the discoveries and hypotheses of modern science concerning the nature of man.

What does modern science have to say about the nature of man? There are, of course, all sorts of disagreements and divergencies in the views of individual scientists. But I think it is true to say that one view is steadily gaining ground, so that it bids fair to become established scientific doctrine. This is the view that we can give a complete account of man *in purely physico-chemical terms*. This view has received a tremendous impetus in the last decade from the new subject of molecular biology, a subject which promises to unravel the physical and chemical mechanisms which lie at the basis of life. Before that time, it received great encouragement from pioneering work in neurophysiology pointing to the likelihood of a purely electro-chemical account of the working of the brain. I think it is fair to say that those scientists who still reject the physico-chemical account of man do so primarily for philosophical, or moral, or religious reasons, and only secondarily, and half-heartedly, for reasons of scientific detail. This is not to say that in the future new evidence and new problems may not come to light which will force science to reconsider the physico-chemical view of man. But at present the drift of scientific thought is clearly set towards the physico-chemical hypothesis. And we have nothing better to go on than the present.

For me, then, and for many philosophers who think like me, the moral is clear. We must try to work out an account of the nature of mind which is compatible with the view that man is nothing but a physico-chemical mechanism.

[1] Inaugural lecture of the Challis Professor of Philosophy at the University of Sydney (1965); slightly amended (1968).

And in this paper I shall be concerned to do just this: to sketch (in barest outline) what may be called a Materialist or Physicalist account of the mind.

But before doing this I should like to go back and consider a criticism of my position which must inevitably occur to some. What reason have I, it may be asked, for taking my stand on science? Even granting that I am right about what is the currently dominant scientific view of man, why should we concede science a special authority to decide questions about the nature of man? What of the authority of philosophy, of religion, of morality, or even of literature and art? Why do I set the authority of science above all these? Why this 'scientism'?

It seems to me that the answer to this question is very simple. If we consider the search for truth, in all its fields, we find that it is only in science that men versed in their subject can, after investigation that is more or less prolonged, and which may in some cases extend beyond a single human lifetime, reach substantial agreement about what is the case. It is only as a result of scientific investigation that we ever seem to reach an intellectual consensus about controversial matters.

In the Epistle Dedicatory to his *De Corpore* Hobbes wrote of William Harvey, the discoverer of the circulation of the blood, that he was 'the only man I know, that conquering envy, hath established a new doctrine in his life-time'.

Before Copernicus, Galileo and Harvey, Hobbes remarks, 'there was nothing certain in natural philosophy.'

And, we might add, with the exception of mathematics, there was nothing certain in any other learned discipline.

These remarks of Hobbes are incredibly revealing. They show us what a watershed in the intellectual history of the human race the seventeenth century was. Before that time inquiry proceeded, as it were, in the dark. Men could not hope to see their doctrine *established*, that is to say, accepted by the vast majority of those properly versed in the subject under discussion. There was no intellectual consensus. Since that time, it has become a commonplace to see new doctrines, sometimes of the most far-reaching kind, established to the satisfaction of the learned, often within the lifetime of their first proponents. Science has provided us with a method of deciding disputed questions. This is not to say, of course, that the consensus of those who are learned and competent in a subject cannot be mistaken. Of course such a consensus can be mistaken. Sometimes it has been mistaken. But, granting fallibility, what better authority have we than such a consensus?

Now this is of the utmost importance. For in philosophy, in religion, in such disciplines as literary criticism, in moral questions in so far as they are thought to be matters of truth and falsity, there has been a notable failure to achieve an intellectual consensus about disputed questions among the learned. Must we not then attach a peculiar authority to the discipline that can achieve a consensus? And if it presents us with a certain vision of the nature of man, is this not a powerful reason for accepting that vision?

I will not take up here the deeper question *why* it is that the methods of science have enabled us to achieve an intellectual consensus about so many disputed matters. That question, I think, could receive no brief or uncontroversial answer. I am resting my argument on the simple and uncontroversial fact that, as a result of scientific investigation, such a consensus has been achieved.

It may be replied – it often is replied – that while science is all very well in its own sphere – the sphere of the physical, perhaps – there are matters of fact on which it is not competent to pronounce. And among such matters, it may be claimed, is the question what is the whole nature of man. But I cannot see that this reply has much force. Science has provided us with an island of truths, or, perhaps one should say, a raft of truths, to bear us up on the sea of our disputatious ignorance. There may have to be revisions and refinements, new results may set old findings in a new perspective, but what science has given us will not be altogether superseded. Must we not therefore appeal to these relative certainties for guidance when we come to consider uncertainties elsewhere? Perhaps science cannot help us to decide whether or not there is a God, whether or not human beings have immortal souls, or whether or not the will is free. But if science cannot assist us, what can? I conclude that it is the scientific vision of man, and not the philosophical or religious or artistic or moral vision of man, that is the best clue we have to the nature of man. And it is rational to argue from the best evidence we have.

Having in this way attempted to justify my procedure, I turn back to my subject: the attempt to work out an account of mind, or, if you prefer, of mental process, within the framework of the physico-chemical, or, as we may call it, the Materialist view of man.

Now there is one account of mental process that is at once attractive to any philosopher sympathetic to a Materialist view of man: this is Behaviourism. Formulated originally by a psychologist, J. B. Watson, it attracted widespread interest and considerable support from scientifically oriented philosophers. Traditional philosophy had tended to think of the mind as a rather mysterious inward arena that lay behind, and was responsible for, the outward or physical behaviour of our bodies. Descartes thought of this inner arena as a *spiritual substance,* and it was this conception of the mind as spiritual object that Gilbert Ryle attacked, apparently in the interest of Behaviourism, in his important book *The Concept of Mind.* He ridiculed the Cartesian view as the dogma of 'the ghost in the machine'. The mind was not something behind the behaviour of the body, it was simply part of that physical behaviour. My anger with you is not some modification of a spiritual substance which somehow brings about aggressive behaviour; rather it is the aggressive behaviour itself; my addressing strong words to you, striking you, turning my back on you, and so on. Thought is not an inner process that lies behind, and brings about, the words I speak and write: it is my speaking and writing. The mind is not an inner arena, it is outward act.

It is clear that such a view of mind fits in very well with a completely Materialistic or Physicalist view of man. If there is no need to draw a distinction between mental processes and their expression in physical behaviour, but if instead the mental processes are identified with their so-called 'expressions', then the existence of mind stands in no conflict with the view that man is nothing but a physico-chemical mechanism.

However, the version of Behaviourism that I have just sketched is a very crude version, and its crudity lays it open to obvious objections. One obvious difficulty is that it is our common experience that there can be mental processes going on although there is no behaviour occurring that could possibly be treated as expressions of these processes. A man may be angry, but give no bodily sign; he may think, but say or do nothing at all.

In my view, the most plausible attempt to refine Behaviourism with a view to meeting this objection was made by introducing the notion of *a disposition to behave.* (Dispositions to behave play a particularly important part in Ryle's account of the mind.) Let us consider the general notion of disposition first. Brittleness is a disposition, a disposition possessed by materials like glass. Brittle materials are those which, when subjected to relatively small forces, break or shatter easily. But breaking and shattering easily is not brittleness, rather it is the *manifestation* of brittleness. Brittleness itself is the tendency or liability of the material to break or shatter easily. A piece of glass may never shatter or break throughout its whole history, but it is still the case that it is brittle: it is liable to shatter or break if dropped quite a small way or hit quite lightly. Now a disposition to *behave* is simply a tendency or liability of a person to behave in a certain way under certain circumstances. The brittleness of glass is a disposition that the glass retains throughout its history, but clearly there could also be dispositions that come and go. The dispositions to behave that are of interest to the Behaviourist are for the most part, of this temporary character.

Now how did Ryle and others use the notion of a disposition to behave to meet the obvious objection to Behaviourism that there can be mental processes going on although the subject is engaging in no relevant behaviour? Their strategy was to argue that in such cases, although the subject was not behaving in any relevant way, he or she was *disposed* to behave in some relevant way. The glass does not shatter, but it is still brittle. The man does not behave, but he does have a disposition to behave. We can say he thinks although he does not speak or act because at that time he was disposed to speak or act in a certain way. *If* he had been asked, perhaps, he would have spoken or acted. We can say he is angry although he does not behave angrily, because he is disposed so to behave. *If* only one more word had been addressed to him, he would have burst out. And so on. In this way it was hoped that Behaviourism could be squared with the obvious facts.

It is very important to see just how these thinkers conceived of dispositions. I quote from Ryle

> To possess a dispositional property *is not to be in a particular state, or to undergo a particular change*; it is to be bound or liable to be in a particular state, or to undergo a particular change, when a particular condition is realised. (*The Concept of Mind*, p. 43, my italics.)

So to explain the breaking of a lightly struck glass on a particular occasion by saying it was brittle is, on this view of dispositions, simply to say that the glass broke because it is the sort of thing that regularly breaks when quite lightly struck. The breaking was the normal behaviour, or not abnormal behaviour, of such a thing. The brittleness is not to be conceived of as a *cause* for the breakage, or even, more vaguely, a *factor* in bringing about the breaking. Brittleness is just the fact that things of that sort break easily.

But although in this way the Behaviourists did something to deal with the objection that mental processes can occur in the absence of behaviour, it seems clear, now that the shouting and the dust have died, that they did not do enough. When I think, but my thoughts do not issue in any action, it seems as obvious as anything is obvious that there is something actually going on in me which constitutes my thought. It is not simply that I would speak or act if some conditions that are unfulfilled were to be fulfilled. Something is currently going on, in the strongest and most literal sense of 'going on', and this something is my thought. Rylean Behaviourism denies this, and so it is unsatisfactory as a theory of mind. Yet I know of no version of Behaviourism that is more satisfactory. The moral for those of us who wish to take a purely physicalistic view of man is that we must look for some other account of the nature of mind and of mental processes.

But perhaps we need not grieve too deeply about the failure of Behaviourism to produce a satisfactory theory of mind. Behaviourism is a profoundly unnatural account of mental processes. If somebody speaks and acts in certain ways it is natural to speak of this speech and action as the *expression* of his thought. It is not at all natural to speak of his speech and action as identical with his thought. We naturally think of the thought as something quite distinct from the speech and action which, under suitable circumstances, brings the speech and action about. Thoughts are not to be identified with behaviour, we think, they lie behind behaviour. A man's behaviour constitutes the *reason* we have for attributing certain mental processes to him, but the behaviour cannot be identified with the mental processes.

This suggests a very interesting line of thought about the mind. Behaviourism is certainly wrong, but perhaps it is not altogether wrong. Perhaps the Behaviourists are wrong in identifying the mind and mental occurrences with behaviour, but perhaps they are right in thinking that our notion of a mind and of individual mental states is *logically tied to behaviour*. For perhaps what we mean by a mental state is some state of the person which, under suitable circumstances, *brings about* a certain range of behaviour. Perhaps mind can be defined not as behaviour, but rather as the inner *cause* of certain behaviour. Thought is not speech under suitable circumstances, rather it is something within the person which, in suitable circumstances, brings about speech. And, in fact, I believe that this is the true account, or, at any rate, a true first account, of what we mean by a mental state.

How does this line of thought link up with a purely physicalist view of man? The position is, I think, that while it does not make such a physicalist view inevitable, it does make it *possible*. It does not entail, but it is compatible with, a purely physicalist view of man. For if our notion of the mind and mental states is nothing but that of a cause within the person of certain ranges of behaviour, then it becomes a scientific question, and not a question of logical analysis, what in fact the intrinsic nature of that cause is. The cause might be, as Descartes thought it was, a spiritual substance working through the pineal gland to produce the complex bodily behaviour of which men are capable. It might be breath, or specially smooth and mobile atoms dispersed throughout the body; it might be many other things. But in fact the verdict of modern science seems to be that the sole cause of mind-betokening behaviour in man and the higher animals is the physico-chemical workings of the central nervous system. And so, assuming we have correctly characterised our concept of a mental state as nothing but the cause of certain sorts of behaviour, then we can identify these mental states with purely physical states of the central nervous system.

At this point we may stop and go back to the Behaviourists' dispositions. We saw that, according to them, the brittleness of glass or, to take another example, the elasticity of rubber, is not a state of the glass or the rubber, but is simply the fact that things of that sort behave in the way they do. But now let us consider how a scientist would think about brittleness or elasticity. Faced with the phenomenon of breakage under relatively small impacts, or the phenomenon of stretching when a force is applied followed by contraction when the force is removed, he will assume that there is some current *state* of the glass or the rubber which is responsible for the characteristic behaviour of samples of these two materials. At the beginning he will not know what this state is, but he will endeavour to find out, and he may succeed in finding out. And when he has found out he will very likely make remarks of this sort: 'We have discovered that the brittleness of glass is in fact a certain sort of pattern in the molecules of the glass.' That is to say, he will *identify* brittleness with the state of the glass that is responsible for the liability of the glass to break. For him, a disposition of an object is a state of the object. What makes the state of brittleness is the fact that it gives rise to the characteristic manifestations of brittleness. But the disposition itself is distinct from its manifestations: it is the state of the glass that gives rise to these manifestations in suitable circumstances.

You will see that this way of looking at dispositions is very different from that of Ryle and the Behaviourists. The great difference is this: If we treat dispositions as actual states, as I have suggested that scientists do, even if states whose intrinsic nature may yet have to be discovered, then we can say that dispositions are actual *causes*, or causal factors, which, in suitable circumstances, actually bring about those happenings which are the manifestations of the disposition. A certain molecular constitution of glass which constitutes its brittleness is actually *responsible* for the fact that, when the glass is struck, it breaks.

Now I shall not argue the matter here, because the detail of the argument is technical and difficult,[2] but I believe that the view of dispositions as states, which is the view that is natural to science, is the correct one. I believe it can be shown quite strictly that, to the extent that we admit the notion of dispositions at all, we are committed to the view that they are actual *states* of the object that has the disposition. I may add that I think that the same holds for the closely connected notions of capacities and powers. Here I will simply assume this step in my argument.

But perhaps it can be seen that the rejection of the idea that mind is simply a certain range of man's behaviour in favour of the view that mind is rather the inner *cause* of that range of man's behaviour is bound up with the rejection of the Rylean view of dispositions in favour of one that treats disposition as states of objects and so as having actual causal power. The Behaviourists were wrong to identify the mind with behaviour. They were not so far off the mark when they tried to deal with cases where mental happenings occur in the absence of behaviour by saying that these are dispositions to behave. But in order to reach a correct view, I am suggesting, they would have to conceive of these dispositions as actual *states* of the person who has the disposition, states that have actual power to bring about behaviour in suitable circumstances. But to do this is to abandon the central inspiration of Behaviourism: that in talking about the mind we do not have to go behind outward behaviour to inner states.

And so two separate but interlocking lines of thought have pushed me in the same direction. The first line of thought is that it goes profoundly against the grain to think of the mind as behaviour. The

[2] It is presented in my book *A Materialist Theory of the Mind* (1968) ch. 6, sec. vi.

mind is, rather, that which stands behind and brings about our complex behaviour. The second line of thought is that the Behaviourists' dispositions, properly conceived, are really states that underlie behaviour, and, under suitable circumstances, bring about behaviour. Putting these two together, we reach the conception of a mental state as *a state of the person apt for producing certain ranges of behaviour*. This formula: a mental state is a state of the person apt for producing certain ranges of behaviour, I believe to be a very illuminating way of looking at the concept of a mental state. I have found it very fruitful in the search for detailed logical analyses of the individual mental concepts.

Now, I do not think that Hegel's dialectic has much to tell us about the nature of reality. But I think that human thought often moves in a dialectical way, from thesis to antithesis and then to the synthesis. Perhaps thought about the mind is a case in point. I have already said that classical philosophy tended to think of the mind as an inner arena of some sort. This we may call the Thesis. Behaviourism moved to the opposite extreme: the mind was seen as outward behaviour. This is the Antithesis. My proposed Synthesis is that the mind is properly conceived as an inner principle, but a principle that is identified in terms of the outward behaviour it is apt for bringing about. This way of looking at the mind and mental states does not itself entail a Materialist or Physicalist view of man, for nothing is said in this analysis about the intrinsic nature of these mental states. But if we have, as I have asserted that we do have, general scientific grounds for thinking that man is nothing but a physical mechanism, we can go on to argue that the mental states are in fact nothing but physical states of the central nervous system.

Along these lines, then, I would look for an account of the mind that is compatible with a purely Materialist theory of man. I have tried to carry out this programme in detail in *A Materialist Theory of the Mind*. There are, as may be imagined, all sorts of powerful objections that can be made to this view. But in the rest of this paper I propose to do only one thing. I will develop one very important objection to my view of the mind – an objection felt by many philosophers – and then try to show how the objection should be met.

The view that our notion of mind is nothing but that of an inner principle apt for bringing about certain sorts of behaviour may be thought to share a certain weakness with Behaviourism. Modern philosophers have put the point about Behaviourism by saying that although Behaviourism may be a satisfactory account of the mind from an *other-person point of view*, it will not do as a *first-person* account. To explain. In our encounters with other people, all we ever observe is their behaviour: their actions, their speech, and so on. And so, if we simply consider other people, Behaviourism might seem to do full justice to the facts. But the trouble about Behaviourism is that it seems so unsatisfactory as applied to our *own* case. In our own case, we seem to be aware of so much more than mere behaviour.

Suppose that now we conceive of the mind as an inner principle apt for bringing about certain sorts of behaviour. This again fits the other-person cases very well. Bodily behaviour of a very sophisticated sort is observed, quite different from the behaviour that ordinary physical objects display. It is inferred that this behaviour must spring from a very special sort of inner cause in the object that exhibits this behaviour. This inner cause is christened 'the mind', and those who take a physicalist view of man argue that it is simply the central nervous system of the body observed. Compare this with the case of glass. Certain characteristic behaviour is observed: the breaking and shattering of the material when acted upon by relatively small forces. A special inner state of the glass is postulated to explain this behaviour. Those who take a purely physicalist view of glass then argue that this state is a *natural* state of the glass. It is, perhaps, an arrangement of its molecules, and not, say, the peculiarly malevolent disposition of the demons that dwell in glass.

But when we turn to our own case, the position may seem less plausible. We are conscious, we have experiences. Now can we say that to be conscious, to have experiences, is simply for something to go on within us apt for the causing of certain sorts of behaviour? Such an account does not seem to do any justice to the phenomena. And so it seems that our account of the mind, like Behaviourism, will fail to do justice to the first-person case.

In order to understand the objection better it may be helpful to consider a particular case. If you have driven for a very long distance without a break, you may have had experience of a curious state of automatism, which can occur in these conditions. One can suddenly 'come to' and realise that one has driven for long distances without being aware of what one was doing, or, indeed, without being aware of anything. One has kept the car on the road, used the brake and the clutch perhaps, yet all without any awareness of what one was doing.

Now, if we consider this case it is obvious that *in some sense* mental processes are still going on when one is in such an automatic state. Unless one's will was still operating in some way, and unless one was still perceiving in some way, the car would not still be on the road. Yet, of course, *something* mental is lacking. Now, I think, when it is alleged that an account of mind as an inner principle apt for the production of certain sorts of behaviour leaves out consciousness or experience, what is alleged to have been left out is just whatever is missing in the automatic driving case. It is conceded that an account of mental processes as states of the person apt for the production of certain sorts of behaviour may very possibly be adequate to deal with such cases as that of automatic driving. It may be adequate to deal with most of the mental processes of animals, who perhaps spend a good deal of their lives in this state of automatism. But, it is contended, it cannot deal with the consciousness that we normally enjoy.

I will now try to sketch an answer to this important and powerful objection. Let us begin in an apparently unlikely place, and consider the way that an account of mental processes of the sort I am giving would deal with *sense-perception*.

Now psychologists, in particular, have long realised that there is a very close logical tie between sense-perception and *selective behaviour*. Suppose we want to decide whether an animal can perceive the difference between red and green. We might give the animal a choice between two pathways, over one of which a red light shines and over the other of which a green light shines. If the animal happens by chance to choose the green pathway we reward it; if it happens to choose the other pathway we do not reward it. If, after some trials, the animal systematically takes the green-lighted pathway, and if we become assured that the only relevant differences in the two pathways are the differences in the colour of the lights, we are entitled to say that the animal can see this colour difference. Using its eyes, it selects between red-lighted and green-lighted pathways. So we say it can see the difference between red and green.

Now a Behaviourist would be tempted to say that the animal's regularly selecting the green-lighted pathway *was* its perception of the colour difference. But this is unsatisfactory, because we all want to say that perception is something that goes on within the person or animal – within its mind – although, of course, this mental event is normally *caused* by the operation of the environment upon the organism. Suppose, however, that we speak instead of *capacities* for selective behaviour towards the current environment, and suppose we think of these capacities, like dispositions, as actual inner states of the organism. We can then think of the animal's perception as a state within the animal apt, if the animal is so impelled, for selective behaviour between the red- and green-lighted pathways.

In general, we can think of perceptions as inner states or events apt for the production of certain sorts of selective behaviour towards our environment. To perceive is like acquiring a key to a door. You do not have to use the key: you can put it in your pocket and never bother about the door. But if you do want to open the door the key may be essential. The blind man is a man who does not acquire certain keys, and, as a result, is not able to operate in his environment in the way that somebody who has his sight can operate. It seems, then, a very promising view to take of perceptions that they are inner states defined by the sorts of selective behaviour that they enable the perceiver to exhibit, if so impelled.

Now how is this discussion of perception related to the question of consciousness or experience, the sort of thing that the driver who is in a state of automatism has not got, but which we normally do have? Simply this. My proposal is that consciousness, in this sense of the word, is nothing but *perception or awareness of the state of our own mind*. The driver in a state of automatism perceives, or is aware of, the road. If he did not, the car would be in a ditch. But he is not currently aware of his awareness of the road. He perceives the road, but he does not perceive his perceiving, or anything else that is going on in his mind. He is not, as we normally are, conscious of what is going on in his mind.

And so I conceive of consciousness or experience, in this sense of the words, in the way that Locke and Kant conceived it, as like perception. Kant, in a striking phrase, spoke of 'inner sense'. We cannot directly observe the minds of others, but each of us has the power to observe directly our own minds. and 'perceive' what is going on there. The driver in the automatic state is one whose 'inner eye' is shut: who is not currently aware of what is going on in his own mind.

Now if this account is along the right lines, why should we not give an account of this inner observation along the same lines as we have already given of perception? Why should we not conceive of it as an inner state, a state in this case directed towards other inner states and not to the environment, which enables us, if we are so impelled, to behave in a selective way *towards our own states of mind*? One who is aware, or conscious, of his thoughts or his emotions is one who has the capacity to make discriminations between his different mental states. His capacity might be exhibited in words.

He might say that he was in an angry state of mind when, and only when, he *was* in an angry state of mind. But such verbal behaviour would be the mere *expression* or *result* of the awareness. The awareness itself would be an inner state: the sort of inner state that gave the man a capacity for such behavioural expressions.

So I have argued that consciousness of our own mental state may be assimilated to *perception* of our own mental state, and that, like other perceptions, it may then be conceived of as an inner state or event giving a capacity for selective behaviour, in this case selective behaviour towards our own mental state. All this is meant to be simply a logical analysis of consciousness, and none of it entails, although it does not rule out, a purely physicalist account of what these inner states are. But if we are convinced, on general scientific grounds, that a purely physical account of man is likely to be the true one, then there seems to be no bar to our identifying these inner states with purely physical states of the central nervous system. And so consciousness of our own mental state becomes simply the scanning of one part of our central nervous system by another. Consciousness is a self-scanning mechanism in the central nervous system.

As I have emphasised before, I have done no more than sketch a programme for a philosophy of mind. There are all sorts of expansions and elucidations to be made, and all sorts of doubts and difficulties to be stated and overcome. But I hope I have done enough to show that a purely physicalist theory of the mind is an exciting and plausible intellectual option.

PART TWO

Initial Criticism and Clarification

V Materialism as a scientific hypothesis

U. T. Place

In discussing the logical status of the thesis that sensations are processes in the brain, J. J. C. Smart[1] contends that I was partly right and partly wrong in maintaining that this thesis could and should be interpreted as a straightforward scientific hypothesis.[2] He argues that in so far as the issue is between a brain-process thesis and a heart, liver, or kidney thesis the issue is empirical and can be decided by experiment. But in so far as the issue is between materialism on the one hand and epiphenomenalism, psycho-physical parallelism, interactionism, and so forth, on the other, the issue is non-empirical. I shall argue that Smart is partly right and partly wrong in maintaining that the issue between the kind of materialism which both he and I would wish to defend and the rival doctrines of epiphenomenalism, psycho-physical parallelism, interactionism, and so forth, is a non-empirical issue.

In my own paper on this topic[3] I argued that there are certain logical conditions which must be satisfied to enable us to say that a process or event observed in one way is the same process or event as that observed in (or inferred from) another set of observations made under quite different conditions.[4] In that paper I suggested only one logical criterion, namely, that the process or event observed in or inferred from the second set of observations should provide us with an explanation, not of the process or event observed in the first

[1] Paper III. The reference is to remarks on pp. 65–6. I should say that I am in substantial agreement with the remainder of Smart's paper.

[2] Paper II.

[3] Ibid., pp. 47–8.

[4] This problem is discussed in more general terms in two papers by Feigl. In 'The Mind–Body Problem', *Revue Internationale de Philosophie*, IV (1950), reprinted in *Readings in the Philosophy of Science*, ed. H. Feigl and M. Brodbeck (New York 1953) pp. 612–26, the relevant passage will be found, in the latter volume, on pp. 621–3. See also pp. 438–45 of 'The "Mental" and the "Physical" ', *Minnesota Studies in the Philosophy of Science*, II, pp. 370–497.

set of observations, but of the very fact that such observations are made. I illustrated this point by comparing the case where the movements of the sun and the moon observed astronomically are used to explain the movement of the tides observed geophysically with the case where observations interpreted in terms of the motion of electric charges are used to explain, not a separate event called 'lightning', but the fact that we see and hear the sort of things we do on a stormy night.[5] I would now want to add to this the rather obvious additional criterion that the two sets of observations must refer to the same point in space and time, allowing for such things as the time taken by the transmission of light and sound, distortions in the transmitting media, the personal equation of the observer, and differences in the precision with which location is specified in the two sets of observations.

For the purposes of the present argument it does not matter whether this account of the logical criteria used to establish the identity of an event described in terms of two different procedures of observation is correct or not. What is important is that there must be some logical criteria which we use in deciding whether two sets of correlated observations refer to the same event or to two separate but causally related events. The problem of deciding what these criteria are is a logical problem which cannot be decided by experiment in any ordinary sense of the term; and since we cannot be certain that the criteria are satisfied in the case of sensations and brain processes unless we know what the criteria are, the issue is to that extent a philosophical issue. Moreover, even if we agree on the

[5] Feigl, in *Readings in the Philosophy of Science*, p. 623, gives another example, that of temperature and molecular movement, which brings out the same point, although Feigl's interpretation of it differs from my own. He distinguishes between the identity of things observed under different conditions, as in the case of the same mountain observed from different viewpoints by different observers, and the identity of concepts, as in the case of 2^3 and $\sqrt{64}$ (p. 622). The identity of things is established empirically, while the identity of concepts is established either deductively, as in the case of 2^3 and $\sqrt{64}$, or empirically, as in the case of temperature and molecular motion, by the empirical verification of a scientific theory within which it is possible to define one concept in terms of the other. I prefer to regard the temperature, lightning, and sensation-brain-process cases as examples of a special variety of the identity of things in which an identity is asserted between a state, process, or event and the micro-processes of which it is composed. I suspect, however, that the difference between Feigl's position and my own on this point is not as fundamental as it appears at first sight.

nature of these logical criteria, it is still open to the philosopher to question the logical propriety of applying them in the case of sensations and brain processes.

For the sake of argument, however, let us assume that these philosophical issues have been settled and that they have been settled in favour of the materialist hypothesis. We now find ourselves faced with a purely empirical issue, namely, whether there is in fact a physiological process, be it in the brain, the heart, the liver, the kidney or the big toe, which satisfies the logical criteria required to establish its identity with the sensation process. As it happens, we already know enough to be quite sure that, if there is such a process, it must be situated in the brain, and even within the brain there are extensive areas that can be ruled out with virtual certainty as possible loci of consciousness – areas, for example, where brain lesions produce motor disturbances without any change in consciousness other than an awareness of the disability itself and emotional reactions to the problems it creates. But the empirical problem is not, as Smart seems to think, simply a matter of determining the precise anatomical location of this physiological process. It is still an open question whether there is, even in this relatively circumscribed area, a process which satisfies the logical criteria required to establish its identity with the sensation process.[6] Even assuming that we know what these criteria are and are satisfied that they are applicable in this case, we cannot regard the question as finally settled until a process satisfying the necessary criteria has been discovered or until we are sure that we know enough about the brain to be certain that no such process exists.

Until such time as this issue is settled by further psycho-

---

[6] We certainly cannot say that a process has been discovered which satisfies the criteria I have suggested, that is, a process an understanding of which enables us to explain the peculiarities of sensations, mental images, and dreams as reported by the individual in whom they occur. We can, of course, explain a great many of the peculiarities of sensation in terms of the stimulus pattern impinging on the receptors, the anatomy and physiology of receptor organs, and the cerebral projection of afferent nerve fibres; but what we want, if I am right, and what we have not yet got, is the clear identification of a process in the brain which 'incorporates' a relatively small part of the total stimulus pattern impinging on the receptors at any one moment in the way that the sensation process does that is capable of assuming forms determined by factors endogenous to the brain as in dreams and mental imagery, and that has the sort of function in the individual's thought processes and his adaptation to his environment which his sensations and mental imagery appear to have.

physiological research, materialism remains an empirical hypothesis
– the hypothesis that there exists, presumably in the brain, a physiological process which satisfies the logical criteria required to establish
its identity with the sensation process. If this hypothesis is confirmed,
the need disappears for alternative theories designed to explain the
relationship between sensation, considered as an independent non-
physiological process, and the physiological processes with which it
is correlated. Theories like epiphenomenalism could then only be
made tenable by refusing to accept the logical criteria put forward
as establishing the identity of a process characterised by reference to
two entirely different observation procedures or their application to
the case of brain processes and sensation. Given a solution of the
logical issues favourable to materialism, these theories can be ruled
out on empirical grounds in a way that Gosse's theory of creation[7]
cannot be ruled out.

In practice, of course, those who object to the materialist hypothesis are much more likely, and indeed would be much better
advised, to make their stand among the logical issues I have mentioned than to accept the logical criteria put forward as establishing
the identity of a physiological process with the sensation process and
pin their hopes on the failure of scientific research to discover a
process satisfying these criteria. It is among these philosophical issues
that the real battle will be fought. To this extent Smart is right when
he says that the issue between materialism on the one hand and
epiphenomenalism, psycho-physical parallelism, and so forth, on the
other will not be decided by a programme of experimental research.
But this does not affect my contention that materialism can and
should be treated as a straightforward scientific hypothesis. It may
be that the logical criteria for establishing the identity of the object
of two types of observation are logically inapplicable to the case of
sensations and brain processes. If so, I am just plain wrong in claiming that materialism can be treated as a scientific hypothesis; but if
the criteria are applicable, I am right. I am not partly right and
partly wrong.

[7] Smart, Paper III, p. 66.

VI 'Sensations and brain processes': A reply to J. J. C. Smart

J. T. Stevenson

J. J. C. Smart in his article, 'Sensations and brain processes', (Paper III) attempts to show that there are no cogent philosophical arguments against the thesis that sensations are identical with brain processes, and that there is no reason to believe that there are any 'nomological danglers' and hence irreducible psycho-physical laws.[1] I shall attempt to show that, given Smart's thesis concerning the relations between sensations and brain processes, it follows that there *are* nomological danglers and laws whereby they dangle. And, as I shall show, this fact has some rather surprising consequences.

Before proceeding with the argument, however, there are two points of clarification to be made. The first is that Smart does not claim that 'sensation' means, or can be translated as, or is synonymous with 'brain process'. He is quite emphatic on this point, and many of his replies to the standard philosophical objections to this thesis depend on it.

The second point concerns Smart's use of the word 'is' in his statement 'A sensation *is* a brain process.' The word 'is' might be used in its predicative sense as in 'The table *is* brown.' We can safely put this interpretation aside. The use of 'is' as in the following passage is the one that might raise difficulty for the interpretation I shall give.

> Modern physical science tells us that lightning *is* a certain kind of electrical discharge due to ionisation of clouds of water vapour in the atmosphere. This, it is now believed, is what the true nature of lightning *is*. . . . There is one thing, a flash of lightning, *which is*

[1] Smart takes the expression 'nomological dangler' from Feigl, but uses it in such a way that sensations are examples of nomological danglers (cf. p. 54, above). The laws whereby the 'nomological danglers dangle' are, on Smart's usage, psycho-physical laws. I shall, for the sake of convenience, follow Smart's terminology.

described scientifically as an electrical discharge to the earth from a cloud of ionised water molecules. . . . We say that what lightning *really is*, what its *true nature* as revealed by science *is*, is an electrical discharge. (P. 57; italics mine.)

Quite frankly, I am not sure what to make of phrases like 'The *true nature* of *x* is . . .' or '*x really* is . . .'; nor am I sure that statements like this are scientific statements. But at any rate, either 'is' is being used in this passage in the sense of 'is strictly identical with' or it is not. If it is being used in that sense, we can pass on to a consideration of the notion of strict identity. If it is not, then it is irrelevant, for it is quite certain that Smart's main thesis is that sensations are *strictly identical* with brain processes. He tells us 'When I say that a sensation is a brain process or that lightning is an electrical discharge, I am using 'is' in the sense of strict identity' (p. 56). But what does it mean to say '*x* is strictly identical with *y*'? A clear meaning is given to this expression by Leibniz's principle of the identity of indiscernibles as formulated in standard logic text books:

$$(x = y) =_{df} (F) (Fx \equiv Fy)$$

That is to say, *x* is strictly identical with *y* if and only if every property of *x* is a property of *y*, and conversely. And, I suggest, this is the only clear meaning that can be given to Smart's contention that sensations are strictly identical with brain processes.[2]

Now Smart's claim is that although 'sensation' is not synonymous with 'brain process', nevertheless sensations are strictly identical with brain processes. Let us, for purposes of illustration, consider the following example that Smart himself uses.

It happens to be the case that the Morning Star is strictly identical with the Evening Star: they are one and the same thing, namely, the planet Venus. But 'Morning Star' does not mean the same as 'Evening Star': the two terms are not synonymous. A traditional and clearer way of stating this is to say that 'Morning Star' does not have the same sense, or intension, or *connotation* as 'Evening Star'. 'Morning Star' connotes several properties, including one which can roughly be expressed as 'appearing in the morning', whereas 'Evening Star' connotes among other things 'appearing in the evening'. It is very important to notice, however, that the Morning Star has precisely the same properties as the Evening Star: the Morning Star (that is, Venus) not only appears in the morning

[2] There is ample evidence in Smart's paper to support my interpretation. (See especially pp. 56, 57, 58 and 63.)

but also appears in the evening; and the Evening Star (again Venus) not only appears in the evening but also appears in the morning. Now the fact I wish to bring out by means of the example is this: if it is true that 'Morning Star' does in fact connote 'appearing in the morning' and also that the Morning Star is indeed strictly identical with the Evening Star, then it follows that the Evening Star appears in the morning. If the Morning Star is strictly identical with the Evening Star, this implies that the Evening Star has *all* the properties of the Morning Star, including the defining properties for 'Morning Star'.

In general terms the point is this: if 'A' connotes R,S,T and 'B' does not connote R,S,T but, say, X,Y,Z, then 'A' is not synonymous with 'B'. Now if 'A' is not synonymous with 'B', and if, nevertheless, A is strictly identical with B, then both A and B have precisely the same properties, including all the defining properties in question, namely, R,S,T,X,Y and Z. Moreover, if every A is strictly identical with some B or other, say B', B" . . .; then if B', B" . . . exist, A's exist.

Let us now turn to Smart's thesis. Smart wishes to assert at least three propositions: (1) 'Sensation' is not synonymous with 'brain process' or any other word in the materialist's preferred vocabulary. (2) Sensations are strictly identical with brain processes. (3) There exist brain processes which are identical with sensations.

In the light of the foregoing, it should be clear that from (1), (2), and (3), it follows (a) that there are sensations, and (b) that the properties which are connoted by 'brain process' and also those that are connoted by 'sensation' are possessed by one and the same thing, namely, whatever is referred to by both 'sensation' and 'brain process'. Thus *we have not got rid of the danglers*. For sensations were nomological danglers in virtue of certain properties which they had, and we have in *no way* eliminated these properties. In fact, by insisting (1) that 'sensation' is not synonymous with 'brain process', (2) that sensations are strictly identical with brain processes, and (3) that there are brain processes which are identical with sensations, we have ensured that there are just as many danglers as there were before we accepted the strict identity of sensations and brain processes. Indeed, on Smart's thesis it turns out that brain processes are danglers, for now brain processes have all those properties that made sensations danglers. Furthermore, we still have laws which are in all essential respects just like psycho-physical laws, as the following argument shows.

Let us distinguish two sorts of properties, M-properties and P-properties. M-properties are all and only those properties which the materialist wishes to allow in his physicalistic scheme. Among these M-properties will be the defining properties for 'brain process'. P-properties are those defining properties for 'sensation' which prevent us from defining 'sensation' in terms of M-properties.

Now on Smart's thesis P-properties cannot be reduced to M-properties; that is, the words for the alleged P-properties cannot be defined in terms of M-properties.[2] For if the words for P-properties are definable in terms of M-properties without remainder, then 'sensation' is definable in terms of M-properties, because it is *only* these troublesome P-properties which prevent us from defining 'sensation' in terms of M-properties. But if 'sensation' is definable in terms of M-properties, then 'sensation' is synonymous with some word or words in the materialist's preferred vocabulary; and hence one of Smart's original propositions, namely (1), is false. But it will not do to deny (1), for Smart has taken great pains to assure us that 'sensation' is *not* synonymous with any words in his preferred vocabulary. Therefore, P-properties can only be related to M-properties in a non-logical way; that is, any connection between them will be synthetic.

Thus a consequence of Smart's theory is that, instead of the usual psycho-physical laws stating that a certain sensation occurs if and only if a certain brain process occurs, we are *now* to say that a brain process has P-properties if and only if it has certain M-properties. But it is still a contingent matter of fact, to be discovered by some sort of empirical investigation, that wherever a brain process has a certain conjunction of M-properties it also has certain P-properties. And to state this relation is to state a generalisation which is, in all essential respects, just like a psycho-physical law relating sensations to brain processes. The only difference is that we have to deal with certain properties of sensations rather than sensations themselves.

Moreover, we shall probably still have the ordinary psycho-physical laws, for presumably not all brain processes will be sensations. There must be some law, then, concerning *which* brain processes are sensations. This law would state: 'Whenever such-and-such a brain process occurs, there is a sensation.' And does not this look very much like an ordinary psycho-physical law?

There are two ways in which we might try to avoid the conclusions I have drawn. First, we might assert the proposition (4) 'There

---

[2] In replying to an objection put to him by Professor Max Black, Smart attempts to define colour words in physicalist terms. There is no need to go into details here, for my argument shows what is wrong with any such attempt on his part.

are no P-properties.' But this will not do because (4), (2), and the definition of 'P-property' imply the contradictory of (3). The argument to show this is as follows. If there are no P-properties, there are no sensations. For 'P-property' is just a way of referring to those defining properties for 'sensation' which prevent us from defining 'sensation' in terms of M-properties; and if these properties do not exist it follows that sensations do not exist. If there are no sensations, there are no brain processes which are identical with sensations. For sensations are, according to (2), strictly identical with certain brain processes; it follows, therefore, that if the one does not exist, the other does not exist. Hence, to get rid of P-properties by denying their existence would require us to drop the thesis that sensations are strictly identical with brain processes or to admit that those brain processes which are identical with sensations do not exist. But to accept the first alternative would be to destroy Smart's thesis, and to accept the second would be to make it pointless. Therefore it will not do to deny the existence of P-properties.

Second, we might try to conjure away P-properties by claiming (5) 'All P-properties are strictly identical with certain M-properties even though the words for P-properties are not definable in terms of M-properties.' I am not sure that such a hypothesis is intelligible. But if it is, a reapplication of my main argument shows that it follows that there are still P-properties and they retain all their properties. Thus the new danglers would be the properties of P-properties. And the same line of argument can be extended as long as it makes sense to talk of the properties of properties of properties, and so forth. At any point where such talk is no longer significant, (5) can no longer be completely formulated. For, *ex hypothesi*, there are no P_{n+1}-properties which prevent us from defining the words for P_n-properties in terms of M_n-properties. Thus (5) would amount to a statement that P-properties are reducible to M-properties. And I have already replied to this hypothesis.

Now in his article Smart has made the following claim:

> If it be agreed that there are no cogent philosophical arguments which force us to accept dualism, and if the brain-process theory and dualism are equally consistent with the facts, then the principles of parsimony and simplicity seem to me to be overwhelmingly in favour of the brain-process theory. (P. 66; italics mine.)

But, as I have shown, the brain-process theory is not parsimonious of laws: on the brain-process theory we would have at least as many laws as on a dualist theory. One reason, then, for preferring the brain-process theory has been removed.

It might still seem, however, that Smart's theory is parsimonious of *substances*. Yet even this is doubtful, for on his theory brain processes turn out to have just those properties which have led some people to postulate that sensations are processes involving non-material substances. Thus the very least that we would have to say, if we are going to discuss substances at all, is that there are two radically different *kinds* of material substance – the one involved in ordinary processes, and the one involved in certain brain processes – which is hardly more parsimonious than saying that there are two different kinds of substance. Moreover, the issue between Smart's materialistic monism and ordinary dualism turns out to be mainly verbal: the criteria which serve to differentiate the one kind of material substance from the other are *precisely* the criteria which are usually used to differentiate material from non-material substance.

I conclude, then, that one form of materialism, namely Smart's, has no advantage over one ordinary form of dualism, and is, indeed, in all important respects, precisely equivalent to it.[4]

[4] I should like to acknowledge the invaluable assistance of Mr K. E. Lehrer on a number of points in this paper.

VII Further remarks on sensations and brain processes

J. J. C. Smart

In a discussion of my article 'Sensations and brain processes' J. T.
Stevenson distinguishes two sorts of properties.[1] M-properties are
those properties, for example of brain processes, which I can allow
in my physicalist scheme. P-properties are those properties of sensations which prevent us from defining 'sensation' in terms of M-
properties. Stevenson then points out that some of these P-properties
will be nomological danglers, that is, connected to M-properties by
ultimate psycho-physical laws, and so I am not any better off in
this respect than is the traditional dualist. My reply is that I do not
admit that there are any such P-properties. The way in which I
avoid admitting P-properties is indicated in my reply to Objection 3
in the original article, but I did not make myself sufficiently clear.

On my view sensation reports are neutral between materialism
and dualism: they are roughly equivalent to something of the form
'What is going on in me is like what goes on in me when . . .', where
the dots are replaced by a description of stimulus conditions. Sensation statements differ from the corresponding brain-process statements in their great openness or topic-neutrality. The main reason
why sensation statements cànnot be translated into the corresponding
brain-process statements is similar to the reason why 'someone telephoned' cannot be translated into 'the doctor telephoned', even
though it was the doctor who telephoned. Another reason, which is
less important for the present argument, is that we have to some
extent given sensation reports a special logic, for example in respect
of incorrigibility. As Wittgenstein has often pointed out, the logic
of part of our language can depend on facts about the world, and it
just is the case that what a man says about his sensations is more
patent to us than are the processes he reports. But a difference in
logic need not imply a distinction in ontology, as the example of

[1] See Paper VI.

nation statements and citizen statements perhaps shows. Nations are nothing over and above citizens. Let us, however, return to the more important reason for the non-translatability of sensation statements into brain-process statements. Sensation reports are not materialistic statements any more than in the above example 'someone telephoned' is a medical statement. Nevertheless the fact that makes it true, that the doctor telephoned, is a medical fact. Although 'someone telephoned' is not a medical statement, it is not a non-medical statement. Similarly, although sensation reports are not materialistic statements, they are not immaterialistic; they are quite neutral. Stevenson will ask me how then I distinguish the class of sensations. I reply that they are the things, whatever they are, that are reported in a certain recognisable class of utterances. Nor is there a need for ultimate laws which state which of our brain processes are sensations.[2] We can distinguish the ones which are sensations as those which can in suitable circumstances be the specific causal conditions of those behavioural reactions which are sensation reports.

I was, I fear, misleadingly epigrammatic when I said that sensations, as 'raw feels', are colourless in the way in which *something* is colourless.[3] Consider the statement 'Something is in the box.' The thing in the box certainly has features, though they are not indicated in the statement above. Perhaps it has the features of being a biscuit and of being cracked. Similarly, sensations do have features, namely neurophysiological ones, but these features, save perhaps for some topic-neutral ones like waxing and waning, are not immediately apprehended or mentioned in the sensation reports. I derive some support for this from the elusiveness of 'raw feels', our inability to describe sensations except by reference to stimulus conditions.

Stevenson may still be right in saying that I cannot in the end avoid admitting P-properties, but he has not convinced me yet. I have here tried to elucidate and amplify that part of my paper which was designed to allow me to deny the existence of P-properties.[4]

[2] P. 90: 'Moreover . . . psycho-physical law.'
[3] P. 61.
[4] There are some additional points which I should have liked to make. I have omitted them because I have made them in a note in the *Australasian Journal of Philosophy*, xxxviii (1960) pp. 252–4, in reply to discussions of my views by G. Pitcher and W. D. Joske, *AJP*, xxxviii (1960) pp. 150–60.

VIII Smart on sensations
Kurt Baier

Smart argues that sensations are brain processes.[1] I wish to show that at least as far as pains are concerned Smart's theory is untenable. Smart tries to show that 'I have a pain' means something which makes it true to say that it is a report of a brain process. In support of this analysis, he makes two connected claims, one concerning the nature of the issue between Dualism and Materialism, the other concerning the bearing on this issue of the way we talk.

Concerning the first claim, he says that the main issue between Materialism and Dualism is whether, over and above physical entities and processes, there are also irreducibly psychical ones.[2] This issue, according to Smart, is metaphysical, that is, incapable of being settled by reference to empirical fact or linguistic considerations.[3] It can therefore be settled simply by reference to principles, such as the principles of parsimony and simplicity, which decide the intrinsic preferability of one metaphysical system over another. These principles speak clearly and decisively in favour of Materialism, because the assumption of one single kind of entity and process is simpler and more parsimonious than the assumption of two.[4]

Concerning the second claim, Smart admits that the issue between Dualism and Materialism could not, however, be purely metaphysical, in his sense, if linguistic considerations told against one or the other.[5] On the face of it, linguistic considerations seem to tell against Materialism, for there are in our language certain types of utterance, normally called 'reports of sensations or experiences', 'introspective reports' or 'talk about our state of consciousness'[6] which, from their very meaning, appear to be reports of 'something irreducibly psychical'.[7] According to Smart, however, they are not

---

[1] Paper III. All page references are to this, unless otherwise specified. Cf. also Papers II and V; and Feigl, 'The Mind–Body Problem in the Development of Logical Empiricism', in *Readings in the Philosophy of Science*, pp. 612–26. See also my article 'Pains', *Australasian Journal of Philosophy*, XL (1962) pp. 1–23.

[2] Pp. 53, 54, 55, 63.   [3] Pp. 62–3, 65–6.   [4] P. 66.
[5] Pp. 62, 65–6.   [6] Pp. 55, 61, 63, 64.   [7] P. 53.

really such reports. Contrary to what the Dualist believes, they leave
open the question what sort of thing it is they report, whether something physical or something psychical. The Dualist misunderstands
the difference between 'introspective reports' and 'talk about the
environment'.[8] He thinks the difference is that introspective reports,
from their very meaning, are reports of something irreducibly
psychical, whereas reports about the environment, from their very
meaning, are reports of something physical. In fact, however, Smart
argues, the difference is more involved: whereas talk about the
environment, from its very meaning, must be said to report physical
processes, introspective talk is not, from its very meaning, committed
on the question what sorts of things it reports. Applying his theory
about introspective reports to reports of pains, Smart suggests the
following definition 'X has a pain' means 'There is something going
on which is like what is going on when, e.g. someone is sticking a pin
into X.'[9] The words (says Smart) ' "there is something going on
which is like what is going on when" are all quasi-logical or topic-
neutral words. This explains why the ancient Greek peasant's reports
about his sensations can be neutral between dualistic metaphysics
and my materialistic metaphysics. It explains how sensations can
be brain processes and yet how those who report them need
know nothing about brain processes. For he reports them only very
abstractedly as "something going on which is like what is going on
when . . ." Similarly a person may say "someone is in the room",
thus reporting truly that the doctor is in the room, even though he
has never heard of doctors.'[10]

Suppose we are savages who know nothing about doctors. A
visitor comes, looks deeply into our eyes, and we get better. If we
say, 'an angel came', we commit ourselves to the view that the
visitation was something supernatural. If we say 'someone came',
we leave open the question what kind of visitor it was. Later, when
we learn about doctors and their astonishing ways, we realise that the
'someone' who called was not an angel but a doctor. The Dualist
makes two mistakes, a linguistic and a metaphysical one. The
linguistic one is to think that 'I have a pain' functions somewhat
like 'an angel came', which implies belief in the supernatural,
whereas it functions rather like 'someone came', which is agnostic
on this point. Secondly, he believes in pains, i.e. in something
psychical, which is rather like believing in angels, i.e. in something
supernatural. According to Smart, however, the best metaphysical
view is that there is nothing in the world but physical entities. Belief

[8] P. 64.   [9] P. 64.   [10] P. 60.

in psychical entities is as unnecessary as belief in angels, ghosts and demons.

Smart's view is therefore not merely that there are no psychic entities and processes, but also that our way of speaking does not imply that there are. This is important, for we could not make the 'metaphysical discovery', that sensations are identical with brain processes, i.e. that Materialism is more parsimonious and simpler than Dualism, unless the possibility of such a discovery were allowed for in our ordinary way of speaking. If Smart's view is correct, then the Dualist is wrong in thinking that talk about the material world is on a par with talk about our minds. If Smart is right, then there is one kind of talk, 'talk about the environment', which is frankly and committedly about physical processes, another kind of talk, 'introspective reports', which is, as far as our rules of language go, non-committal about the nature of what it reports (and which is, in 'metaphysical fact', reporting physical processes),[11] but no sort of sensible talk which is frankly and committedly about psychic fact.

Our first question must therefore be: What exactly does it mean to say that being a remark of a certain sort, say, talk about the environment, implies that its subject-matter is something physical? Whatever else it may mean, it must mean at least this, that its subject-matter is something *public*. The opposite holds for the corresponding contention that being a remark of a certain sort (e.g. an introspective report) does not imply that its subject-matter is something physical but leaves the question open. Whatever else that contention may mean, it must mean at least this, that such an introspective report could conceivably be, though it might very well not be, about something physical, hence about something public.

I shall try to show that introspective reports are necessarily about something private, and that being about something private is *incompatible with* being about something public. If I am right in this then Smart fails in his attempt to show that introspective reports, such as 'I have a pain', *leave open* the question whether they are about something physical or not. I shall further suggest that the phrase 'being about something psychic or mental', whatever else it may mean, must mean at least 'being about something private'. If that is so, then introspective reports, far from leaving open the question whether they are about something physical or about something psychic, are as necessarily about something irreducibly psychic as talk about the environment is about something irreducibly physical.

There can be no doubt that being an introspective report implies

[11] Pp. 61–2.

being about something *private*. Of course, 'something private' is here
used in a technical sense. To avoid confusions between the technical
and the ordinary senses of 'something private', we must make clear
to ourselves precisely what we mean by this term. We must say that
'I have a pain' is about 'something private', because in making this
remark we report something which is *necessarily owned*, that is, 'had
by someone', for it would be self-contradictory to assert the existence
of unfelt pains or pains which no sentient being has; we report something which is *necessarily exclusive or unsharable*, for when you and
I have the same pain, we do not share *one* pain, but we have one
each; something which is *necessarily imperceptible by the senses*, for
it makes no sense to say that someone saw, heard, smelled, touched,
or tasted his or anyone else's pain; something *necessarily asymmetrical*, for whereas it makes no sense to say 'I could see (or hear)
that *I* had a pain', it makes quite good sense to say 'I could see (or
hear) that *he* had a pain'; something about the possession of which
the person who claims to possess it could not possibly examine, consider, or weigh any evidence, although other people could, for it does
not make sense to say, 'I must have a pain in my tooth or else my
cheek would not be so swollen', etc., but this is quite good sense when
said about another; and lastly it is something about which the person
whose private state it is has final epistemological authority, for it does
not make sense to say 'I have a pain unless I am mistaken.'

Thus 'privacy' in the technical sense under discussion involves
the peculiar epistemological authority which I have discussed in my
paper 'Pains'.[12] It is perhaps misleading to speak of this authority
as 'incorrigibility', for it is not true that a person may never be
mistaken about whether or not he has something which is private
in this sense. A person may for instance think, at a given moment
when he does not feel any pain, that he still has the intermittent
toothache which has plagued him for some time, and therefore
expect further twinges in the near future, but be mistaken in this
expectation and consequently in his belief that he still has the intermittent toothache. Rather, this epistemological authority is based
on his being the person necessarily in the best position to discover
his mistake or to confirm his belief, if the concept allows for this.

The two other features of privacy are closely connected with and
explain this authority. One is the necessary 'imperceptibility' of
anything private. Of course, 'imperceptibility' here does not imply
that, like some of the theoretical entities of science, what is private
cannot be 'the object of one or other of the five senses'. For both

[12] *Australasian Journal of Philosophy*, XL (1962) pp. 3–6.

sensations and sense-data are private in the required sense, but sense-data – though not sensations such as pains – *must* be 'objects of one or other of the senses', else we could not distinguish, as we do, between e.g. visual and olfactory sense-data. Rather, what is private is imperceptible because there can be no question of a misperception or hallucination, although, of course, unlike the theoretical entities of science, what is private can be 'had' or 'experienced'.

The other feature of 'privacy' is the radical asymmetry in all epistemological matters. How radical this is can be seen by a comparison of what is private with' something public to which we have 'privileged access', as in 'I feel something in my eye' or 'I feel ill'. In such cases, there is limited asymmetry in that the speaker has *a way of coming to know* not open to others. However, privileged access does not involve the epistemological authority granted the speaker in matters which are 'private'. Nor does it necessarily involve the 'necessary and unsharable ownership' characteristic of things 'private', although it may do so, as in 'smile', or 'illness', but not in 'something (e.g. a beam) in my eye' or 'barbed wire in my foot'. Although we have privileged access to these things, they are public, because the method of *establishing* their existence and nature is symmetrical, the same for the person concerned as for others. The person concerned does not have *altogether* different ways of coming to know and to establish these matters, but merely an additional, privileged way of doing so. It follows that there is sense in *proving* to a person that something to which he has privileged access, e.g. whether he is ill, is other than he thinks, but there is no sense in trying to prove to a person that something 'private to him' is other than he thinks. The doctor, looking at the thermometer, may say to the patient, 'You *must* be feeling hot', but he cannot say this in an attempt *to prove this to an incredulous patient*, for this is something 'private to the patient' about which he has epistemological authority.

If, therefore, a remark is of a type implying that it is wholly about something private, it cannot also be about something public. This does not mean that a given remark could not be about something private and *also* about something public, for one and the same remark may be of a type having two quite different kinds of subject-matter. Of course, it would then be about two things, not one, and it would not be a 'pure' introspective report, but a remark both about one's state of consciousness and about the material or physical world. Such a remark would not *leave* open the question whether it was about something physical *or* about something psychic, but would imply that it was about both. I conclude that Smart's position is untenable.

I mention two errors, interesting on their own account, which may be at least partly responsible for Smart's paradoxical conclusions. The first is to think that, owing to our ignorance of physiology, introspective reports are 'abstract',[13] 'extremely open',[14] 'general',[15] and that all their logical peculiarities are due to this. As our physiological knowledge increases, these faults will be remedied, and at the same time the logical peculiarities of introspective remarks will vanish. They will eventually be replaced by talk about the environment. The second and connected error is to think that the logical differences between introspective reports and talk about the environment are differences only in vocabulary, in the 'logic' of the two languages, or perhaps psychological differences in attitude, such as the difference between 'talking uninhibitedly' and 'talking guardedly',[16] but that none of these amounts to differences in type of subject-matter, such as the differences between 'something physical' and 'something psychic'.

Concerning the first point, in reply to the objection 'that sensations are private, brain processes are *public*',[17] Smart says that this only shows 'that the language of introspective reports has a different logic from the language of material processes',[18] the implication being that this is of no great importance. To the unstated but clearly envisaged objection that introspective reports carry final epistemological *authority*, whereas talk about brain processes does not, Smart replies, 'It is obvious that until the brain-process theory is much improved and widely accepted there will be no *criteria* for saying "Smith has an experience of such-and-such a sort" *except* Smith's introspective reports. So we have adopted a rule of language that (normally) what Smith says goes.'[19]

The wholly untenable implications of this paragraph are that while our physiological knowledge is small, Smith's introspective *report* is the only public criterion for saying that Smith has a certain experience, and that as our physiological knowledge expands, there will become available further public criteria. And when that state has been reached, the present rule of language, which holds for introspective reports, namely that what the speaker says goes, will be replaced by the rules of public language holding for talk about the environment.

However, this is simply a confusion of the privacy of the subject-

---

[13] P. 60.   [14] P. 64.   [15] P. 64.   [16] P. 64.
[17] P. 62.   [18] P. 63.   [19] P. 63.

matter and the availability of external evidence. Let us distinguish
·four types of talk (1) talk about 'private' experiences by their owner,
that is, introspective reports, (2) talk about someone's 'experiences'
by other people, (3) talk about brain processes by their 'owner', (4)
talk about brain processes by other people. The first two are about
something private, the second two about something public. No
increase in physiological knowledge, no improvement in brain-
process theory can have the slightest tendency to replace the first
two by the second two. Before the invention of the thermometer,
one could say only whether the room or the soup or the bath was
hot, medium or cold, and whether one felt hot or cold or comfortable. Temperature talk may be an improvement on hot–cold–
tepid talk, and may eventually replace it. But surely it is not designed
to be an improvement on, and can never replace, hot–cold–comfortable talk. Looking at the thermometer, a man can say with considerable reliability that the room temperature is 85, or that his body
temperature is 103. If he has experience in this field, he may even
venture to say, *going by his feeling alone*, what the temperature of
the room or his body is. And he may be good or bad at this game.
His telling the room or body temperature in this way is, however,
quite compatible with his saying that *although* the room is hot and
he has a temperature, he *feels* cold. The first two remarks are,
respectively, thermometer-based and feeling-based claims *about the
environment*, the third remark is not about the environment but
about his feelings. The introduction of the thermometer cannot
replace our introspective reports of our feeling hot, cold, or comfortable.

But, Smart might object, what about thermometer-based talk
about feeling hot, cold, or comfortable? Surely, that is talk whose
reliability constantly increases with the increase of our knowledge
of physiology. Well, there is such talk, but it is not talk about the
environment: it is talk about experiences, type (2) above. It differs
importantly from introspective reports, but not in subject-matter.
The respects in which it differs are in the relation of the person who
makes it to the experience talked about, in what it is based on, and
in what evidence may legitimately be considered. At no stage of
the increase of our physiological knowledge do we switch from introspective reports to this sort of talk. Both types of talk existed long
before physiology was invented. The ancient Greek peasant, without
knowing anything about physiology, was able to talk about his
fellows' pains as well as his own. Even in the highly misleading sense
of 'criterion' used by Smart, it is not true that, say, Agamemnon's

introspective report was the only criterion Thersites could have for saying that the former had 'experiences' of a certain sort. When he stepped on Agamemnon's foot and Agamemnon exclaimed, in Greek, 'Ouch, watch where you are going, you fool', Thersites was in a position to tell what sort of experience the other was having. He did not need to ask Agamemnon for his introspective report, and it would have added little. When he beat his child or removed another peasant's tooth with a hammer, their behaviour constituted 'criteria' (i.e. evidence) just as good as their introspective reports.

Thus physiology does not provide *the only* evidence of an experience apart from introspective reports, and such evidence never constitutes a logical criterion. Of course, our physiological evidence may one day become so good that *we* prefer to believe that the introspective reporter is lying rather than abandon our physiological theory. We shall then be able to do better, on the basis of physiological evidence, what we are already doing, not so well, on the basis of other sorts of evidence, such as telling when someone is a malingerer. To say that one day our physiological knowledge will increase to such an extent that we shall be able to make absolutely reliable encephalograph-based claims about people's experiences is only to say that, if carefully checked, our encephalograph-based claims about 'experiences' will always be *correct*, i.e. will *make the same claims* as *truthful* introspective reports. If correct encephalograph-based claims about Smith's experiences contradict Smith's introspective reports, we shall be entitled to infer that he is *lying*. In that sense, what Smith says will no longer go. But we cannot of course infer that he is making a mistake, for that is nonsense.

We must, therefore, keep apart two quite different rules of language, 'What Smith *says* goes' and 'What Smith *thinks* goes'. The former rule does not hold always, even now, and increase in physiological knowledge will probably enable us more and more to keep a check on people's veracity. The latter rule holds now and will continue to hold, quite irrespective of the increase in physiological knowledge. For suppose we have the best possible physiological evidence to the effect that no one can have a pain in whose brain the process xyz is not going on. However good the evidence may be, such a physiological theory can never be used to show to the sufferer that he was mistaken in thinking that he had a pain, for such a mistake is inconceivable. The sufferer's epistemological authority must therefore be better than the best physiological theory can ever be. Physiology can therefore never provide a person with more than *evidence* that someone else is having an experience of one sort or another. It can never lay down independent and overriding *criteria* for saying that someone is having an experience of a certain sort. Talk about brain processes therefore must be about something other than talk about experiences. Hence, introspective reports and brain-process talk cannot be merely different ways of talking about the same thing.

There is consequently no close analogy between talking about a flash of lightning and talking about the experience of having a pain. Smart maintains that a flash of lightning is identical with an electric discharge. Now this is true only in the trivial and misleading sense in which Leonardo's 'Last Supper' is identical with, is really, is nothing but, a small portion of the church wall on which it is painted, or the collection of atoms of which it is 'composed'. But even if I am wrong and a flash of lightning really is in some more important sense identical with an electrical discharge, the 'experience' of having a pain cannot be identical with a brain process. When I seem to see a flash of lightning, then, if I must admit that there was no electric discharge I must also admit that there was no flash of lightning, and that I was the victim of an optical illusion or of a hallucination. But no one can admit, however good the physiological evidence which contradicts his claim, that he was the victim of a pain illusion or hallucination. Admittedly, this bald assertion requires some qualifications, but they do not dispose of my point. A person may for instance have to admit that he merely dreamt he had a pain. But that is merely an admission that he mis-remembered. He has to admit that he wrongly believed, at t_2, that he had a pain at t_1. He does not admit that he wrongly believed, at t_1, that he had a pain at t_1. A man may be so confused or mad that he does not know what he has, but that tells as much *against* the possibility of his *discovering* his mistake as *for having made* it.

Smart's second error concerns the subject-matter of introspective reports. According to him the introspective report 'I have a pain' means 'Something is going on which is like what is going on when, i.e. which *feels as though*, someone were sticking a pin into me.' It differs from the corresponding remark about the environment, 'I feel a pin being stuck into me',[20] in various purely linguistic ways which, together, do not amount to implying a fundamental difference in subject-matter, such as the difference between 'being about something irreducibly psychic' and 'being about a physical or material process' would be. These purely linguistic differences are

[20] P. 64.

the following. Talk about the environment is uninhibited, going beyond the evidence of the senses, comparatively naïve,[21] couched in a variety of languages, such as the language of material processes, perception statements, stimulus language, all of which, however, are parts of material object language,[22] having a 'public' logic, and therefore implying that the subject-matter is the physical world. Introspective reports, on the other hand, are inhibited and comparatively sophisticated in that they withhold certain epithets, disinhibit certain descriptive reactions which the naïve person is tempted to make,[23] are couched in the language of introspective reports, which has a private logic[24] but is just as much a part of material object language (because there is no such thing as phenomenal language),[25] all of which amounts to no more than the fact that such remarks leave it open whether they are about something physical or something psychic.

Enough has been said to show that this characterisation of the linguistic differences between introspective reports and talk about the environment is untenable. The 'private' logic attaches not merely to introspective reports but also to physiologically based statements about *another* person's 'experiences'. It is not a function of our ignorance, but a function of this type of subject-matter. These points clearly show that the distinction between 'being about something

---

[21] P. 64.

[22] Pp. 61, 64. See also Smart, 'Sensations and Brain Processes: A Rejoinder to Dr Pitcher and Mr Joske', *Australasian Journal of Philosophy*, XXXVIII (1960) p. 254.

[23] P. 64. Here Smart conflates and confuses a large number of distinctions: the distinction between what the naïve and what the sophisticated person is tempted to say about the environment, what does and does not go beyond the evidence, what the cautious but naïve person, the cautious and sophisticated person, the reckless or irresponsible and naïve, the reckless or irresponsible but sophisticated person is *likely* to claim, what any sort of person is *entitled* to claim on the basis of given evidence, what constitutes a *responsibility-disclaiming* opinion, what constitutes a *fully committed assertion*, and what words are signs of these. All these distinctions are distinctions between different ways of talking about the environment. They are completely irrelevant to the distinction between talking about the environment and talking about one's state of consciousness. Smart is simply misled by the fact that 'It *feels as though* someone is sticking a pin into me' can be used for talking about pins or for talking about feelings. None of the distinctions he alludes to, even if he had got them right, would make any difference to the fact that when I talk about pains, I am not talking, in however roundabout a way, about pins.

[24] P. 63.   [25] P. 61.

physical' and 'being about something psychic or mental', which is logically connected with the distinction between 'being public' and 'being private', is firmly embedded in the way we talk. Smart is therefore wrong in thinking that introspective reports leave open the question whether they are reports of something private or of something public; hence in thinking that they leave open the question whether or not they are reports of something irreducibly psychic; hence in thinking that there is room for the 'metaphysical discovery' that sensations are identical with brain processes. Hence Smart's thesis is untenable.

A doubt may linger. Is there really no room for this metaphysical discovery? Is not Smart right in saying that 'the ordinary man when he reports an experience is reporting that something is going on, but he leaves it open as to what sort of thing is going on, whether in a material solid medium, or perhaps in some sort of gaseous medium, or even perhaps in some sort of non-spatial medium (if this makes sense)'?[26] Surely, it will be said, Smart is right: the ordinary man is wholly uncommitted on the question whether, *as the dualist holds*, 'experiences are something over and above material processes, that is, they are a sort of ghost stuff (or perhaps ripples in an underlying ghost stuff)',[27] or whether, *as Smart holds*, 'experiences are not to be identified with ghost stuff but with brain stuff'.[28] It would indeed be foolish to maintain that the ordinary man is committed on this issue, but this issue is very different from the one discussed so far: how the logical differences between introspective reports and talk about the environment are to be characterised. The fact that the ordinary man leaves open the question of solid versus gaseous (or non-spatial) medium is irrelevant to whether he leaves open the question of public versus private subject-matter.

Exactly what is this issue anyway, on which the ordinary man is uncommitted? Its nonsensical ring is a sure indication that the issue is between *verbal* formulations of high-level scientific theories. If I say 'the light from the setting sun nearly blinded me when I drove home', I am not implying anything about the solidity or gaseousness, spatiality or non-spatiality of the medium in which the light is 'travelling' from the sun into my eyes. For all the ordinary man cares, it may really be rippling along in some ghost light-ether. But the fact that *we do leave open* the question of the nature of the medium in which the process occurs implies that *we do not leave open* the question whether what we are talking about is physical or psychic. We imply, on the contrary, that what we are talking about

[26] P. 62. [27] P. 64. [28] P. 64.

is something physical. The question of the nature of the medium in which a process goes on can be asked only if it is assumed that what is talked about is something physical. Otherwise the discovery of the non-existence of the light-ether, and the like, could tend to show that light etc. is something psychic. On Smart's definition, 'being something psychic' has come to mean 'being something public going on in a medium which does not have *all* the properties of something going on in a *material* medium'. On this view, certain physical theories could well support Monistic Idealism rather than Monistic Materialism.

IX Brain processes and incorrigibility

J. J. C. Smart

I wish to consider an argument put forward by Professor Baier in his 'Smart on sensations' (Paper VIII). The argument is directed against the thesis, which I wish to defend, that sensations are in fact brain processes.[1]

The objection is briefly as follows. Reports of sensations, unlike any statements that a 'physiologist could make, are incorrigible. No physiological evidence, say from a gadget attached to my skull, could make me withdraw the statement that I have a pain when as a matter of fact I feel a pain. For example the gadget might show no suitable similarities of cerebral processes on the various occasions on which I felt a pain.

What should I say about such a possibility? I concede to Baier that I mishandled this objection in my original article. Let me try to do better. I must, I think, agree with Baier that if the sort of situation which we have just envisaged did in fact come about, then I should have to reject the brain-process thesis, and would perhaps espouse dualism. If I felt a pain I could not reject the assertion that I had a pain. My reply is that I do not think that any such situation would in fact occur. It should be recalled that I put forward the brain-process thesis as a factual identification, not as a logically necessary one. I did, of course, as Baier recognises, assert that in ordinary language reports of sensations are *neutral* between materialism and dualism. This enables me to explain the relative incorrigibility of sensation reports as compared with the findings of physiology. The sensation report is neutral between materialism and dualism and so is compatible with any outcome of the envisaged physiological experiment.

Baier points out quite correctly that 'I have a pain' cannot be strictly translated on the lines I suggested, as 'what is going on in me is like what goes on in me when a pin is stuck into me'. As he

[1] See my Papers III and VII, and my notes in *Australasian Journal of Philosophy*, xxxviii (1960) pp. 252-4.

points out, pains have nothing essentially to do with pins. However, my intention was to give the rubric 'what is going on in me is like what is going on in me when . . .', not as providing the framework for a strict translation, but as merely giving the general purport of sensation reports. Their purport is to report likenesses and unlikenesses of certain internal processes without saying wherein these likenesses and unlikenesses consist. There is no need to learn the word 'pain' by having a pin stuck into one. A child may be introducd to the word 'pain' when he accidentally grazes his knee. But sensation talk must be learned by reference to some environmental stimulus situation or another. Or at least this is so with visual experiences and the like. With pains there is also the possibility of specifying the internal processes by reference not only to typical environmental causes but also by reference to typical behavioural reactions, e.g. grimacing. Something of the sort is needed. I agree that it need not be pins. Compare the way in which the proper name 'Moses' can be introduced in various ways, such as via the description 'the man who led the Israelites out of Egypt' or the description 'the man who as a baby was found among the bulrushes'. No particular description is necessary, but at least one or another must be used.[2]

Let me now move from defence to offence. There is something very puzzling about the notion of incorrigible first-person reports, and this is just as much so for a dualist as it is for a materialist. You cannot get rid of logical puzzles by shifting them to the realm of the ghostly. Both the materialist and the dualist, and indeed most behaviourists also,[3] will want to say that the sincere reporting of a sensation is one thing and the sensation reported is another thing. Now, as Hume said, what is distinguishable is separable. It is therefore logically possible that someone should sincerely report an experience and yet that the experience should not occur. (Very nearly the same argument has been independently and simultaneously produced by D. M. Armstrong, as I discovered in correspondence with him. There is a hint of a similar argument, though in a reversed form, in Norman Malcolm's discussion of Wittgenstein's *Philosophical Investigations* in the *Philosophical Review*, LXIII (1954) on p. 556, lines 13–14. This in effect argues from the in-

[2] See the account of proper names in C. B. Martin, *Religious Belief* (Ithaca, N.Y. 1959) pp. 45–51.
[3] The only behaviourist who would escape this would be one who analysed a sensation as simply that part of behaviour which was the sensation report itself.

corrigibility of sensation reports to the untenability of Strawson's view about sensations. I think, however, that it can also be turned against Wittgenstein as interpreted by Malcolm. The argument is also closely related to the argument used by A. I. Melden, and discussed by Baier in his article 'Pains',[4] against the view that volitions are causes of actions.)

The argument of the previous paragraph therefore seems to show that not even sincere reports of immediate experience can be absolutely incorrigible. There is something surprising about this conclusion, but it is hard to see how it could be avoided. It could be said, perhaps, as Baier does in his 'Pains' article in a different connection, that contingently connected things can be referred to by logically connected terms, as is shown by the example of 'father' and 'son'. Now though the use which Baier has made of this move is, in the context in which it occurs in his paper, a good and defensible one, I do not think that it would help in the present connection. You could adopt the artificial convention of making the correctness of a report a criterion of its sincerity, but then this move would ensure that a man who sincerely reported a bruised toenail had a bruised toenail. I conclude that dualism, and for that matter most forms of behaviourism too, is in as bad a state about incorrigibility, if absolute incorrigibility should indeed be a fact, as is the brain-process theory.

[4] *Australasian Journal of Philosophy*, XL (1962) pp. 19–20.

PART THREE

Location and Leibniz's Law

X Could mental states be brain processes?

Jerome Shaffer

In recent discussions of the relation between mental states and brain processes, a view that has received much support is the Identity Theory. Its adherents[1] allow that expressions that refer to mental states differ in their meaning from expressions that refer to brain processes, but they claim that the actual existents picked out by the former expressions turn out, as a matter of empirical fact, to be identical with those picked out by the latter expressions. I wish to examine this theory. For convenience, I shall refer to mental states, e.g. feeling pain, having an after-image, thinking about a problem, considering some proposition, etc., as *C-states*, and I shall refer to whatever brain process may be going on at the same time that some mental state is occurring as a *B-process*. My main contentions will be (1) that C-states cannot be identical with B-processes because they do not occur in the same place, (2) that there is nothing to stop us from making the Identity Theory correct by adopting a convention for locating C-states, and (3) that the question whether it would be useful to adopt such a convention depends upon empirical facts which are at present unknown.

I

Before pointing out why the Identity Theory is incorrect, I wish to defend it against some standard objections. These objections arise from the failure to see that it is *de facto* identity, not identity of meaning, that is intended. Descartes, for example, concluded that the mental and the physical could not be identical, had to be separate and distinct substances, because of such facts as these: (1) that the concept of the mental is a quite different concept from the concept of the physical, (2) that someone might be sure of the existence of his mental process while raising doubts about the

[1] Cf. Place, Paper II; Feigl, 'The "Mental" and the "Physical" ', *Minnesota Studies in the Philosophy of Science*, II, pp. 370–497; J. J. C. Smart, Paper III; Hilary Putnam, 'Minds and Machines', *Dimensions of Mind*, pp. 148–79.

existence of his body, and (3) that God could make the mind exist in separation from the body. But none of these facts supports Descartes's conclusion that mental things cannot be identical with physical things. They show only, what is admitted by Identity Theorists, that we cannot know *a priori* that the mental and physical are identical. Compare the case of the expressions 'human being' and 'featherless biped'. The same facts hold, namely (1) that the concept of a human being is a quite different concept from the concept of a featherless biped, (2) that someone might be sure of the existence of human beings while raising doubts about the existence of featherless bipeds, and (3) that God could have made human beings exist as separate things from featherless bipeds. Yet none of these considerations rules out the possibility that, as a matter of pure empirical fact, human beings turn out to be identical with featherless bipeds, in the sense that the two classes are coextensional, such that anything which is a member of the one class turns out to be a member of the other also. The same goes for C-states and B-processes. Identity Theorists claim only that anything which is a C-state turns out, in fact, to be a B-process also. To put the thesis in Cartesian language, it is claimed that there is only one set of substances, physical substances, and this one set has some members that can be referred to by both physical and mental expressions. None of Descartes's considerations rules out this possibility.

Nor is it a legitimate objection to the Identity Theory that where one expression is used we cannot always substitute the other and preserve the truth-value. For it is a necessary consequence of the fact that C-state expressions and B-process expressions differ in meaning that in at least two familiar cases what we can assert about the one we may not be able to assert about the other. First there is the case of the so-called verbs of intentionality: it may be true that a particular C-state is remembered or expected, for example, but false that a particular B-process is remembered or expected. Secondly there is the case of modal statements: it is true that C-states are necessarily C-states but false that B-processes are necessarily C-states. Thus that two things are *de facto* identical does not imply that any truth about the one will be a truth about the other.

II

Are C-states in fact identical with B-processes? There are a number of criteria that must be met if we wish to show that they are. For one thing, we must show that the two exist during the same time interval, for if there were some time in which one existed but the other did not, that would settle conclusively that they were not identical. For example, if we had reason to think that the object referred to by the expression 'the Evening Star' did not exist in the morning, then we would have reason to think that the Evening Star was not identical with the Morning Star. This coexistence requirement seems to be met in the case of C-states and their correlated B-processes. If future discoveries in neurology and psychology were to lead us to think that they occurred at somewhat different times, then we could certainly rule out the Identity Theory.

A further condition to be met for identifying C-states with B-processes is that, at any given time, both must be located in the same place. If it can be shown that one is not found in the place where the other is found, then it has been shown that they are not identical. It would be just like showing that the object referred to by the expression 'the Evening Star' was not, in the morning, in the place where the object referred to by the expression 'the Morning Star' was located; that would show they were not identical.

Is the spatial requirement met by C-states and B-processes? Do they occur in the same place? No. B-processes are, in a perfectly clear sense, located where the brain is, in a particular region of physical space. But it is not true that C-states occur in the brain, or inside the body at all, for that matter. To be sure, I may have a pain in my leg or in my head; we do locate sensations in the body. But that is not to say that we give location to the *state of consciousness* that I have when I am having a sensation. The pain is in my leg, but it is not the case that my state of being-aware-of-a-pain-in-my-leg is also in my leg. Neither is it in my head. In the case of thoughts, there is no temptation to give them location, nor to give location to the mental state of being aware of a thought. In fact, it makes no sense at all to talk about C-states as being located somewhere in the body. We would not understand someone who pointed to a place in his body and claimed that it was there that his entertaining of a thought or having of an after-image was located. It would make no more sense than to claim that his entertaining of a thought was cubical or a micrometer in diameter.

The fact that it makes no sense to speak of C-states occurring in a volume occupied by a brain means that the Identity Theory cannot be correct. For it is a necessary condition for saying that something is identical with some particular physical object, state, or process

that the thing be located in the place where the particular physical
object, state, or process is. If it is not there, it cannot be identical
with what is there. Here we have something that distinguishes the
mind–body case from such examples of identity as men with featherless bipeds, Morning Star with Evening Star, water with H_2O,
lightning with electrical discharge, etc. To consider another example,
it has been discovered that light rays are electromagnetic radiations
of certain wavelengths. The Identity Theorist would claim that '*every*
argument for *or against* identification would apply equally in the
mind–body case and in the light–electromagnetism case.'[2] But this is
incorrect. There are ways of locating rays of light and ways of locating
electromagnetic radiations, and it turns out that wherever one is
located the other is also. But this cannot be said in the mind–body case.

To do justice to the Identity Theory, however, we cannot let the
matter rest here. For it is not entirely correct to say that C-states
are not located in the brain. That would give the false impression
that they were not in the brain because they were somewhere else.
Furthermore, how would one show that they were not in the brain?
Do we even understand the claim that they are not in the brain?
If it makes no sense to speak of C-states as in the brain, then it makes
no sense to speak of them as not in the brain either. The fact of the
matter is that we have no rules in our language either for asserting
that C-states have a particular location or for denying that they have
a particular location. So we have here a case in which it is senseless
to apply the criterion of same location. But the Identity Theory still
will not do, because if it is senseless to apply one of the criteria for
identity then it is also senseless to claim that there is identity.

III

At this point the Identity Theorist may make the following suggestion:

> We may easily adopt a convention (which is not a change in our
> present rules for the use of experience words but an addition to
> them) whereby it would make sense to talk of an experience in
> terms appropriate to physical process.[3]

A convention we might adopt would be something like this: for any
C-state, if it has a corresponding B-process, it will be said to be
located in that place where its corresponding B-process is located.
Given this convention, it then becomes a matter for empirical

[2] Putnam in *Dimensions of Mind*, p. 171.
[3] Smart, p. 62, above.

investigation whether any C-state has location in space and where that location, if any, is. The outcome of such an investigation could be settled, at least in principle, with as much exactness as we like.

If we were to adopt such a convention, we should run into the following difficulty, raised by Richard B. Brandt:

Even if one does decide to locate them in the brain, it is possible to hold that the brain-volume contains *both* physical events *and* these other events, and to deny that they are one and the same thing.[4]

Brandt does not give examples, but it is easy to do so. Suppose we set up a magnetic field and then put a physical object into it. Then one and the same volume would contain two different things, a physical object and a magnetic field. Why should we say there are two things there, rather than one, a physical object with a particular magnetic property or in a particular magnetic state? Here we need a further necessary condition for identity, in addition to being in the same place at the same time. The presence of the one must be an (empirically) necessary condition for the presence of the other. In the case of the physical object and the magnetic field it is clear that neither one is an empirically necessary condition for the other; take away one and the other would still remain. In the case of C-states and B-processes we have assumed that investigations will show that you cannot have one without the other. If that turns out to be the case, then the third necessary condition of identity will have been met.

The three conditions for identity so far discussed are jointly sufficient. If all three are met, then B-processes and C-states are identical; if it is likely that all three are met, then it is likely that B-processes and C-states are identical. There is no room for any alternative. If B-processes and C-states did not exist at the same time or did not exist at the same place, then a case could be made for saying that they were functionally dependent but different. But if we assume that it will turn out to be the case that they must exist in the same place at the same time, we should be unreasonable to hold out for some other theory – a Causal theory, a Parallelist theory, or the like.

The crucial question, then, is whether we are free simply to adopt a convention for locating C-states in space. Compare the case of adopting a convention for locating fictional characters in space. Suppose we said that since it makes no sense at present to ask where, for example, Snow White is in physical space right now, we shall adopt a convention for assigning location. For any fictional character, it will be correct to say that it is, was, and always will be located in

[4] Richard B. Brandt, 'Doubts about the Identity Theory', *Dimensions of Mind*, p. 66.

the place where its creator was when he first thought of the character. We could now point to a place and say, 'There is where the fictional character Snow White is.' But it is obvious that this could not be a way of locating an object, but only an elliptical way of saying that this is where his creator was. The reason that this could not be a convention for locating fictional objects in space does not depend upon the particular convention we might choose. Any convention of this sort would be absurd because there is no room in the concept of fictional characters for such a convention. This is because it is self-contradictory to speak of a non-existent thing like a fictional character as having some actual location in physical space. The very meaning of 'fictional character' depends upon the contrast with things that actually do have spatial location. Hence we are not free, in this case, simply to adopt a convention for locating, which we can add to our present rules governing expressions that refer to fictional characters.

In the case of C-states it seems to me that room does exist for the adoption of such a convention. There is nothing in the way we teach the use of C-state expressions that rules out their having spatial location, no direct contrast with things that actually do have spatial location. So we can adopt an additional rule that would allow us to locate C-states in space. This is, of course, to change the meanings of expressions that refer to C-states, to change our concept of C-states. It is a change that is consistent with our present rules and that allows us to keep the rest of the concept intact, but it is still a change in the concept. There is, however, no change in the extension of the terms; everything that is a C-state as it is ordinarily conceived will also be a C-state as the concept has been modified, and vice versa. The only difference is that it will now make sense to ask about the physical location of C-states.

Given this modified concept of C-states, the criteria for *de facto* identity of C-states and B-processes have been met. Those things and just those things referred to by C-state expressions will be referred to by B-process expressions. It would be as unreasonable to hold that the world contains C-states in addition to B-processes as it would be to hold that the world contains featherless bipeds in addition to human beings (assuming the two classes are coextensive) or water in addition to H_2O. Of course it is logically possible that there be disembodied C-states, with no corresponding B-processes. That is to say, an Identity Theory that uses the modified concept of C-states is a genuine empirical hypothesis, like the hypothesis that human beings are featherless bipeds and that water is H_2O.

IV

In this section I wish to discuss the objection that nothing at all would be gained by so altering our concept of C-states that the identity would hold. This objection is referred to by Smart as 'the one I am least confident of having satisfactorily met' (p. 59, foot-note). The objection may be put in the following way. For it to be a factual discovery that C-states and B-states are identical, each must have some feature peculiar to itself by which it may be identified as a C-state or as a B-process; but then are we not at least committed to 'the existence of irreducibly psychic *properties*' (p. 59)?

In trying to deal with this objection, Smart thinks he must show that psychic properties must be *defined* in terms of physical properties. He attempts to define C-states in the following way. He maintains that when a person reports the occurrence of a C-state, say the having of a yellowish-orange after-image,

> ... he is saying something like this: '*There is something going on which is like what is going on when* I have my eyes open, am awake, and there is an orange illuminated in good light in front of me, that is, when I really see an orange' (p. 60).

Thus Smart attempts to represent the special features of first-person present-tense reports as nothing but rather indefinite assertions which, if made definite (although the speaker may not know enough physiology to make them definite himself), would turn out to be ordinary assertions about B-processes.

The difficulty with such a definition is that it leaves no room for the fact that we are sometimes justified in the reports we make about our own C-states although we have no information at all about B-processes, not even indefinite information. How could one report even the minimal something going on unless one noticed something? And since it obviously is the case that we can notice something even when we notice nothing in our nervous system, it obviously is the case that some other feature must be noticed which entitles us to say that something is going on.

In general, it is hopeless to expect to be able to *define* psychic properties in terms of physical properties, and still hold, as Identity Theorists do, that it is a factual discovery that C-states and B-processes are identical. Unless there are special features that allow us independently to identify C-states, we can never be in a position to discover their *de facto* identity with B-processes.

I see no reason why the Identity Theorist should be disconcerted by admitting that psychic properties are different from physical properties. For to say that psychic properties are different from physical properties is simply a way of saying that mentalistic expressions have different meanings and different conditions for ascription from physicalistic expressions. It is a fact about the world that both sets of expressions have application (how could that be denied?), but this is a fact from which the Identity Theory begins, not a fact that destroys it. Furthermore, that psychic and physical properties are different does not in any way imply that they are 'irreducibly' different. To take a classic case, the property of having a certain temperature must be different from the property of having a certain mean kinetic energy, or else it could never have been discovered that they were related in particular ways, ways which we indicate when we say that temperature has been reduced to mean kinetic energy. In general, for one property to be reducible to another, they must be different; something cannot be reducible to itself.

But still one might ask what is to be gained by altering our concept of C-states so as to be able to assert their *de facto* identity with B-processes? It does seem to me that one now does have a simpler conceptual scheme. The traditional Dualistic theories admitted two distinct classes of entities and events, physical entities and physical events on the one hand and mental entities and events on the other. On the Identity Theory there is only one set of entities and events, the physical, and it is just these entities and events which turn out to be what is referred to when people use mentalistic expressions. This is analogous to the discovery that water and steam are not different substances but the same substance in different states. It is perfectly true that not all physical processes will be identical with C-states, only neural processes of a particular sort. And that subset of physical processes will have special features, those which are the logically necessary features of C-states. For example, (1) there will be one and only one person in the world who would know of the existence of a particular C-state even if he lacked any of the grounds that anyone else might have for knowing of the existence of that state, and (2) the one and only privileged person could not fail to know of its existence, if it occurred at all. These are features of C-states and, if C-states turn out to be identical with B-processes, then they will be features of B-processes. Thus the simplification presented by the Identity Theory has its price. One class of physical events will have the familiar and undeniable features of C-states. These features may be, in some sense, reducible to physicalistic features, but they are not thereby eliminated from the scheme of things. Only extra entities are eliminated.

V

The question whether the conceptual revision proposed by Identity Theorists should be accepted or not cannot be determined solely by philosophers. It is in part an empirical question, to be judged in terms of future discoveries in neurology and psychology. Take the similar case of water and H_2O. Imagine the debates that must have raged when it was discovered that water could be replaced by definite proportions of hydrogen and oxygen. Were the water, on the one hand, and the two gases, on the other, merely successive states of some further, underlying thing (cf. Double Aspect theory)? Did the one produce the other (cf. Interaction theories)? Was the one a mere shadowy appearance of the other (cf. Epiphenomenalism)? Was there mere correlation of the one disappearing as the other appeared (cf. Parallelism)? Or was the water *identical* with the combination of the two? The adoption of new uses for such terms as 'element', 'compound', and 'analysis' did not amount merely to trivial solution that simply begged the question in favour of the claim of identity. For it was an empirical discovery that certain substances are 'compounds' of specific 'elements', the discovery that a particular set of terms can be used to represent and describe these substances in such a way as to tie together a large range of phenomena, yield predictions, and furnish explanations. From a knowledge of the chemical constituents and their proportions we can predict and explain many features of the compound – mass, density, spectral patterns, radioactive properties, and frequently much of its physical and chemical behaviour. It is such fruits as these that make plausible the identification of substances with the chemical combination of their constituents.

In the case of the Identity Theory, the linguistic innovation consists in modifying our concept of C-states by giving criteria for the spatial location of C-states. Only future discoveries in neurophysiology can tell us how fruitful this innovation might be. If, for example, we never get beyond the point of having gross, brute correlations between C-states and B-processes, then I can see no advantage in the claim that they are identical. But suppose we can, some day, discover certain physical features which distinguish the physical processes that are identical with C-states from those which are not; suppose we can break down B-processes into structures that correspond to the internal structures of C-states; suppose that detailed theories could be worked out for showing that, given the particular

neural variables, we get one C-state rather than another and we can
infer new C-states from novel configurations of B-processes. If these
developments occur, then, as in the example from chemistry, it would
be unreasonable to hold out against the Identity Theory. For we
would have not merely gross correlations of C-states and B-processes
but precisely the detailed kind of point-for-point correlations that
entitles us in other cases to say that one property, state, or thing has
been reduced to another. The value of thinking of C-states in this
new way, as having location in the brain, would have been shown by
empirical discoveries. But this is not to say that it would have been
an empirical discovery that C-states were located in the brain.

If we were to accept the Identity Theory with its new concept of
C-states, the question would still remain of what the exact relation
is between C-states and B-processes. One possibility, although not
the only one, is that of a macro–micro relation. Even here there
are alternatives. One would be that C-states were composed of
neural components, analogous to the physicist's particles or the
chemist's elements. If it seems strange to think that C-states might
be made up of physical components, remember that even the claim
that water is 'composed' of hydrogen and oxygen or of a swarm
of subatomic particles requires new concepts of composition and
components. A different macro–micro relation might be used, such
that C-states consisted of B-processes without being composed of
them; such would be the case if a field theory of neural behaviour
were adopted. This would be analogous to the claim that a ray of
light consists of wave-motion, that a bolt of lightning consists of
an electrical discharge. A half-way house, here, might be a claim
analogous to the claim that temperature consists of the mean kinetic
energy of the molecules. I suspect that none of these details could
be settled until we had a good deal more information about the
brain.

If someone were to insist on knowing what the relation is between
B-processes and C-states as we conceive them now (in contrast to
how we might, some day, more usefully conceive them), then part
of the answer is that they are not identical, since the spatial criterion
is not met. Another part of the answer is that, if present information
is a reliable guide, they occur simultaneously and are conjoined in
a regular, lawlike way. Another part of the answer consists in seeing
in detail how this case is like and unlike other cases, e.g. two independent mechanisms, two objects interacting in the same system, a
process and its by-products, looking at something from inside of it
and from the outside, etc. I doubt if more than this can be done.

XI The identity of mind and body

James Cornman

'Could mental states be brain processes?' This is the title question of an article by Jerome Shaffer.[1] Before attempting to answer this question we should first consider what kind of question it is. That is, what kind of approach is required in order to arrive at a satisfactory answer? Is it, for example, an empirical question? That is, is arriving at a satisfactory answer an empirical matter? Shaffer seems to think that it is and also that those who hold the Identity Theory, i.e. the theory that mental states are identical with certain physical processes such as brain processes, consider the problem expressed by the question to be a matter of empirical fact. But let us see whether it is or not.

One necessary condition of the identity of mental phenomena with some kind of physical phenomena is that there be, using Feigl's terminology, a one-to-one 'simultaneity-correspondence between the mental and the physical'. However, this one-to-one correspondence need not be between each mental phenomenon and some one physical phenomenon. It might be between each mental phenomenon and some group of physical phenomena or between each of a kind of physical phenomena and some group of mental phenomena. Thus, for example, it might be that each mental phenomenon is in a one-to-one simultaneity-correspondence with some particular group of brain processes. Assuming that we are interested in a version of the Identity Theory that postulates a one-to-one simultaneity-correspondence between mental phenomena and brain processes, how could we discover whether or not the above-mentioned necessary condition has been met? Certainly we should do so by an empirical investigation in which we tried to correlate the different brain processes of persons with the different mental phenomena they described themselves as experiencing. Thus, this much of the question concerning the correctness of the Identity Theory is a matter of empirical fact. But this would decide the issue only with regard to

[1] Paper X.

one necessary condition of the theory's correctness. The rest of the answer is not an empirical matter.

To show this let me point out that there is at least one other proposed solution to the mind–body problem that has as a necessary condition the above one-to-one simultaneity-correspondence. This kind of correspondence is a necessary condition not only of the Identity Theory, but also of Psycho-Physical Parallelism, which is the theory that although mental phenomena are distinct from and causally independent of physical phenomena, there is nevertheless some kind of a one-to-one simultaneity-correspondence between the mental and the physical. Thus one necessary condition of Parallelism is the same kind of one-to-one correspondence that is a necessary condition of the Identity Theory.

Given that the required one-to-one correspondence has been empirically established, what further must we do to decide between the Identity Theory and Parallelism? We exhaust all the empirical means available in deciding upon the truth of the above-mentioned necessary condition. It might for that reason be suggested that this is the perfect place to employ Occam's razor as a means of justifying the Identity Theory. However, aside from the question of when Occam's razor is applicable, there are certain conceptual difficulties involved in the Identity Theory which at least delay the application of the razor.

The central conceptual problem for the Identity Theory arises, I believe, from the fact that mental phenomena seem to have properties inappropriate to physical phenomena, and physical phenomena seem to have properties inappropriate to mental phenomena. However, the particular way in which the problem arises depends upon which version of the Identity Theory is at issue. Shaffer, I believe, holds one species of the materialistic version, i.e. the view that mental phenomena are not only identical with brain processes but are in some important sense reducible to brain processes. J. J. C. Smart, who also holds this view, has considered the objection that raises the problem for the materialistic version. As Smart puts it, the objection grants that 'it may be possible to get out of asserting the existence of irreducibly psychic processes, but not out of asserting the existence of irreducibly psychic *properties*'.[2] Thus, the objection goes, although sensations may be identical with brain processes and thus there would be no irreducibly psychic processes, nevertheless these brain processes would have two quite different sorts of properties, physical and psychic. Thus even assuming, for example,

[2] Paper III, p. 59.

that the sentence 'I see a yellowish-orange after-image' is a report about some brain process, that brain process would have the property of 'being a yellowish-orange after-image'. If this is a property it is certainly a psychic property, that is, a property that lies outside a materialistic framework.

Smart, however, thinks that he has a way of doing away with psychic properties. What he proposes is that, although a sentence such as 'I see a yellowish-orange after-image' is a report about some brain process, it does not, as some others think, attribute some psychic property to the brain process. To show that it does not Smart provides what I take to be a rough translation of the sentence. Thus the adequacy of Smart's claim rests upon the adequacy of translations such as he provides. He claims that when 'a person says "I see a yellowish-orange after-image", he is saying something like this: "*There is something going on which is like what is going on when* I have my eyes open, am awake, and there is an orange illuminated in good light in front of me, that is, when I really see an orange"' (p. 60).

Will this translation solve the problem? Shaffer thinks not. He has two reasons. He says, first,

> The difficulty with such a definition is that it leaves no room for the fact that we are sometimes justified in the reports we make about our own [mental states] although we have no information at all about [physical processes], not even indefinite information (p. 119).

This objection assumes that we can have information about our own mental states without having any information about any physical process. However, this is where it goes wrong. For if, as Smart believes, all mental states are indeed brain processes, then when we have information about mental states we thereby have information about brain processes. We do not have, of course, the information one finds in physiology, but still information, albeit of a different kind, about brain processes.

Shaffer's second objection to Smart's translation is:

> In general, it is hopeless to expect to be able to define psychic properties in terms of physical properties and still hold, as Identity Theorists do, that is a factual discovery that [mental states] and [brain processes] are identical (p. 119).

Shaffer here, I take it, is accusing Smart of holding two inconsistent theses: that the verification of his version of the Identity Theory is an empirical matter, and that psychic properties are definable in terms of physical properties. Surely it is true that psychic properties are not definable in terms of the physiological properties of brain processes, because it is a factual, i.e. empirical, discovery whether or not there is some variety of a one-to-one simultaneity-correspondence between mental phenomena and brain processes. But there is nothing inconsistent in the twofold claim that an empirical discovery is a necessary condition of the justification of the theory that mental phenomena and brain processes are identical, and that psychic properties are definable within a physicalistic framework, *unless* the definitions are in terms of physiological properties of brain processes. However, as Smart states, his translation is not in terms of any physical properties. That is, it attributes neither a psychic nor a physical property to the appropriate brain process because it does not attribute any specified kind of property at all. The sentence as translated merely refers to something going on that is *in some unspecified way* like other things that go on under certain conditions. Thus, if Smart is correct, he can consistently assert both his translation and that the Identity Theory involves an empirical discovery. Thus, I think, Smart can avoid Shaffer's objections.

However, there are objections he cannot avoid. To see this, let us examine his translation of 'I see a yellowish-orange after-image'. Whereas the original sentence, call it P_1, seems to specify in some respect what is going on, the translation, call it M, does not. The consequence of this is that, although P_1 is a sufficient condition of M, it is not a necessary condition, because there is a sentence that implies M but does not imply P_1. Such a sentence is P_2: 'I see a roughly spherical shape'. Thus M does not mean P_1. To avoid this problem we might try to translate P_1 into M', which would refer not merely to an orange but to some n number of things that have only one thing in common, their yellowish-orange colour. Thus, since not all of the n things would be spherical or any other one specific shape, then P_2 would be eliminated. However, we would have a related problem because there is a sentence such as 'I see a coloured after-image' (P_3) which implies M' but does not imply P_1. Thus M' does not mean P_1. I believe that any other emendations of M would fail in a similar manner because the crucial part of M: 'there is something going on', is just too general. Psychic properties cannot be eliminated by this kind of translation, nor, I believe, by any other.

But even if the Identity Theorist is faced with the ineliminability of psychic properties, does he have an insoluble problem, as Smart seems to think? Shaffer thinks not. He claims that the Identity

Theorist should not be 'disconcerted by admitting that psychic properties are different from physical properties' (p. 120). However, I am not sure what his reasons are. Surely, if the Identity Theorist wishes to work within a physicalistic framework as Smart does, there is a problem concerning those psychic properties which at least seems to lie outside a physicalistic framework. And if no translation of psychological expressions that would show them to be within such a framework succeeds, then a materialistic version of the Identity Theory such as Smart's would seem to fail.

However, not all versions of the Identity Theory are materialistic. Neither a Double Aspect version nor an Idealistic version is faced with Smart's problem, and both, so far as I can see, are as compatible with the requirements of science as the Materialistic version is. Have we then the right to conclude that at least some versions of the Identity Theory can be justified by application of Occam's razor? Not yet, I think, because there remains a conceptual problem facing any version of the Identity Theory.

In general we accept the principle of the identity of indiscernibles as the criterion of identity. That is, we say that two non-synonymous names or descriptions refer to the same thing if and only if a predicate is truly predicted of one if and only if it is also truly predicted of the other. Let us apply this to predicates that are relevant to the Identity Theory. For example, we can talk about intense, unbearable, nagging, or throbbing pains. And yellow, dim, fading, or circular after-images. And dogmatic, false, profound, or unconscious beliefs. On the other hand we can also discuss publicly observable, spatially located, swift, irreversible physical processes. Thus if the Identity Theory is correct, it seems that we should sometimes be able to say truthfully that physical processes such as brain processes are dim or fading or nagging or false, and that mental phenomena such as after-images are publicly observable or physical or spatially located or swift.

However, there surely is some doubt about whether these expressions can be truthfully used. They seem to be in some sense meaningless. Utilising Gilbert Ryle's concept of a category mistake, we can say that the above expressions are meaningless in the sense that they commit a category mistake; i.e. in forming these expressions we have predicated predicates, appropriate to one logical category, of expressions that belong to a different logical category. This is surely a conceptual mistake. Consequently, because what would appear to be a necessary condition of the truth of the Identity Theory involves a category mistake, the Identity Theory, unlike the competing dualistic theories, seems to be in serious conceptual difficulty. Thus we cannot, it would seem, arrive at the Identity Theory via Occam's razor. Shaffer suggests that we need only adopt a new rule of language, one which prescribes that a mental state is 'located in that place where its corresponding [brain] process is located (p. 116). If this one new rule were adopted, Shaffer believes that the identity of mental states and brain processes could then be empirically established, because the criterion of identity, he claims, is that brain processes and neutral states be identical if and only if they exist at the same time and same place, and each is an empirically necessary condition for the presence of the other. Given the new rule, and since the other two conditions of identity can be empirically established, the Identity Theory can be either verified or falsified empirically.

But if, as assumed above, the identity of indiscernibles is the ultimate criterion of identity, then Shaffer would seem to have no right to adopt a convention that would make it possible for brain processes and mental states to be identical, because if, as argued above, each has properties not truly attributable to the other, then, by Leibniz's principle, they are not identical. The conclusion, then, is that the adoption of merely this one rule, as Shaffer suggests, is surely not enough.

But, perhaps, to avoid this problem we could adopt rules that would eliminate all the category mistakes involved in the Identity Theory. This would surely be legitimate if, as Smart seems to think, all that is required is that we adopt new rules for the application of the appropriate expressions without changing the present rules (p. 62). That is, if the situation is such that there are no rules for the application of these expressions which in any way forbid the required addition, then no change in existing rules is needed. However, if the formation of the relevant expressions involves category mistakes – a statement which, to be sure, has been no more than intuitively justified – then what is needed is not merely the addition of new rules but the change of old ones, because category mistakes are violations of rules for application of expressions. And this kind of conceptual change in order to justify a philosophical theory is surely not legitimate.

Have we then reached the point at which we must conclude that the Identity Theory, no matter which version, is doomed to failure because of insoluble conceptual difficulties? There is, I think, one possible way to avoid this conclusion. The above attempts to save the Identity Theory fail because they proceed on the assumption that the theory is mistaken if it fails to meet the requirements of the principle of the identity of indiscernibles. However, this assumption may not be warranted. An equivalent way to express this principle is that, for any x and y, x and y are *not* identical if and only if some property ϕ is such that 'ϕx' is true and 'ϕy' is false, or, conversely, 'ϕx' is false and 'ϕy' is true. From this we can see that one necessary condition of applying this principle to some x and y is that both 'ϕx' and 'ϕy' have a truth-value. But this necessary condition cannot be met if either 'ϕx' or 'ϕy' involves a category mistake. In such cases, then, the principle does not apply. Another way to show this is that if we apply this principle in such a case, then whatever the expressions in question refer to would fail to be identical and also fail to be not identical, which is surely mistaken. Because the principle does not apply in such cases, it is at least possible that if two terms are in different logical categories they both refer to the same thing.

To show that this kind of identity, which I shall call 'cross-category identity', is not unusual, let me cite what seems to be a widely accepted case of cross-category identity. We talk of the temperature of a gas as being identical with the mean kinetic energy of the gas molecules. But although we can say that the temperature of a certain gas is 80° centigrade, it is surely in some sense a mistake to say that the mean kinetic energy of the gas molecules is 80° centigrade. If this mistake is what I have called a category mistake, then this is a case of cross-category identity. If it is also a category mistake to talk of a fading or dim brain process, then we have some grounds for thinking that the identity of mind and body would be a cross-category identity, and, therefore, that the Identity Theory need not involve conceptual difficulties. The next project, then, for an Identity Theorist might well be to develop further the concept of a category and to work out further in what cases the application of the concept of cross-category identity is justified.

XII Shaffer on the identity of mental states and brain processes

Robert Coburn

In 'Could mental states be brain processes?' (Paper X) Jerome Shaffer undertakes to examine a much-discussed view of the relation between 'mental states' or 'states of consciousness' and brain processes. According to this view – roughly speaking – whether or not expressions that refer to mental states pick out the same 'things' as do expressions that refer to brain processes is a more or less straightforward empirical question, a question which can be decided by, and only by, further scientific (especially neurophysiological) research. In the course of his examination of this view, Shaffer considers a number of difficulties which arise in connection with it, and having done so, he concludes that though some of these difficulties are more serious than others, none of them is really insurmountable. Unfortunately, his treatment of what he takes to be the central difficulty with the view in question is, I believe, seriously defective, and my purpose in the present note is to indicate wherein, in my judgement, its defects lie.

The difficulty to which I refer arises, according to Shaffer, from the following two facts (1) that 'a necessary condition for saying that something is identical with some particular physical object, state, or process [is] that the thing be located in the place where the particular physical object, state, or process is' (pp. 115–16, and (2) that 'we have no rules in our language either for asserting that C-states [i.e. mental states] have a particular location or for denying that they have a particular location' (p. 116). Indeed, Shaffer insists that the difficulty these facts engender renders the theory that mental states *are* identical with brain processes *a priori* false. However, the difficulty can nonetheless be surmounted by a certain manœuvre, and thus a slightly modified version of the so-called 'Identity Theory' rendered empirical and hence possibly true. The manœuvre is simply to adopt certain 'spatial conventions' that would enable us to decide questions concerning the locations in physical space of items like A's experience of pain in his left calf, the condition B is in when he can be said to be having an after-image, C's 'state of being aware of a thought' (p. 115), etc – in short, mental states in general. Accordingly, the modified Identity Theory which Shaffer holds to express a straightforward empirical possibility is the theory that, as it might be put, 'mental states' rather than mental states are identical with brain processes, where the scare-quotes serve to indicate that the expressions which in ordinary speech refer to mental states are now understood to be governed by 'spatial conventions', and hence that the concept of a mental state that finds expression in the modified theory is slightly different from the concept expressed in (current) everyday discourse.

Now it might be thought from what I have so far said that the main defect in Shaffer's treatment of the difficulty in question lies in his simply having begged the question as to the possibility of making the manœuvre indicated. In fact, however, this question is not begged. By way of defending the possibility of this manœuvre, Shaffer draws a contrast between two quite different types of entity: mental states and fictional characters. The latter, he maintains, are clearly the sort of thing we could not, by the adoption of certain conventions, decide to locate in physical space. This is so because, as he says, 'there is no room in the concept of fictional characters' (p. 118) for a spatial convention; and there is 'no room' because 'it is self-contradictory to speak of a non-existent thing like a fictional character as having some actual location in physical space' (p. 118). In the case of mental states, by contrast, it is perfectly possible to adopt such conventions because their adoption is plainly consistent with the rules that currently govern expressions referring to such states. The addition of such rules will, he concedes, alter our concepts of mental states; but they will alter them only apparently by *adding* something to these concepts inasmuch as the alteration of such a concept effected by the adoption of a spatial convention 'allows us to keep the rest of the concept intact' (p. 118).

This defence of the possibility of the manœuvre under consideration, however, seems to me inadequate, and my objections to Shaffer's treatment of the difficulty in question spring essentially from this source. The first of these objections is as follows. Let us suppose that certain neural events are discovered to be (causally) necessary and sufficient conditions for the occurrence of such and such a type of pain experience. And let us further suppose that the convention is adopted of 'locating' such experiences at the point(s)

in the brain where these neural events take place. Now let us ask
what consequences such a convention would carry. One such consequence would be, I submit, that pain experiences of the type in
question would be rendered 'public' entities in the sense that no
person would be in any better position essentially than any other
for determining with certainty whether such an experience was
occurring. This is so because the idea that something should be going
on in such and such a place and yet that one person should occupy
an intrinsically privileged epistemological position *vis-à-vis* that
occurrence is prima facie absurd. But if 'publicising' all mental states
in the sense indicated is a consequence of adopting spatial conventions for the expressions that refer to such states, surely it is false
that adopting such conventions is consistent with the rules which
govern such expressions under current semantic conditions, and *a
fortiori* false that the sort of conceptual changes Shaffer insists are
necessary to keep the Identity Theory from lapsing into *a priori*
falsehood would leave our mental concepts essentially intact. For
surely it is an essential feature of e.g. the language of pain that pain
experiences are not 'public' in the above sense, but rather are such
that if a person says (denies) he is having a pain experience, then –
provided he is sincere and has got the right words – he is (isn't)
in pain.

My second objection to Shaffer's treatment of the difficulty in
question turns upon the fact that a necessary condition for the
applicability of at least many mental concepts is the presence of
certain 'surroundings' – behavioural or otherwise. Consider the concept of remembering, for example. In its primary, entailment sense,
the concept is inapplicable unless the event (say) allegedly remembered took place. Again, a person cannot – at least under ordinary
conditions – be said to feel depressed without exhibiting some
depressive behaviour. Nor, of course, can a person intend to write a
cheque for $100 in the absence of a number of social institutions.
Now the objection to which considerations like these give rise is
simply this. If Shaffer intends the expression 'mental states' to cover
such things as 'states of remembering', 'states of intending', etc.,
then once again it would seem that any 'spatial conventions' adoption of which would render it logically possible to identify mental
states with brain processes will be inconsistent with the rules that
currently govern expressions referring to such states. For how could
an experience of (say) remembering such and such events be thought
of as located in the brain unless such an experience were also conceived as possible independently of any particular surrounding cir-

cumstances, and as detectable – at least in principle – independently of any knowledge of such surrounding circumstances?

It should be said that this latter objection may very well be inapplicable when put in this way. For, as I have suggested by stating the objection hypothetically, Shaffer may not intend the expression 'mental states' to cover as wide a ground as might seem necessary for the objection to take hold. However, since he nowhere explicitly indicates any restrictions on the applicability of the phrase – he explains his use of it only by enumerating several cases which fall under it (see p. 113) – the objection seems hardly unfair. But in any case, if the central point of the objection is well taken, then even were Shaffer to restrict mental states to feelings of pain, experiences of after-images, and the like, thereby excluding from consideration ostensibly less thoroughly 'internal' items, it would seem necessary for him to refute the Wittgensteinian contention that even such things as pains are logically connected with behaviour of various sorts. For apart from such a refutation, the objection on a slightly different formulation could still be argued, and argued persuasively, to hold.

It might be thought, of course, that Shaffer could concede both objections without serious harm to his position. After all, it might be said, all that my objections show at best is that the conceptual changes involved in the adoption of 'spatial conventions' to govern expressions referring to mental states are more far-reaching than Shaffer realises. But why should this fact be thought devastating to the stand Shaffer takes *vis-à-vis* the Identity Theory? The answer to this reply, however, is not far to seek. Once the character of the conceptual changes involved is seen, the idea of identifying mental states conceived as localisable items with brain processes loses much of its fascination and point. For even were neurophysiology to develop in the ways Identity Theorists say would justify us in identifying 'mental states' with brain processes, there would still exist unreduced experiences of pain e.g. in the ordinary sense of these words; hence no significant ontological simplification would be effected by the identification to which such developments would allegedly point.

XIII Mental events and the brain

Jerome Shaffer

When J. J. C. Smart propounded his version of the Identity Theory,[1] he confessed that he found the most powerful objection to his theory to be as follows. Even if we can establish the *de facto* identity of mental events and neural events, do we not still have to admit the existence of mental features (to pin down one side of the *de facto* identity)? Are we not then still committed to something irreducibly mental? If so, we have the 'nomological danglers' which are incompatible with the thoroughgoing materialism Smart wishes to establish. Smart's attempt to deal with this objection has been criticised by me[2] and by others,[3] and Smart has replied to some of these criticisms.[4] I wish to reconsider this objection to Smart's theory, especially in the light of some recent criticisms[5] of my own paper.

On the Identity Theory, the having of an after-image, the feeling of a pain, or the occurrence of a thought is claimed to be identical, as a matter of empirical fact, with some event occurring in the brain. The two occurrences are held to be identical in the same sense that a flash of lightning is held to be identical with a particular sort of electrical discharge, i.e. not that the terms referring to them are synonymous but that the terms happen to pick out, refer to, or denote one and the same event.

Now there are serious problems concerning whether mental and brain events *could* be identical. I shall return to this issue at the end of this discussion. But assuming it could be shown that they are identical, there still is a problem here for Smart's materialism. For if

[1] Paper III.
[2] See Paper X.
[3] See Papers VI, VIII and XI; also George Pitcher, 'Sensations and Brain Processes: A Reply to Professor Smart', *Australasian Journal of Philosophy*, xxxviii (1960) pp. 150–7.
[4] See Papers VII and IX; also 'Sensations and Brain Processes: A Rejoinder to Dr Pitcher and Mr Joske', *Australasian Journal of Philosophy*, xxxviii (1960) pp. 252–4.
[5] Papers XI and XII.

it is an *empirical* identity, then how we identify mental events will have to be different from how we identify brain events; if they were identified in the same way, then they would not be logically independent. Now suppose we identified mental events by noticing the occurrence of some peculiarly *mental feature*. Then we would still be left with some irreducibly non-physical aspects, and this Smart would find objectionable.

So the new task, for Smart, is to give some account, in non-mentalistic terms, of what we report when we report the having of a thought or after-image or pain. According to Smart, all such reports are of the following form: there is now occurring an internal process, x, such that x is like what goes on when a particular physical stimulus affects me. Thus to report an orange after-image is to report 'something going on which is like what is going on when I have my eyes open, am awake, and there is an orange illuminated in good light in front of me, that is, when I really see an orange'.[6] In this definition there appear only physicalistic terms and logical terms; there are no peculiarly mental terms in it. But there are no terms describing brain events either. So it can turn out to be the case that the 'something going on' which is reported is factually identical with a particular event. Whatever will be found to be common to such situations will be, of course, for science to determine, if it can; that the common internal process is a brain process is merely an empirical conjecture. This is the way Smart replies to the charge that he is still left with an irreducibly mental feature.[7]

At the heart, then, of Smart's Identity Theory is the suggestion that mental events are definable as the concomitants or products of certain physical stimulus conditions or anything that is just like those concomitants or products. Now there are some very serious difficulties in this view. In the first place, I am inclined to think the definition could not be completed. Indefinitely many factors would be relevant in stating the causally sufficient conditions for, say, seeing an orange, to use the example of the after-image cited above. Any one of these could prevent the final brain event from occurring. We would have to mention 'normal' conditions and 'normal' subjects, or speak of 'all other things being equal', and that would be to admit that we could not actually complete the translation. Secondly, even if the translation could be completed in theory, it would be so filled with complicated assertions about propagation of energy, media,

[6] P. 60, above.

[7] This is clearly pointed out in Cornman's paper (p. 126, above) as well as in some recent replies of Smart (cited above).

nerves, etc., that it is unbelievable that such things would be part of what the ordinary man *means* when he reports a mental event (or even what the neurophysiologist means).

What leads Smart to think that mental events can be defined in terms of the stimulus conditions that are their causes? His reason is that 'sensation talk must be learned by reference to some environmental stimulus situation or another.'[8] But while this latter claim seems sensible enough, it does not follow that *what* is learned in some environmental stimulus situation is definable in terms of that environment stimulus situation. We might learn what the expression 'seeing stars' means by being hit on the head, but to know how the expression is learned is not to know the meaning; a blind man might know how the meaning of the expression is learned, but still not know the meaning. Smart's purported analyses of the meanings of mental terms are, at best, instructions for coming to learn the meanings of these terms, rules for the obtaining of examples to be used in ostensive definitions.

I have shown that Smart's account of the meaning of reports of sensations is defective. I now wish to give a general argument why no such materialistic manoeuvring can succeed, showing that we cannot avoid admitting at the least the existence of *non-physical properties or features*, even if we give up non-physical *events* as a different class from physical *events*.

Let us take the case where a person reports the having of some mental event, the having of an after-image, a thought, or a sensation of pain. Now such a person has surely noticed that *something* has occurred, and he has surely noticed that this something has *some* features (or how could he report it was an after-image rather than a sensation of pain?). Now it seems to me obvious that, in many cases at least, the person does not notice any *physical* features – he does not notice that his brain is in some particular state, nor does he notice any external physical stimulus, nor any physical event between the stimulus and the neurological response. Yet he does notice *some* feature. Hence he must notice something other than a physical feature. The noticing of some non-physical feature is the only way to explain how anything is noticed at all.

In my earlier discussion of Smart's views (Paper X), I had put this point ambiguously by saying that we could have information about our own mental events without having information about our physical events. Cornman claims that I beg the question here against the Identity Theory: he says, 'If, as Smart believes, all mental states

8 P. 108, above.

are indeed brain processes, then when we have information about· mental states we thereby have information about brain processes' (p. 125). I think Cornman is right here. That is why I now wish to put the point in terms of *noticing*. I may have noticed a person at a party, but from the fact that the person turns out to be the best-dressed woman in America it does not follow that I noticed this feature of the person. Similarly, from the fact that the event I notice turns out to be a brain event (if the Identity Theory is correct) it does not follow that I noticed a neurological feature, nor a physical feature of any sort. Hence when I claim that a person may notice the occurrence of a mental event without noticing the occurrence of anything physical, I cannot be accused of begging the question against the Identity Theory.

If my argument is correct, Smart must conclude that when a person reports the having of some mental event, the person must have noticed the occurrence of some non-physical feature. In some of Smart's recent replies, he suggests two ways he might try to avoid this conclusion. (1) He construes the reporter of a mental event to be noticing a similarity between two brain events, but says that the person may not notice the respect in which the events are similar.[9] My point is that it is most implausible to think that, at least in most cases of reporting mental events, the person notices anything at all about his brain. (2) He sometimes hints that the report of a mental event is merely a behavioural response and therefore not a case of noticing at all. Thus, at one point, in discussing how a person might report a similarity without being able to say in what respect they are similar, Smart says, 'Thinking cybernetically it is indeed easier to envisage the nervous system as being able to react to likenesses of its internal processes without being able to issue descriptions of these likenesses.'[10] And at another point, in trying to describe the difference between those brain events which are identical with mental events and those which are not, he says, 'We can distinguish the ones which are sensations as those which can in suitable circumstances be the specific causal conditions of those behaviour reactions which are sensation reports.'[11] Although he admits to being 'very receptive' to this view of the report as a mere expression or reaction, he cannot accept it.[12] And surely he is right in rejecting it, for such a view cannot account for the obvious fact that 'I now have an

---

[9] P. 61, above; *Australasian Journal of Philosophy*, xxxviii (1960) p. 253.
[10] *Australasian Journal of Philosophy*, xxxviii (1960) p. 253.
[11] P. 94, above.   [12] P. 55, above.

orange after-image' can be used to make true or false statements
and, therefore, can be used to make a genuine report.

If the above remarks are sound, then we must admit, at the
very least, the existence of non-physical properties or non-physical
features. Are they 'irreducibly different' from physical properties,
the 'nomological danglers' that Smart is so fearful of? Not necessarily. Suppose we are able to discover psychological laws that govern
mental phenomena. And suppose we are able to deduce these and
other psychological laws from neurophysiological laws, via the
empirically determined correspondences of the mental and neural.
Furthermore, suppose we are able to predict the occurrence of
further mental states not included in our original empirically determined correspondences on the basis of the occurrence of neural
states. Will we not then be in a position to give a complete explanation of psychological phenomena and psychological laws in terms
of the physical? And if we now adopt conventions that will allow
us to speak of mental events as having location in the brain, then
we will indeed have shown that psychology is reducible to physiology
and the mental reducible to the physical. The properties would still
be different properties, but they would no longer be *irreducibly*
different.[13]

So far in this discussion I have assumed it could turn out that
mental events and brain events are identical. I wish to consider this
assumption now with respect to a recent criticism that has been
made by Coburn (Paper XII). I had argued that the Identity Theory
must be rejected on *a priori* grounds. If mental and brain events
were identical, they would have to occur in the same place. But it
makes no sense to say of some mental event, a thought for example,
that it occurred in some particular part of the brain. Hence the
identity cannot hold. However, I further suggested that we could
adopt a convention for the locating of mental events in the brain
which would rule out this *a priori* objection. The consequence of
adopting this convention would be to change our concept of a mental
event, but, I claimed, there was nothing in our present concept that
ruled out the adoption of such a convention.

Coburn argues that such a convention could not be adopted. If we
take mental events to be locatable in space, then they would be
' "public" entities in the sense that no person would be in any better
position essentially than any other for determining with certainty

[13] This sort of empirical reduction is discussed at length by Ernest Nagel
in *The Structure of Science* (New York 1961) chs 11 and 12; cf. esp.
p. 366.

whether such an experience was occurring' (p. 132). If Coburn is right in saying that mental events would then become '*public*' in this sense, I would agree that a convention for locating them in space could not be adopted. But why should one think that they would become 'public'? Coburn's reason is that 'the idea that something should be going on in such and such a place and yet that one person should occupy an intrinsically privileged epistemological position *vis-à-vis* that occurrence is prima facie absurd' (p. 132). But is that true? Mental events can occur at such and such a *time* and still be private. Why is *temporal* location possible but not *spatial* location? I see no absurdity in adopting such a convention.

As I pointed out in the paper Coburn discusses (p. 120), mental events will have certain public aspects if we accept the Identity Theory. Brain events are public events, and if mental events are identical with them then there will be a respect in which mental events are public too. And conversely, of course, there will be a respect in which brain events are private. That is to say, there will be this class of events which will be known to occur either on the basis of neurological observations or by introspection. There will still be privileged access to these events, but there will also be public access to them. The event I know to have occurred on the basis of introspection will turn out to be one and the same as the event you know to have occurred by neurological observation. This is possible because one and the same event will have both physical and non-physical features. Therefore there will be physiological criteria for its occurring; in addition the person concerned will be in a position to report its occurrence without appeal to these physiological criteria.

But suppose there is a conflict between neurological observation and introspection? Then we will have an *empirical* refutation of the Identity Theory.[14]

[14] Cf. Smart, p. 107, above.

XIV Comment: 'Mental events and the brain'

Paul Feyerabend

Shaffer's note (Paper XIII) and the preceding discussion to which it refers show very clearly the dilemma of any identity hypothesis concerning mental events and brain processes. Such hypotheses are usually put forth by physiologically inclined thinkers who want also to be empiricists. Being physiologically inclined, they want to assert the *material* character of mental processes. Being empiricists, they want their assertion to be a testable statement about *mental* processes. They try to combine the two tendencies in an empirical statement of the form:

X is a mental process of kind $A \equiv$
$$X \text{ is a central process of kind } \alpha \quad \text{(H)}$$

But this hypothesis backfires. It not only implies, as it is intended to imply, that mental events have physical features; it also seems to imply (if read from the right to the left) that some physical events, viz. central processes, have non-physical features. It thereby replaces a dualism of events by a dualism of features. Moreover, this consequence seems to be the result of the way in which the physiologist has *formulated* his thesis. Even if he is a convinced monist he seems to be forced, by the very content of his thesis of monism, to acknowledge the correctness of a *dualistic* point of view.

For a dualist this predicament is proof of the untenability of monism. But surely he is too rash in drawing this conclusion! H implies dualism. Hence, dualism will be true *provided* H is true. However, if *monism* is correct, then H is false: there are then *no* mental processes in the usual (non-materialistic) sense. This shows that the discussion of the content of H regarded as an empirical hypothesis is not at all sufficient for deciding the issue between monism and dualism. It also shows *that the monist misstates his case when defending* H.

The proper procedure for him to adopt is to develop his theory without any recourse to existent terminology. If he wants to use H at all, he ought to use it for *redefining* 'mental process' (if he intends to perpetuate ancient terminology, that is). The empirical character of his theory is not endangered thereby. After all, a physiological theory of epilepsy does not become an empty tautology on account of the fact that it does not make use of the phrase – or of the notion – 'possessed by the devil', 'devil' here occurring in its *theological* sense. There are enough independent predictions available, many more predictions in fact than the mentalist could ever provide – or would even be willing to provide (think only of the tremendous field of the physiology of perception).

However, so it is usually objected, unless a connection is established with previous language, we do not know what we are talking about, and we are therefore not able to formulate our observational results. This objection assumes that the terms of a general point of view and of a corresponding language can obtain meaning only by being related to the terms of some other point of view that is familiar and known by all. Now if that is indeed the case, then how did the latter point of view and the latter language ever obtain its familiarity? And if it could obtain its familiarity without help 'from outside', as it obviously did, then there is no reason to assume that a different point of view cannot do equally well. (Besides, we learn the ordinary idiom when we are small children; is it assumed that a grown-up physiologist will be incapable of doing what a small child does quite well?) Moreover, observational results always have to be formulated with respect to a certain background of theory (with respect to a certain language-game, to use more fashionable terminology). There is no reason why physiology should not by itself be capable of forming such a background. We have to conclude, then, that the reasonableness – and the success – of a purely physiological approach to human beings is not at all dependent on the outcome of an analysis of H.

'Bridge-laws' such as H play a most important role within the current theory of explanation and reduction. If our comments above are correct, then it follows that these theories are inadequate as measures of the success of theory construction.

XV Materialism and the mind–body problem

Paul Feyerabend

This paper has a twofold purpose. First, it defends materialism against a certain type of attack which seems to be based upon a truism but which is nevertheless completely off the mark. And secondly it intends to put philosophy in its proper place. It occurs only too often that attempts to arrive at a coherent picture of the world are held up by philosophical bickering and are perhaps even given up before they can show their merits. It seems to me that those who originate such attempts ought to be a little less afraid of difficulties; that they ought to look through the arguments which are presented against them; and that they ought to recognise their irrelevance. Having disregarded irrelevant objections they ought then to proceed to the much more rewarding task of developing their point of view *in detail,* to examine its fruitfulness and thereby to get fresh insight, not only into some generalities, but into very concrete and detailed processes. To encourage such development from the abstract to the concrete, to contribute to the invention of further ideas, this is the proper task of a philosophy which aspires to be more than a hindrance to progress.

The crudest form of materialism will be taken as the basis of argument. If *it* can successfully evade the objections of some philosophers, then a more refined doctrine will be even less troubled.

Materialism, as it will be discussed here, assumes that the only entities existing in the world are atoms, aggregates of atoms and that the only properties and relations are the properties of, and the relations between such aggregates. A simple atomism such as the theory of Democritus will be sufficient for our purpose. The refinements of the kinetic theory, or of the quantum theory, are outside the domain of discussion. And the question is: Will such a cosmology give a correct account of human beings?

The following reason is put forth why this question must be answered in the negative: human beings, apart from being material, have *experiences*; they *think*; they *feel* pain; etc., etc. These processes cannot be analysed in a materialistic fashion. Hence, a materialistic psychology is bound to fail.

The most decisive part of this argument consists in the assertion that experiences, thoughts, etc., are not material processes. It is customary to support this assertion in the following manner.

There are statements which can be made about pains, thoughts, etc., which cannot be made about material processes; and there are other statements which can be made about material processes but which cannot be made about pains, thoughts, etc. This impossibility exists because the attempt to form such statements would lead to results which are either *false*, or else to results which are *meaningless*.

Let us consider meaninglessness first. Whether or not a statement is meaningful depends on the grammatical rules guiding the corresponding sentence. The argument appeals to such rules. It points out that the materialist, in stating his thesis, is violating them. Note that the particular *words* he uses are of no relevance here. Whatever the *words* employed by him, the resulting *system of rules* would have a structure incompatible with the structure of the idiom in which we usually describe pains and thoughts. This incompatibility is taken to refute the materialist.

It is evident that this argument is incomplete. An incompatibility between the materialistic language and the rules implicit in some other idiom will criticise the former only if the latter can be shown to possess certain advantages. Nor is it sufficient to point out that the idiom on which the comparison is based is in *common use*. This is an irrelevant historical accident. Is it really believed that a vigorous propaganda campaign which makes everyone speak the materialistic language will turn materialism into a correct doctrine? The choice of the language that is supposed to be the basis of criticism must be supported by better reasons.

As far as I am aware there is only one further reason that has been offered: it is the *practical success* of ordinary English which makes it a safe basis for argument. 'Our common stock of words' writes J. L. Austin ('A Plea for Excuses') 'embodies all the distinctions men have found worth drawing, and the connections they have found worth marking, in the lifetime of many generations: these surely are likely to be more numerous, more sound, since they have stood up to the long test of the survival of the fittest, and more subtle . . . than any that you or I are likely to think up . . .'[1] This reason is

[1] *Proceedings of the Aristotelian Society*, 1956–7. .Article reprinted in *Philosophical Papers*, ed. Urmson and Warnock (Oxford 1961) p. 130.

very similar to, and almost identical with, a certain point of view in the philosophy of science. Ever since Newton it has been assumed that a theory which is confirmed to a very high degree is to be preferred to more tentative general ideas and it has been, and still is, believed that such general ideas must be removed in order not to hinder the course of factual discovery. 'For if the possibility of hypotheses', writes Newton (reply to a letter by P. Pardies), 'is to be the test of truth and reality of things, I see not how certainty can be obtained in any science; since numerous hypotheses may be devised, which shall seem to overcome new difficulties.'[2] I mention this parallel in order to show that philosophical points of view which prima facie seem to bear the stamp of revolutionary discoveries, especially to those who are not too well acquainted with the history of ideas, may in the end turn out to be nothing but uncritical repetitions of age-old prejudices. However, it must also be emphasised, in all fairness to the scientists, that the parallel does not go very far. Scientific theories are constructed in such a way that they can be *tested*. Every application of the theory is at the same time a most sensitive investigation of its validity. This being the case there is indeed some reason to trust a theory that has been in use for a considerable time and to look with suspicion at new and vague ideas. The suspicion is mistaken, of course, as I shall try to point out presently. Still, it is not completely foolish to have such an attitude. At least prima facie there seems to be a grain of reason in it.

The situation is very different with 'common idioms'. First of all, such idioms are adapted not to *facts*, but to *beliefs*. If these beliefs are widely accepted; if they are intimately connected with the fears and the hopes of the community in which they occur; if they are defended, and reinforced with the help of powerful institutions; if one's whole life is somehow carried out in accordance with them – then the language representing them will be regarded as most successful. At the same time it is clear that the question of the truth of the beliefs has not been touched.

The second reason why the success of a 'common' idiom is not at all on the same level as is the success of a scientific theory lies in the fact that the use of such an idiom, *even in concrete observational situations*, can hardly ever be regarded as a *test*. There is no attempt, as there is in the sciences, to conquer new fields and to try the theory in them. And even on familiar ground one can never be sure whether certain features of the descriptive statements used are *confronted*

---

[2] *Isaac Newton's Papers and Letters on Natural Philosophy*, ed. I. B. Cohen (Cambridge 1958) p. 106.

with facts, and are thereby *examined*; or whether they do not simply function as *accompanying noises*. Some more recent analyses concerning the nature of facts seem to show that the latter is the case. It is clear that the argument from success is then inapplicable.

Assume thirdly – and now I am well aware that I am arguing contrary to fact – that the idiom to which reference is made in the above argument *is* used in a testable fashion and that the parallel, alluded to above, with scientific method is a legitimate one. Is it *then* possible to reject materialism by reference to the success of a non-materialistic language?

The answer is NO and the reason, which I have explained in detail in my 'Explanation, Reduction, and Empiricism' (in vol. III of the *Minnesota Studies in the Philosophy of Science*)[3] as well as in 'Problems of Empiricism' (in vol. II of the *Pittsburgh Studies in the Philosophy of Science*),[4] is as follows: in order to discuss the weaknesses of an all-pervasive system of thought such as is expressed by the 'common' idiom, it is not sufficient to compare it with 'the facts'. Many such facts are formulated in terms of the idiom and therefore already prejudiced in its favour. Also there are many facts which are inaccessible, *for empirical reasons*, to a person speaking a certain idiom and which become accessible only if a different idiom is introduced. This being the case, the construction of alternative points of view and of alternative languages which radically differ from the established usage, far from precipitating confusion, *is a necessary part of the examination of this usage* and must be carried out *before* a final judgement can be made. More concretely: if you want to find out whether there *are* pains, thoughts, feelings in the sense indicated by the common usage of these words, then you must become (among other things) a materialist. Trying to eliminate materialism by reference to the common idiom, therefore, means putting the cart before the horse.

The argument presented so far has some further features which are in need of criticism. Let us take it for granted that incompatibility with ordinary (or other) usage and the meaninglessness arising from it is a sufficient reason for eliminating a point of view. Then it must still be made clear that while the grammar of the *primitive terms* of the point of view may be incompatible with accepted usage, the grammar of the *defined terms* need not be so incompatible. The same applies to the 'grain' of both: it has sometimes been objected that a sensation is a very simple thing, whereas a collection of atoms

[3] (Minneapolis 1962).　　　　[4] (Pittsburgh 1963).

has a much more complex structure (it is 'spotty'). This is correct. But there are still *properties* of such collections which do not participate in their 'grain'. The density of a fluid is an example. The fluid itself has the same 'grain' as a heap of atoms. The density has not. It ceases to be applicable in domains where the fine structure of the fluid becomes apparent. There are infinitely many other properties of this kind. The defender of the customary point of view has therefore much too simple an idea of the capabilities of materialism. He overlooks that materialism might even be able to provide him with the synonyms he wants; he overlooks that the materialistic doctrine might be able to satisfy his (*irrelevant*) demand for at least partial agreement of grammar.

While the argument from meaninglessness is wholly based upon language, the argument from falsity is not. That a thought cannot be a material process is, so it is believed, established *by observation*. It is by observation that we discover the difference between the one and the other and refute materialism. We now turn to an examination of this argument.

To start with we must admit that the difference does exist. Introspection does indicate, in a most decisive fashion, that my present thought of Aldebaran is not localised whereas Aldebaran is localised; that this thought has no colour whereas Aldebaran has a very definite colour; that this thought has no parts whereas Aldebaran consists of many parts exhibiting different physical properties. Is this character of the introspective result proof to the effect that thoughts cannot be material?

The answer is NO and the argument is the truism that what *appears to be* different does not need to *be* different. Is not the seen table very different from the felt table? Is not the heard sound very different from its mechanical manifestations (Chladni's figures; Kundt's tube, etc., etc.)? And if despite this difference of appearance we are allowed to make an identification, postulating an object in the outer world (the physical table, the physical sound), then why should the observed difference between a thought and the impression of a brain prevent us from making another identification, postulating this time an object in the inner (material) world, viz. a brain process? It is of course quite possible that such a postulate will run into trouble and that it will be refuted by independent tests (just as the earlier identification of comets with atmospheric phenomena was refuted by independent tests). The point is that the prima facie observed difference between thoughts and the appearance of brain processes does *not* constitute such trouble. It is also correct that a language which is based upon the assumption that the identification has already been carried out would differ significantly from ordinary English. But this fact can be used as an argument against the identification only *after* it has been shown that the new language is *inferior* to ordinary English. And such disproof should be based upon the *fully* developed materialistic idiom and *not* on the bits and pieces of materialese which are available to the philosophers of today. It took a considerable time for ordinary English to reach its present stage of complexity and sophistication. The materialistic philosopher must be given *at least* as much time. As a matter of fact he will need more time as he intends to develop a language which is fully testable, which gives a coherent account of the most familiar facts about human beings *as well as* of thousands more recondite facts which have been unearthed by the physiologists. I also admit that there are people for whom even the reality of the external world and the identifications leading to it constitute a grave problem. My answer is that I do not address *them*, but that I presuppose a minimum of reason in my readers; I assume they are realists. And assuming this I try to point out that their realism need not be restricted to processes outside their skin – unless of course one already *presupposes* what is to be established by the argument, that things inside the skin are very different from what goes on outside. Considering all this I conclude that the argument from observation is invalid.

It is quite entertaining to speculate about some results of an identification of what is observed by introspection with brain processes. Observation of micro-processes in the brain is a notoriously difficult affair. Only very rarely is it possible to investigate them in the living organism. Observation of dead tissue, on the other hand, is applied to a structure that may differ significantly from the living brain. To solve the problems arising from this apparent inaccessibility of processes in the living brain we need only realise that the living brain *is already connected with a most sensitive instrument* – the living human organism. Observation of the reactions of this organism, introspection included, may therefore be much more reliable sources of information concerning the living brain than any other 'more direct' method. Using a suitable identification-hypothesis one might even be able to say that introspection leads to a *direct observation* of an otherwise quite inaccessible and very complex process *in the brain*.

Against what has been said above it might be, and has been, objected that in the case of thoughts, sensations, feelings, the distinction between what they *are* and what they *appear to be* does not apply. Mental processes are things with which we are *directly acquainted*. Unlike physical objects whose structure must be unveiled by experimental research and about whose nature we can make only more or less plausible conjectures, they can be known completely, and with certainty. Essence and appearance coincide here, and we are therefore entitled to take what they seem to be as a direct indication of what they are. This objection must now be investigated in some detail.

In order to deal with all the prejudices operating in the present case, let us approach the matter at a snail's pace. What are the reasons for defending a doctrine like the one we have just outlined? If the materialist is correct, then the doctrine is false. It *is* then possible to test statements of introspection by physiological examination of the brain, and reject them as being based upon an introspective mistake. Is such a possibility to be denied? The doctrine we are discussing at the present moment thinks it is. And the argument is somewhat as follows.

When I am in pain, then there is no doubt, no possibility of a mistake. This certainty is not simply a psychological affair, it is not due to the fact that I am too strongly convinced to be persuaded of the opposite. It is much more related to a logical certainty: there is no possibility whatever of criticising the statement. I might not show any physiological symptoms – but I never meant to include them into my assertion. I might not even show pain behaviour – but this is not part of the content of my statement either. Now if the difference between essence and appearance were applicable in the case of pains, then such certainty could not be obtained. It *can* be obtained as has just been demonstrated. Hence, the difference does not apply and the postulation of a common object for mental processes and impressions of physiological processes cannot be carried out.

The first question which arises in connection with this argument concerns the *source* of this certainty of statements concerning mental processes. The answer is very simple: it is their *lack of content* which is the source of their certainty. Statements about physical objects possess a very rich content. They are vulnerable because of the existence of this content. Thus, the statement 'there is a table in front of me' leads to predictions concerning my tactual sensations; the behaviour of other material objects (a glass of brandy put in a certain position will remain in this position and will not fall to the ground; a ball thrown in a certain direction will be deflected; the behaviour of other people (they will walk around the table; point out objects on its surface), etc. Failure of any one of these predictions may force me to withdraw the statement. This is not the case with statements concerning thoughts, sensations, feelings; or at least there is the impression that the same kind of vulnerability does not obtain here. The reason is that their content is so much poorer. No prediction, no retrodiction can be inferred from them, and the need to withdraw them can therefore not arise. (Of course, lack of content is only a *necessary* condition of their empirical certainty; in order to have the character they possess, statements about mental events must also be such that in the appropriate circumstances their production can be achieved with complete ease; they must be *observational* statements. *This* characteristic they share with many statements concerning physical objects.)

The second question is how statements about physical objects *obtain* their rich content and how it is that the content of mental statements as represented in the current argument is so much poorer.

One fairly popular answer is by reference to the 'grammar' of mental statements and of physical statements respectively. We mean by pains, thoughts, etc., processes which are accessible only to one individual and which have nothing to do with the state of his body. The content of 'pain', or of 'thinking of Vienna' is low because 'pain', 'thought' are mental terms. If the content of these terms were enriched, and thereby made similar to the content of 'table', they would cease to function in the peculiar way in which mental terms do as a matter of fact function, and 'pain', for example, would then cease to mean what is meant by an ordinary individual who in the face of the absence of physiological symptoms, of behavioural expression, of suppressed conflicts still maintains that he is in pain. This answer may be correct, and it will be taken to be correct for the sake of argument. However, in order to defeat the materialist it must also be shown that a language structured in this way will describe the world more correctly, and more efficiently, than any language the materialist could develop. No such proof is available. The argument from 'common' usage and, for that matter, from any established usage is therefore irrelevant.

There is only one point on which this argument may possess some force, and this point concerns the use of *words*: having shown that a materialistic pain and an 'ordinary' pain would be two very different things indeed, the defender of the established usage may forbid the materialist to employ the word 'pain', which for him rightfully belongs to the ordinary idiom. Now, quite apart from the fact that this would mean being very squeamish indeed, and unbearably 'proper' in linguistic matters, the desired procedure *cannot be carried out*. The reason is that changes of meaning occur too frequently, and that they cannot be localised in time. Every interesting discussion, that is every discussion which leads to an advance of knowledge, terminates in a situation where some decisive change of meaning has occurred. Yet it is not possible, or it is only very rarely possible, to say *when* the change took place. Moreover a distinction must be drawn between the *psychological circumstances* of the production of a sentence, and the *meaning* of the statement that is connected with that sentence. A new theory of pains will not change the pains; nor will it change the causal connection between the occurrence of pains and the production of 'I am in pain', except perhaps very *slightly*. It *will* change the meaning of 'I am in pain'. Now it seems to me that observational terms should be correlated with causal antecedents and *not* with meanings. The causal connection between the production of a 'mental' sentence and its 'mental' antecedent is very strong. It has been taught in the very youth. It is the basis of all observation concerning the mind. To sever this connection is a much more laborious affair than a change of connections with meaning. The latter connections change all the time anyway. It is therefore much more sensible to establish a one-to-one connection between observational terms and their causal antecedents, than between such terms and the always variable *meanings*. This procedure has great advantages and can do no harm. An astronomer who wishes to determine the rough shape of the energy output (dependence on frequency) of a star by looking at it will hardly be seduced into thinking that the word 'red' which he uses for announcing his results refers to sensations. Linguistic sensitivity may be of some value. But it should not be used to turn intelligent people into nervous wrecks.

Another reply to the question on p. 149 which is prima facie satisfactory is that we know quite a lot about physical objects and that we know much less about mental events. We use this knowledge not only on the relatively rare occasions when we answer questions involving it, but we infuse it also into the notions with which we describe material objects: a table *is* an object which deflects a ball thrown at it; which supports other objects; which is seen by other people; and so on. We let this knowledge become part of the language we speak by allowing the laws and theories it contains to become the grammatic rules of this language. This reply would seem to be supported by the fact that objects of a relatively unknown kind always give rise to fewer predictions and that the statements con-

cerning them are therefore relatively safe. In many such cases the
only tests available are the reports of others which means that mass
hallucinations can still count as confirming evidence.

Now this reply, however plausible, does not take into account that
a considerable amount is known about mental processes also, and
this not only by the psychologist, or the physiologist, but even by the
common man, be he now British, or a native of ancient Greece, or of
ancient Egypt. Why has *this* knowledge not been incorporated into
the mental notion? Why are these notions still so poor in content?

Before answering the question we must first qualify it. It is quite
incorrect to assume that the relative poverty of mental notions is a
common property of all languages. Quite the contrary, we find that
people have at all times objectivised mental notions in a manner
very similar to the manner in which we today objectivise materialistic
notions. They did this mostly (but not always – the witchcraft theory
of the Azande constituting a most interesting *materialistic* exception)
in an objective-*idealistic* fashion and can therefore be easily criticised,
or smiled about, by some progressive thinkers of today. In our
present discussion such criticism is off the mark. We have *admitted*,
on p. 146, that the materialistic type of objectification may at some
future time run into trouble. What we wanted to defend was the
initial right to carry it out and it was this *initial* right that was
attacked by reference to 'common usage'. Considering this context,
it is important to point out that there is hardly any interesting
language, used by a historical culture, which is built in accordance
with the idea of acquaintance. This idea is nothing but a philosophical invention. It is now time to reveal the motives for such an
invention.

We start the discussion with a still further argument intending
to show that and why the knowledge we may possess about mental
events must not be incorporated into the mental terms and why
their content must be kept low. This argument is apparently factual
and it consists in pointing out *that there is knowledge by acquaintance*, or, alternatively, that there are things which can be known
by acquaintance; we *do* possess direct and full knowledge of our
pains, of our thoughts, of our feelings, at least of those which are
immediately present and not suppressed.

This argument is circular. If we possess knowledge by acquaintance with respect to mental states of affairs, if there seems to be
something 'immediately given', then this is the *result* of the low
content of the statements used for expressing this knowledge. Had
we enriched the notions employed in these statements in a materi-

alistic (or an objective-idealistic) fashion *as we might well have done*, then we would not any longer be able to say that we know mental processes by acquaintance. Just as with material objects we would then be obliged to distinguish between their nature and their appearance, and each judgement concerning a mental process would be open to revision by further physiological (or behavioural) inquiry. The reference to acquaintance cannot therefore justify our reluctance to use the knowledge we possess concerning mental events, their causes, their physiological concomitants (as their physiological content will be called *before* the materialistic move) for enriching the mental notions.

What has just been said deserves repetition. The argument which we attacked was as follows: there is the *fact* of knowledge by acquaintance. This fact refutes materialism which would exclude such a fact. The attack consisted in pointing out that although knowledge by acquaintance may be a fact (which was, however, doubted on p. 151), this fact is the result of certain peculiarities of the language spoken *and therefore alterable*. Materialism (and, for that matter, also an objective spiritualism like the theory of the *ba* or Hegel's spiritualism) recognises the fact and suggests that it be altered. It therefore clearly cannot be refuted by a repetition of the fact. What must be shown is that the *suggestion* is undesirable, and that acquaintance is desirable.

We have here discovered a rather interesting feature of philosophical arguments. The argument from acquaintance presents what seems to be fact of nature, viz. our ability to acquire secure knowledge of our own states of mind. We have tried to show that this alleged fact of nature is the result of the way in which any kind of knowledge (or opinion) concerning the mind has been incorporated, or is being incorporated into the language used for describing facts: this knowledge, this opinion is not used for *enriching* the mental concepts; it is rather used for making predictions in terms of the still unchanged, and poor concepts. Or, to use terms from technical philosophy, this knowledge is interpreted instrumentalistically, and not in a realistic fashion. The alleged fact referred to above is therefore a projection, into the world, of certain peculiarities of our way of building up knowledge. Why do we (or why do philosophers who use the language described) proceed in this fashion?

They proceed in this fashion because they hold a certain philosophical theory. According to this theory, which has a very long history and which influences even the most sophisticated and the most 'progressive' contemporary philosophers (with the possible exception of Popper and Wittgenstein), the world consists of two domains, the domain of the outer, physical world, and the domain of the inner, or mental world. The outer world can be experienced, but only indirectly. Our knowledge of the outer world will therefore forever remain hypothetical. The inner world, the mental world, on the other hand, can be directly experienced. The knowledge gained in this fashion is complete, and absolutely certain. This, I think, is the philosophical theory behind the method we described in the previous paragraph.

Now I am not concerned here with the question of whether this theory is correct or not. It is quite possible that it is true (though I am inclined to doubt this, especially in view of the fact that it presents what should be the result of a decision, viz. the richness or the poverty of the content of a statement and its corresponding property of being either hypothetical, or certain, *as a fact of nature* and thereby confounds the basic distinction between the *ought* and the *is*). What I *am* interested in here is the way in which the theory is *presented*. It is not presented as a hypothesis which is open to criticism and which can be rationally discussed. In a certain sense it is not even presented. It is rather incorporated into the language spoken in a fashion which makes it inaccessible to empirical criticism – whatever the empirical results, they are not used for enriching the mental concepts which will therefore for ever refer to entities knowable by acquaintance.

This procedure has two results. It hides the theory and thereby removes it from criticism. And it creates what looks like a very powerful fact supporting the theory. As the theory is hidden, the philosopher can even *start* with this fact and reason from it, thereby providing a kind of inductive argument for the theory. It is only when we examine what independent support there exists for this alleged fact that we discover that it is not a fact at all but rather a reflection of the way in which empirical results are handled. We discover that 'we were ignorant of our . . . activity and therefore regarded as an alien object what had been constructed by ourselves' (Kuno Fischer in his account of Kant's theory of knowledge).[5]

This is an excellent example of the circularity of philosophical argumentation even in those cases where such argumentation is based upon what seems to be an incontrovertible fact of nature ('inner' nature, that is). This example is a warning that we should not be too impressed by empirical arguments but that we should first investigate the source of their apparent success. Such an investigation

[5] *Immanuel Kant und seine Lehre* (Heidelberg 1889) p. 10.

may discover a fatal circularity and thereby destroy the force of the argument. It is quite obvious that a circularity of this kind cannot be removed by considering further *empirical* evidence. But it can be removed by an examination of the *methodological* tenability of the procedure described. We now give a brief outline of such an examination.

There are some philosophers who agree that the *fact* of acquaintance cannot be used as an argument against the materialist (or any other kind of 'internal realist'). Their reasons are not those given above but rather the realisation that none of the situations described in the ordinary idiom, in any ordinary idiom, can be known by acquaintance. Realising this they will look for arguments which remain valid in the face of adverse facts, and they will therefore appeal to norms rather than to facts. They usually suggest the construction of an *ideal language* containing statements of the desired property. In this they are guided by the idea that our knowledge must possess a solid, that is an incorrigible foundation. The construction of such a language has sometimes been represented as a task of immense difficulty and as worthy of a great mind. I submit that this means vastly overestimating it. Of course, if this task is meant to be the discovery of *already existing* statements of the ordinary language which possess the desired property (Russell's 'canoid patch of colour' indicates that he conceived his task in this fashion), then it is perhaps impossible to carry it out. It may also be impossible to give an account of complex perceptions in terms of simple sensible elements (the investigations of the *Gestalt* school of psychology most definitely indicate that such composition from psychological elements will be an extremely difficult matter). But why should the attempt to find a *safe* observation language be impelled by such inessential restrictions? What we want is a series of observation statements leading to knowledge by acquaintance. Such statements can be obtained *immediately* by a philosophical laboratory assistant, by taking any observation statement and eliminating its predictive and retrodictive content as well as all consequences concerning public events occurring simultaneously. The resulting string of signs will still be observational, it will be uttered on the same objective occasion as was its predecessor, but it will be incorrigible, and the object described by it will be 'known' by acquaintance. This is how acquaintance can be achieved. Now let us investigate some consequences of this procedure.

Such an investigation is hardly ever carried out with due circumspection. What happens usually is this. One starts with a sentence which has a perfectly good meaning, such as 'I am in pain.' One interprets it as a statement concerning what can be known by acquaintance. One overlooks that such an interpretation drastically changes the original meaning of the sentence and one retains in this fashion the illusion that one is still dealing with a meaningful statement. Blinded by this illusion one cannot at all understand the objection of the opponent who takes the move towards the 'given' seriously and who is incapable of getting any sense out of the result. Just investigate the matter in some detail. Being in pain I say 'I am in pain' and, of course, I have some independent idea as to what pains are. They do not reside in tables and chairs; they can be eliminated by taking drugs; they concern only a single human being (hence, being in pain I shall not get alarmed about my dog); they are not contagious (hence, being in pain I shall not warn people to keep away from me). This idea is shared by everyone else and it makes people capable of understanding what I intend to convey. But now I am not supposed to let any one of these ideas contribute to the meaning of the *new* statement, expressed by the same sentence, about the immediately given; I am supposed to free this meaning of all that has just been said; not even the idea that a dreamt pain and a pain really felt are different must now be retained. If all these elements are removed, then what do I mean by the new statement resulting from this semantical canvas-cleaning? I may utter it on the occasion of pain (in the normal sense); I may also utter it in a dream with no pain present, and I may be equally convinced that this is the right thing to do. I may use it metaphorically, connecting it with a thought (in the usual sense) concerning the number two; or I may have been taught (in the usual sense of the word) to utter it when I have pleasant feelings and therefore utter it on these occasions. Clearly all these usages are now legitimate, and all of them describe the 'immediately given pain'. Is it not evident that using this new interpretation of the sentence I am not even in principle able to derive enlightenment from the fact that Herbert has just uttered it? Of course, I can still treat it as a *symptom* of the occurrence of an event which in the ordinary speech would be expressed in the very same fashion, viz. by saying 'I am in pain.' But in this case I provide my own interpretation which is very different from the interpretation we are discussing at the present moment. And we have seen that according to this interpretation the sentence cannot be taken to be the description of anything definite. It therefore means nothing; it cannot be understood by anyone (except in the sense in which a person looking at someone else's distorted face 'understands' what is going on – but then he does his own interpreting); and it is completely inadequate as a 'foundation of knowledge' or as a measure of factual meaning. Now if the given were a reality, then this would mean the end of rational, objective knowledge. Not even revelation could then teach us what admittedly cannot be known in principle. Language and conversation, if it existed, would become comparable to a cat-serenade, all expression, nothing said, nothing understood. Fortunately enough, the 'given' is but the reflection of our own unreason and it can be eliminated by building up language in a more sensible fashion. This finishes our discussion of the argument from acquaintance.

To sum up: we have discussed three arguments against materialism. The first argument points out that materialism is not the ontology of ordinary English. We have given the reasons why this argument would be irrelevant even if ordinary English should turn out to be a highly successful *testable* idiom. The second argument refers to results of observation. We have pointed out that results of observation are in need of *interpretation* and that no reason has been given why a materialistic interpretation should be excluded. The third argument was by reference to the fact of 'acquaintance'. We have shown, first, that this fact is not unchangeable and second that if it were a *fact* knowledge would be impossible. I am not aware of any other philosophical arguments against materialism (clearly all considerations of synonymy or coextensionality belong to what we have above called the first argument). There is, therefore, not a single reason why the attempt to give a purely physiological account of human beings should be abandoned, or why physiologists should leave the 'soul' out of their considerations.

A common feature of all the discussed arguments is this: they try to criticise a theory *before* this theory has been developed in sufficient detail to be able to show its power. And they make established modes of thinking and of expression the basis of this criticism. We have pointed out that the only way of discovering the faults of established modes of thinking is by resolutely trying out a different approach. It would seem to me that the task of philosophy, or of any enterprise interested in the advance, rather than the embalming of knowledge, would be to encourage the development of such new modes of approach, to participate in their improvement rather than to waste time in showing, what is obvious anyway, that they are different from the established ways of thinking.

PART FOUR

The Smart–Malcolm
Symposium on Materialism

XVI Materialism

J. J. C. Smart

First of all let me try to explain what I mean by 'materialism'. I shall then go on to try to defend the doctrine.[1] By 'materialism' I mean the theory that there is nothing in the world over and above those entities which are postulated by physics (or, of course, those entities which will be postulated by future and more adequate physical theories). Thus I do not hold materialism to be wedded to the billiard-ball physics of the nineteenth century. The less visualisable particles of modern physics count as matter. Note that energy counts as matter for my purposes: indeed in modern physics energy and matter are not sharply distinguishable. Nor do I hold that materialism implies determinism. If physics is indeterministic on the micro-level, so must be the materialist's theory. I regard materialism as compatible with a wide range of conceptions of the nature of matter and energy. For example, if matter and energy consist of regions of special curvature of an absolute space-time, with 'worm holes' and what not,[2] this is still compatible with materialism: we can still argue that in the last resort the world is made up entirely of the ultimate entities of physics, namely space-time points.

It will be seen that my conception of materialism is wider than that of Bertrand Russell in his introduction to Lange's *History of Materialism*.[3] But my definition will in some respects be narrower than those of some who have called themselves 'materialists'. I wish

[1] Presented in a symposium on 'Materialism' at the sixtieth annual meeting of the American Philosophical Association, Eastern Division, 27 December 1963.

I wish to thank Dr C. B. Martin and Mr M. C. Bradley, who have commented on an earlier version of this paper. I have made some slight changes, but space prevents me from taking up some of their fundamental objections.

[2] See J. A. Wheeler, 'Curved Empty Space–Time as the Building Material of the Physical World' in *Logic, Methodology and Philosophy of Science*, ed. E. Nagel, P. Suppes and A. Tarski (Stanford, Calif. 1962).

[3] F. A. Lange, *The History of Materialism*, translated by E. C. Thomas, 3rd ed., with an introduction by Bertrand Russell (New York 1925).

to lay down that it is incompatible with materialism that there should be any irreducibly 'emergent' laws or properties, say in biology or psychology. According to the view I propose to defend, there are no irreducible laws or properties in biology, any more than there are in electronics. Given the 'natural history' of a super-heterodyne (its wiring diagram), a physicist is able to explain, using only laws of physics, its mode of behaviour and its properties (for example, the property of being able to receive such and such a radio station which broadcasts on 25 megacycles). Just as electronics gives the physical explanation of the workings of superheterodynes, etc., so biology gives (or approximates to giving) physical and chemical explanations of the workings of organisms or parts of organisms. The biologist needs natural history just as the engineer needs wiring diagrams, but neither needs non-physical laws.[4]

It will now become clear why I define materialism in the way I have done above. I am concerned to deny that in the world there are non-physical entities and non-physical laws. In particular I wish to deny the doctrine of psycho-physical dualism.[5] (I also want to deny any theory of 'emergent properties', since irreducibly non-physical properties are just about as repugnant to me as are irreducibly non-physical entities.)

Popular theologians sometimes argue against materialism by saying that 'you can't put love in a test-tube'. Well you can't put a gravitational field in a test-tube (except in some rather strained sense of these words), but there is nothing incompatible with materialism, as I have defined it, in the notion of a gravitational field.

Similarly, even though love may elude test-tubes, it does not elude materialistic metaphysics, since it can be analysed as a pattern of bodily behaviour or, perhaps better, as the internal state of the human organism that accounts for this behaviour. (A dualist who analyses love as an internal state will perhaps say that it is a soul state, whereas the materialist will say that it is a brain state. It seems to me that much of our ordinary language about the mental is neither dualistic nor materialistic but is neutral between the two. Thus, to say that a locution is not materialistic is not to say that it is immaterialistic.)

---

[4] For a fuller discussion see my paper 'Can Biology Be An Exact Science?', *Synthèse* II (1959) pp. 359–68.

[5] In recent years essentially dualistic theories have been propounded in rather sophisticated forms, for example, by P. F. Strawson, in *Individuals*. That Strawson's view is essentially dualistic can be seen from the fact that he admits that disembodied existence is logically compatible with it.

But what about consciousness? Can we interpret the having of an after-image or of a painful sensation as something material, namely, a brain state or brain process? We seem to be immediately aware of pains and after-images, and we seem to be immediately aware of them as something different from a neurophysiological state or process. For example, the after-image may be green speckled with red, whereas the neurophysiologist looking into our brains would be unlikely to see something green speckled with red. However, if we object to materialism in this way we are victims of a confusion which U. T. Place has called 'the phenomenological fallacy'.[6] To say that an image or sense-datum is green is not to say that the conscious experience of having the image or sense-datum is green. It is to say that it is the sort of experience we have when in normal conditions we look at a green apple, for example. Apples and unripe bananas can be green, but not the experience of seeing them. An image or a sense-datum can be green in a derivative sense, but this need not cause any worry, because, on the view I am defending, images and sense-data are not constituents of the world, though the processes of having an image or a sense-datum are actual processes in the world. The experience of having a green sense-datum is not itself green; it is a process occurring in grey matter. The world contains plumbers, but does not contain the average plumber; it also contains the having of a sense-datum, but does not contain the sense-datum.

It may be objected that, in admitting that apples and unripe bananas can be green, I have admitted colours as emergent properties, not reducible within a physicalist scheme of thought. For a reply to this objection I must, for lack of space, refer to my article 'Colours', *Philosophy*, xxxvi (1961) pp. 128–42. Here colours are elucidated in terms of the discriminatory reactions of normal percipients, and the notion of a normal colour percipient is defined without recourse to the notion of colour. Colour classifications are elucidated as classifications in terms of the highly idiosyncratic discriminatory reactions of a complex neurophysiological mechanism. It is no wonder that these classifications do not correspond to anything simple in physics. (There is no one–one correlation between colour and wave-length, since infinitely many different mixtures of wave-lengths correspond to the same colour, i.e. produce the same discriminatory reaction in a normal percipient.)

When we report that a lemon is yellow we are reacting to the lemon. But when we report that the lemon looks yellow we are

[6] See Paper II.

reacting to our own internal state. When I say 'it looks to me that there is a yellow lemon' I am saying, roughly, that what is going on in me is like what is going on in me when there really is a yellow lemon in front of me, my eyes are open, the light is daylight, and so on. That is, our talk of immediate experience is derivative from our talk about the external world. Furthermore, since our talk of immediate experience is in terms of a typical stimulus situation (and in the case of some words for aches and pains and the like it may, as we shall see, be in terms of some typical *response* situation) we can see that our talk of immediate experience is itself neutral between materialism and dualism. It reports our internal goings-on as like or unlike what internally goes on in typical situations, but the dualist would construe these goings-on as goings-on in an immaterial substance, whereas the materialist would construe these goings-on as taking place inside our skulls.

Our talk about immediate experiences is derivative from our language of physical objects. This is so even with much of our language of bodily sensations and aches and pains. A stabbing pain is the sort of going-on which is like what goes on when a pin is stuck into you. (Trivially, you also have a stabbing pain when a pin is in fact stuck into you, for in this essay I am using 'like' in a sense in which a thing is like itself. That I am using 'like' in this sense can be seen by reflecting on what the analysis of the last paragraph would imply in the case of having a veridical sense-datum of a yellow lemon.) However, some of our sensation words do not seem to work like 'stabbing pain'. Consider 'ache'. Perhaps here the reference to a typical stimulus situation should be replaced by a reference to a typical response situation. Instead of 'what is going on in me is like what goes on in me when a yellow lemon is before me' we could have some such thing as 'what is going on in me is like what goes on in me when I groan, yelp, etc.' In any case it is not inconsistent with the present view to suppose that, when children have got the idea of referring to their own internal goings-on as like or unlike what goes on in some typical situation, they can then in some cases go on simply to classify them as like or unlike one another. (All the aches are more like one another than any of them are to any of the itches, for example.) In other words, they may be able to report some of their internal goings-on as like or unlike one another, and thus to report these goings-on, even when their language is not tied closely to stimulus or response situations. Notice that I am still denying that we introspect any non-physical property such as *achiness*. To say that a process is an ache is simply to classify it with other processes that are felt to be like it, and this class of processes constitutes the aches.

An important objection is now sure to be made. It will be said that anything is like anything else in *some* respect or other. So how can our sensation reports be classifications in terms of likenesses and unlikenesses alone? And if you say that they are likenesses or unlikenesses in virtue of properties that are or are not held in common, will these properties not have to be properties (e.g. *achiness*) that are beyond the conceptual resources of a physicalist theory?

Looked at in the abstract this argument appears impressive, but it becomes less persuasive when we think out, in terms of bits of cybernetic hardware, what it is to recognize likenesses and unlikenesses. Thus, consider a machine for recognising likenesses and unlikenesses between members of a set of round discs, square discs, and triangular discs. It would probably be easier to construct a machine that just told us (on a tape, say) 'like' or 'unlike' than it would be to construct a machine that told us wherein the likenesses consisted, whether in roundness, squareness, or triangularity. Moreover, we may agree that everything is like everything else and still say that some things are much liker than others. Consider the notion of following a rule, which plays so important a part in Wittgenstein's philosophy.[7] Suppose that one man continues the sequence 0, 1, 2, 3, ... up to 1000 and then continues 1001, 1002, 1003, 1004, ... Here we certainly feel like saying that he goes on doing the same thing after 1000 as he did before 1000. Now suppose that a second man goes 0, 1, 2, 3, ... 1000, 1002, 1004, ..., and a third man goes 0, 1, 2, 3, ... 1000, 1001, 1002, 1003, 1005, 1007, 1011, 1013, ... According to Wittgenstein's account, it would seem that the second and third men also could say that they were doing the same thing after 1000 as they did up to 1000. Indeed there are rules to cover these cases too, for example, 'add one up to 1000 and then add twos until 2000, threes until 3000, and so on' and 'add ones up to 1001 and then go up by prime numbers'. These rules are more complicated than the original one; moreover, like even the first rule, they could be divergently interpreted. We can concede Wittgenstein all this. Nevertheless, it does not follow that there is no sense in which some sequences are objectively more like one another than are others. It will not do to say that the continuations of the

[7] *Philosophical Investigations*, translated by G. E. M. Anscombe (Oxford 1953) sections 185 ff.

sequence 0, 1, 2, 3, . . . that go 1002, 1004, 1006, . . . or 1001, 1002, 1003, 1005, 1007, 1011, 1013, . . . are as like what goes before 1000 as is the continuation 1001, 1002, 1003, ... This can be seen if we reflect that a machine built to churn out the symbols of the sequence 0, 1, 2, 3, . . . 1001, 1002, 1003, 1004, . . . could be a simpler machine (i.e. could contain fewer parts) than one built to churn out either of the other two sequences. This indicates that absolute likenesses and unlikeness is something objective, even though it is also a matter of degree.

I conclude, therefore, that it is by no means empty to say that some of our internal processes are like or unlike one another, even though we do not indicate in what respect they are like. This makes our reports of immediate experience quite open or 'topic-neutral', to use a phrase of Ryle's. They do not commit us either to materialism or to dualism, but they are quite *compatible* with the hypothesis which I wish to assert: that the internal goings-on in question are brain processes.[8]

It may be said: But on your view you can have no criterion of correctness when you report a sensation simply as *like* one you had before (cf. Wittgenstein, *Investigations*, section 258). But must I have such a criterion? On my view my internal mechanism is just built so that I react in the way I do. And I may *in fact* react correctly, though I have no criterion for saying that my reaction is correct. That is, when I report my internal processes as alike, it may always, or at least mostly, be the case that they *are* alike. Indeed, on the basis of common-sense psychology, scientific psychology, or perhaps (in the future) electroencephalography, we may gain indirect evidence that our reactions are correct in reporting likenesses of internal processes. A slot machine that puts out a bar of chocolate only when a shilling (or a coin indistinguishable in size and shape from a shilling) is inserted into it certainly has no criterion for the size and shape. But its reactions are veridical: it will not give you a bar of chocolate if you put a sixpence into it.

It is important to realise that, if the view that I wish to defend is correct, conscious experiences must be processes involving millions of neurons, and so their important likenesses and unlikenesses to one

---

[8] Shaffer, in his interesting article 'Mental events and the brain', (Paper XIII) thinks (p. 137) that it is implausible that what we notice in inner experience are brain processes. If my view is correct, we do notice brain processes, though only in a 'topic-neutral' way: we do not notice *that* they are brain processes. I do not find this implausible – not as implausible as non-physical entities or properties, anyway.

another may well be statistical in nature. As P. K. Feyerabend[9] has pointed out, this shows how a sensation (or a brain process) can possess such properties as of being clear or confused (well-defined or ill-defined), as well as why a sensation seems to be a simple entity in a way in which the details of a brain process are not simple. Brain processes can well have statistical properties that cannot even meaningfully be asserted of individual neurons, still less of individual molecules or atoms. Feyerabend compares this case with that of the density of a fluid, the notion of which can be meaningfully applied only to a large statistically homogeneous ensemble of particles and which has no application in the case of a single particle or small group of particles. Notice also that the materialist hypothesis does not imply that there is anything like consciousness in a single atom, or even in a single neuron for that matter. A conscious experience is a very complex process involving vast numbers of neurons. It is a process, not a stuff. The materialist does not need to accept Vogt's crude and preposterous idea that the brain secretes thought much as the liver secretes bile.[10] We can certainly agree with Wittgenstein thus far: that thought is not a *stuff*. Indeed this side of Wittgenstein's thought is particularly attractive: his elucidation of mental concepts in terms of bodily behaviour would, if it were adequate, be perfectly compatible with the sort of physicalist world-view which, for reasons of scientific plausibility, it seems to me necessary to defend. (I differ from Wittgenstein since I wish to elucidate thought as inner process and to keep my hypothesis compatible with a physicalist viewpoint by identifying such inner processes with brain processes.) The trouble with Wittgenstein is that he is too operationalistic.[11]

This can perhaps be brought out by considering something Wittgenstein says in section 293 of his *Philosophical Investigations*. He there argues against the tendency to construe 'the grammar of the expression of sensation on the model of "object and name"'. He says that if we try to do so 'the object drops out of consideration as irrelevant'. I imagine that he would argue equally strongly against the model (more relevant to the present issue) of *process* and name. I am not sure how seriously we are to take the word 'name' here.

---

9 See Paper XV, esp. pp. 145–6, above.

10 See Lange, *History of Materialism*, ii, p. 312.

11 In coming to this conclusion I have been very much influenced by my colleague C. B. Martin. See also H. Putnam, 'Dreaming and "Depth Grammar"', *Analytical Philosophy*, i, ed. R. J. Butler (Oxford 1962) pp. 211–35.

Surely all we need are predicates, e.g. '. . . is a pain'. (Wittgenstein is considering the case of someone who says 'here is a pain' or 'this is a pain'.) Indeed, in a Quinean language there would be no names at all. Suppose, therefore, that we construe the word 'name' rather more widely, so that we can say, for example, that 'electron' is a name of electrons. (More properly we should say that '. . . is an electron' is a predicate true of anything which is an electron.) Now let us apply Wittgenstein's argument of 'the beetle in the box' to electrons (*Investigations*, section 293). A person can see only the beetle in his own box (just as, on the view Wittgenstein is attacking, my pain is something of which only I can be acquainted), but the case with electrons is even worse, since no one at all can literally see an electron. We know of electrons only through their observable effects on macroscopic bodies. Thus Wittgenstein's reasons for saying that pains are not objects would be even stronger reasons for saying that electrons are not objects either.[12]

I have no doubt that Wittgenstein would have been unmoved by this last consideration. For I think he would have been likely to say that electrons are grammatical fictions and that electrons must be understood in terms of galvanometers, etc., just as pains are to be understood in terms of groans, etc. In reply to the question, 'Are you not really a behaviourist in disguise? Aren't you at bottom really saying that everything except human behaviour is a fiction?', he replies: 'If I do speak of a fiction it is of a *grammatical* fiction' (section 307). Certainly, if a philosopher says that pains are grammatical fictions, he is not denying that there are pains. Nevertheless he is denying that pains are anything (to use John Wisdom's useful expression) 'over and above' pain behaviour. Such a philosopher is not a crude behaviourist who denies that there are pains, but surely he can well be said to be a behaviourist of a more sophisticated sort. Why should he be shy of admitting it? Now the very same reasons which lead Wittgenstein to go behaviourist about pains would surely lead him to go instrumentalist (in an analogously sophisticated way) about electrons.

This is not the place to contest instrumentalism about the theoretical entities of physics. But I wish to put forward one consideration which will be followed by an analogous one in the case of sensations. Can we conceive of a universe consisting only of a swarm of electrons, protons, neutrons, etc., that have never and never will come together as constituents of macroscopic objects? It would seem

[12] See the excellent article by Helen Hervey, 'The Private Language Problem', *Philosophical Quarterly*, 7 (1957) pp. 63–79, esp. p. 67.

that we can, even though the supposition might be inconsistent with certain cosmological theories, and it might become inconsistent with physics itself, if physics one day becomes united with cosmology in a unified theory. On this supposition, then, there could be electrons, protons, etc., but no macroscopic objects.[13] On the other hand, there could not be the average plumber without plumbers, or nations without nationals. (In arguing thus I am indebted to C. B. Martin.) It is therefore not clear in what sense electrons and protons could be said to be grammatical fictions. Now let us ask analogously in what sense Wittgenstein could allow that pain experiences are grammatical fictions. It is not evident that there is any clear sense.

Consider this example.[14] In some future state of physiological technology we might be able to keep a human brain alive *in vitro*. Leaving the question of the morality of such an experiment to one side, let us suppose that the experiment is done. By suitable electrodes inserted into appropriate parts of this brain we get it to have the illusion of perceiving things and also to have pains, and feelings of moving its non-existent limbs, and so on. (This brain might even be able to think verbally, for it might have learned a language before it was put *in vitro*, or else, by suitable signals from our electrodes, we might even give it the illusion of learning a language in the normal way.) Here we have the analogue to the case of the world of electrons, etc., but with no macroscopic objects. In the present case we have mental experiences, but no behaviour. This brings out vividly that what is important in psychology is what goes on in the central nervous system, not what goes on in the face, larynx, and limbs. It can of course be agreed that what goes on in the face, larynx, and limbs provides observational data whereby the psychologist can postulate what goes on in the central nervous system. If experiences are postulated on the basis of behaviour, instead of being grammatical fictions out of behaviour, then we can deal with the case of the brain *in vitro*. For whereas grammatical fictions are nothing over and above what they are fictions out of, entities such as are postulated in a hypothesis could still exist even if there had been no possible evidence for them. There could be electrons even if there were no macroscopic bodies, and there could be processes in the central nervous system even if there were no attached

---

[13] An analogous argument, based on a gaseous universe, is used by B. A. O. Williams, 'Mr Strawson on Individuals', *Philosophy*, xxxvi (1961) pp. 309–32; see pp. 321–2.

[14] I gather that Armstrong has also been using this example to make the same point.

body and, hence, no bodily behaviour. Of course I do not wish to deny that in the case of the brain *in vitro* we could have evidence other than that of bodily behaviour: electroencephalographic evidence, for example.[15]

It is true that Wittgenstein is arguing against someone who says that he knows what pain is only from his own case. I am not such a person. I want to say that sensations are postulated processes in other people and *also* processes which, when they occur in ourselves, we can report as like or unlike one another. If we cannot look at the beetle in another person's box, that does not matter; no one can look into any box at all when in the simile the beetle is taken to be not a pain but an electron. We have very good indirect evidence for asserting that all electrons are like one another and unlike, say, protons.

I have suggested that, in spite of his own disclaimer, Wittgenstein is in fact a sort of behaviourist. I have also suggested that such a behaviourism is no more tenable than is an analogous instrumentalism about the theoretical entities of physics. Nevertheless, Wittgenstein's philosophy of mind, if it could be accepted, would be very attractive. For, like the analysis that I am advocating, it would be compatible with materialism: it would not land us with emergent properties or non-physical entities. But even a disguised or Wittgensteinian behaviourism falls down because, as I have argued, it cannot account for the overriding importance of the central nervous system: the example of the brain *in vitro* shows that what is essential to a pain is what goes on in the brain, not what goes on in the arms or legs or larynx or mouth. Furthermore, it is hard to accept the view that so-called 'reports' of inner experience are to be construed as surrogates for behaviour, as if a report of a pain were a wince-substitute. To say that these behaviour surrogates are properly called 'reports' in ordinary language does little to mitigate the paradoxical nature of the theory.

It may be asked why I should demand of a tenable philosophy of mind that it should be compatible with materialism, in the sense in which I have defined it. One reason is as follows. How could a non-physical property or entity suddenly arise in the course of animal evolution? A change in a gene is a change in a complex molecule which causes a change in the biochemistry of the cell. This may lead to changes in the shape or organisation of the developing embryo.

[15] H. Reichenbach in his *Experience and Prediction* (Chicago 1938), in one of the best defences of physicalism in the literature, has put forward a similar account of experiences as postulated things; see sections 19 and 26.

But what sort of chemical process could lead to the springing into existence of something non-physical? No enzyme can catalyse the production of a spook! Perhaps it will be said that the non-physical comes into existence as a by-product: that whenever there is a certain complex physical structure, then, by an irreducible extra-physical law, there is also a non-physical entity. Such laws would be quite outside normal scientific conceptions and quite inexplicable: they would be, in Herbert Feigl's phrase, 'nomological danglers'.[16] To say the very least, we can vastly simplify our cosmological outlook if we can defend a materialistic philosophy of mind.

In defending materialism I have tried to argue that a materialist and yet non-behaviourist account of sensations is perfectly consistent with our ordinary language of sensation reports. (Though I have had space to consider only a selection of the arguments commonly put forward against materialism; for example, I have not considered the argument from the alleged incorrigibility of reports of inner experience. Elsewhere I have argued that, even if such incorrigibility were a fact, it would provide as much of a puzzle to the dualist as it does to the materialist.)[17]

Nevertheless there is also in ordinary language a dualistic overtone: to some extent it enshrines the plain man's metaphysics, which is a dualism of body and soul. We cannot therefore hope (even if we wished) to reconcile *all* of ordinary language with a materialist metaphysics. Or, to put it otherwise, it is hard to decide just where to draw the line between non-metaphysical ordinary language and the plain man's metaphysics. Nevertheless, I think that the attempt to reconcile the hard core of ordinary language with materialism is worth while. For one thing, some features of ordinary language will probably remain constant for a very long time. This is because much of our perception of macroscopic objects depends on innate mechanisms, not on mechanisms that have developed through learning processes. For example, consider our perception of objects as three-dimensional. Again, we shall probably continue indefinitely to need a colour language, anthropocentric though it is. The colour classifications we make depend on the peculiarities of the human visual apparatus, and, so long as we retain our present physiological characteristics, we shall retain our present colour language. With these reservations, however, I am also attracted to P. K. Feyerabend's contention that in defending materialism we do not need to show its

[16] See his paper 'The "Mental" and the "Physical"', *Minnesota Studies in the Philosophy of Science*, II pp. 370–497.
[17] See Paper IX.

consistency with ordinary language, any more than in defending the general theory of relativity we need to show its consistency with Newtonian theory.[18] (Newtonian theory and general relativity are indeed inconsistent with one another: for example, the advance of the perihelion of Mercury is inconsistent with Newtonian theory, but follows from general relativity.). Feyerabend is perhaps therefore right in arguing that the scientific concept of pain does not need to be (and indeed should not be) even extensionally equivalent to the concept of pain in ordinary language. (The concept of a planetary orbit in general relativity does not quite coincide extensionally with that in Newtonian theory, since the orbit of Mercury fits the former but not the latter.) Perhaps, therefore, even if it should be shown that materialism is incompatible with the core of our ordinary language, it could still be defended on the basis of Feyerabend's position. Nevertheless, just as J. K. Galbraith in his book *The Affluent Society* prefers where possible to argue against what he calls 'the conventional wisdom' on its own ground, so I think that it is worth while trying to meet some of my philosophical friends as far as possible on their own ground, which is the analysis of ordinary language. Indeed it seems probable that the ordinary language of perception and of inner experience has more to recommend it than has the conventional wisdom of the last generation of economists: we are not confronted with a rapidly changing universe or with a rapidly changing human physiology in the way in which the economist is faced with a rapidly changing human environment.

[18] And Wilfrid Sellars has argued that what he calls 'the scientific image' should be sharply separated off from 'the manifest image', and would probably say that in the present paper I am wrongly importing elements of the manifest image into the scientific image.

XVII Scientific materialism and the Identity Theory

Norman Malcolm

I

My main topic will be, roughly speaking, the claim that mental events or conscious experiences or inner experiences are brain processes.[1] I hasten to say, however, that I am not going to talk about 'mental events' or 'conscious experiences' or 'inner experiences'. These expressions are almost exclusively philosophers' terms, and I am not sure that I have got the hang of any of them. Philosophers are not in agreement in their use of these terms. One philosopher will say, for example, that a pain in the foot is a mental event, whereas another will say that a pain *in the foot* certainly is not a *mental* event.

I will avoid these expressions, and concentrate on the particular example of *sudden thoughts*. Suddenly remembering an engagement would be an example of suddenly thinking of something. Suddenly realising, in a chess game, that moving this pawn would endanger one's queen, would be another example of a sudden thought. Professor Smart says that he wishes to 'elucidate thought as an inner process',[2] and he adds that he wants to identify 'such inner processes with brain processes'. He surely holds, therefore, that thinking and thoughts, including sudden thoughts, are brain processes. He holds also that conscious experiences (pp. 164 and 165), illusions (p. 167 and aches and pains (p. 162) are brain processes, and that love (p. 160) is a brain state. I will restrict my discussion, however, to sudden thoughts.

My first inclination, when I began to think on this topic, was to believe that Smart's view is false – that a sudden thought certainly is not a brain process. But now I think that I do not know what it

[1] This paper was read at the Sixtieth Annual Meeting of the American Philosophical Association, Eastern Division. It is a reply to Professor Smart's essay 'Materialism' (Paper XVI).

[2] P. 165, above.

means to say that a sudden thought is a brain process. In saying this I imply, of course, that the proponents of this view also do not know what it means. This implication is risky for it might turn out, to my surprise and gratification, that Smart will explain his view with great clarity.

In trying to show that there is real difficulty in seeing what his view means, I will turn to Smart's article 'Sensations and brain processes'.[*] He says there that in holding that a sensation is a brain process he is 'using "is" in the sense of strict identity' (p. 56). 'I wish to make it clear', he says, 'that the brain process doctrine asserts identity in the *strict* sense' (p. 56). I assume that he wishes to say the same about the claimed identity of a thought with a brain process. Unfortunately he does not attempt to define this 'strict sense of identity', and so we have to study his examples.

One of his examples of a 'strict identity' is this: 7 is identical with the smallest prime number greater than 5 (p. 56). We must remember, however, that one feature of 'the identity theory', as I shall call it, is that the alleged identity between thoughts, sensations, etc., and brain processes, is held to be *contingent*. Since the identity of 7 with the smallest prime greater than 5 is *a priori* and relates to timeless objects, it does not provide me with any clue as to how I am to apply the notion of 'strict identity' to temporal events that are *contingently* related. The example is unsatisfactory, therefore, for the purpose of helping me to deal with the question of whether thoughts are or are not 'strictly identical' with certain brain processes.

Let us move to another example. Smart tells us that the sense in which the small boy who stole apples is the same person as the victorious general is *not* the 'strict' sense of 'identity' (p. 56). He thinks there is a mere spatio-temporal continuity between the apple-stealing boy and the general who won the war. From this *non*-example of 'strict identity' I think I obtain a clue as to what he means by it. Consider the following two sentences: 'General de Gaulle is the tallest Frenchman'; 'The victorious general is the small boy who stole apples.' Each of these sentences might be said to express an identity: yet we can see a difference between the two cases. Even though the victorious general *is* the small boy who stole apples, it is possible for the victorious general to be in this room at a time when there is *no* small boy here. In contrast, if General de Gaulle *is* the tallest Frenchman, then General de Gaulle is not in this room unless the tallest Frenchman is here. It would be quite

[*] Paper III.

natural to say that this latter identity (if it holds) is a *strict* identity, and that the other one is not. I believe that Smart would say this. This suggests to me the following rule for his 'strict identity': If something, *x*, is in a certain place at a certain time, then something, *y*, is strictly identical with *x* only if *y* is in that same place at that same time.

If we assume that Smart's use of the expression 'strict identity' is governed by the necessary condition I have stated, we can possibly understand why he is somewhat hesitant about whether to say that the Morning Star is strictly identical with the Evening Star. Smart says to an imaginary opponent: 'You may object that the Morning Star is in a sense not the very same thing as the Evening Star, but only something spatio-temporally continuous with it. That is, you may say that the Morning Star is not the Evening Star in the strict sense of "identity" that I distinguished earlier' (p. 57). Instead of rebutting this objection, Smart moves on to what he calls 'a more plausible example of strict identity'. This suggests to me that Smart is not entirely happy with the case of the stars as an example of strict identity. Why not? Perhaps he has some inclination to feel that the planet that is both the Morning and the Evening Star is not the Morning Star *at the same time* it is the Evening Star. If this were so, the suggested necessary condition for 'strict identity' would not be satisfied. Smart's hesitation is thus a further indication that he wants his use of the expression 'strict identity' to be governed by the rule I have stated.

Let us turn to what Smart calls his 'more plausible' example of strict identity. It is this: Lightning is an electric discharge. Smart avows that this is truly a strict identity (p. 56 and pp. 57–8). This example provides additional evidence that he wants to follow the stated rule. If an electrical discharge occurred in one region of the sky and a flash of lightning occurred simultaneously in a different region of the sky, Smart would have no inclination to assert (I think) that the lightning was strictly identical with the electrical discharge. Or if electrical discharges and corresponding lightning flashes occurred in the same region of the sky, but not at the same time, there normally being a perceptible interval of time between a discharge and a flash, then Smart (I believe) would not wish to hold that there was anything more strict than a systematic correlation (perhaps causal) between electric discharges and lightning.[4]

[4] Place (Paper II) also defends the identity theory. An example that he uses to illustrate the sense of identity in which, according to him, 'con-

I proceed now to take up Smart's claim that a sudden thought is strictly identical with some brain process. It is clear that a brain process has spatial location. A brain process would be a mechanical, chemical or electrical process in the brain substance, or an electric discharge from the brain mass, or something of the sort. As Smart puts it, brain processes take place 'inside our skulls'.[5]

Let us consider an example of a sudden thought. Suppose that when I am in my house I hear the sound of a truck coming up the driveway and it suddenly occurs to me that I have not put out the milk bottles. Now is this sudden thought (which is also a sudden memory) literally inside my skull? I think that in our ordinary use of the terms 'thought' and 'thinking', we attach no meaning to the notion of determining the bodily location of a thought. We do not seriously debate whether someone's sudden thought occurred in his heart, or his throat, or his brain. Indeed, we should not know what the question meant. We should have no idea what to look for to settle this 'question'. We do say such a thing as 'He can't get the thought out of his head'; but this is not taken as giving the location of a thought, any more than the remark 'He still has that girl on the brain' is taken as giving the location of a girl.

It might be replied that *as things are* the bodily location of thoughts is not a meaningful notion; but if massive correlations were discovered between thoughts and brain processes then we might *begin* to locate thoughts in the head. To this I must answer that our philosophical problem *is* about how things are. It is a question about our *present* concepts of thinking and thought, not about some conjectured future concepts.[6]

---

sciousness' could turn out to be a brain process is this: 'A cloud is a mass of water droplets or other particles in suspension' (pp. 44 and 46). I believe that Place would not be ready to hold that this is a genuine identity, *as contrasted with* a systematic and/or causal correlation, if he did not assume that in the very same region of space occupied by a cloud there is, at the very same time, a mass of particles in suspension.

[5] P. 162, above.

[6] Shaffer proposes an ingenious solution to our problem (Paper X). He allows that at present we do not attach any meaning to a bodily location of thoughts. As he puts it, we have no 'rules' for asserting or denying that a particular thought occurred in a certain part of the body. But why could we not *adopt* a rule, he asks? Supposing that there was discovered to be a one-to-one correspondence between thoughts and brain processes, we could *stipulate* that a thought is located where the corresponding brain process is located. Nothing would then stand in the way of saying that thoughts are *identical* with those brain processes! Although filled with

The difficulty I have in understanding Smart's identity theory is the following. Smart wants to use a concept of 'strict identity'. Since there are a multitude of uses of the word 'is', from the mere fact that he tells us that he means 'is' in the sense of 'strict identity' it does not follow that he has explained which use of 'is' he intends. From his examples and non-examples, I surmise that his so-called 'strict identity' is governed by the necessary condition that if x occurs in a certain place at a certain time, then y is strictly identical with x only if y occurs in the same place at the same time. But if x is a brain process and y is a sudden thought, then this condition for strict identity is not (and cannot be) satisfied. Indeed, it does not even make sense to set up a test for it. Suppose we had determined, by means of some instrument, that a certain process occurred inside my skull at the exact moment I had the sudden thought about the milk bottles. How do we make the further test of whether my *thought* occurred inside my skull? For it would have to be a *further* test: it would have to be logically independent of the test for the presence of the brain process, because Smart's thesis is that the identity is *contingent*. But no one has any notion of what it would mean to test for the occurrence of the thought inside my skull *independently* of testing for a brain process. The idea of such a test is not intelligible. Smart's thesis, as I understand it, requires this unintelligible idea. For he is not satisfied with holding that there is a systematic correlation between sudden thoughts and certain brain processes. He wants to take the additional step of holding that there is a 'strict identity'. Now his concept of strict identity either embodies the necessary condition I stated previously, or it does not. If it does not, then I do not know what he means by 'strict identity', over and above systematic correlation. If his concept of strict identity does embody that necessary condition, then his concept of strict identity cannot be meaningfully applied to the relationship between sudden thoughts and brain processes. My conclusion is what I said in the beginning: the identity theory has no clear meaning.

---

admiration for this philosophical technique, I disagree with Shaffer when he says (p. 118) that the adopted convention for the location of thoughts would not have to be merely an elliptical way of speaking of the location of the corresponding brain processes. Considering the origin of the convention, how could it amount to anything else?

II

I turn now to a different consideration. A thought requires circumstances or, in Wittgenstein's word, 'surroundings' (*Umgebung*). Putting a crown on a man's head is a coronation only in certain circumstances.[7] The behaviour of exclaiming 'Oh, I have not put out the milk bottles', or the behaviour of suddenly jumping up, rushing to the kitchen, collecting the bottles and carrying them outside – such behaviour expresses the thought that one has not put out the milk bottles *only in certain circumstances.*

The circumstances necessary for this simple thought are complex. They include the existence of an organised community, of a practice of collecting and distributing milk, of a rule that empty bottles will not be collected unless placed outside the door, and so on. These practices, arrangements and rules could exist only if there was a common language; and this in turn would presuppose shared activities and agreement in the use of language. The thought about the milk bottles requires a background of mutual purpose, activity and understanding.

I assume that if a certain brain process were strictly identical with a certain thought, then the occurrence of that brain process would be an absolutely sufficient condition for the occurrence of that thought. If this assumption is incorrect, then my understanding of what Smart means by 'strict identity' is even *less* than I have believed. In support of this assumption I will point out that Smart has never stated his identity theory in the following way. *In certain circumstances* a particular brain process is identical with a particular thought. His thesis has not carried such a qualification. I believe his thesis is the following: A particular brain process is, *without qualification*, strictly identical with a particular thought. If this thesis were true it would appear to follow that the occurrence of that brain process would be an absolutely sufficient condition for the occurrence of that thought.

I have remarked that a necessary condition for the occurrence of my sudden thought about the milk bottles is the previous existence of various practices, rules and agreements. If the identity theory were true, then the surroundings that are necessary for the existence of my sudden thought would also be necessary for the existence of the brain process with which it is identical.[8] That brain process

---

[7] *Philosophical Investigations*, section 584.
[8] It is easy to commit a fallacy here. The circumstances that I have men-

would not have occurred unless, for example, there was or had been a practice of delivering milk.

This consequence creates a difficulty for those philosophers who, like Smart, hold both to the identity theory and also to the viewpoint that I shall call 'scientific materialism'. According to the latter viewpoint, the furniture of the world 'in the last resort' consists of 'the ultimate entities of physics'.[9] Smart holds that everything in the world is 'explicable in terms of physics'.[10] It does not seem to me that this can be true. My sudden thought about the milk bottles was an occurrence in the world. That thought required a background of common practices, purposes and agreements. But a reference to a practice of e.g. delivering milk could not appear in a proposition of physics. The word 'electron' is a term of physics, but the phrase 'a practice of delivering milk' is not. There could not be an explanation of the occurrence of my thought (an explanation taking account of all the necessary circumstances) which was stated solely in terms of the entities and laws of physics.

My sudden thought about the milk bottles is not unique in requiring surroundings. The same holds for any other thought. No thought would be explicable wholly in the terms of physics (and/or biology) because the circumstances that form the 'stage-setting' for a thought cannot be described in the terms of physics.

Now if I am right on this point, and if the identity theory were true, it would follow that none of those *brain processes* that are identical with thoughts could be given a purely physical explanation. A philosopher who holds both to the identity theory and to scientific materialism is forced, I think, into the self-defeating position of conceding that many brain processes are not explicable solely in terms of physics.[11] The position is self-defeating because such a

---

tioned are *conceptually* necessary for the occurrence of my thought. If the identity theory were true it would not follow that they were *conceptually* necessary for the occurrence of the brain process that is identical with that thought. But it would follow that those circumstances were necessary for the occurrence of the brain process *in the sense* that the brain process *would not* have occurred in the absence of those circumstances.

[9] P. 159, above.

[10] P. 54, above.

[11] I believe this argument is pretty similar to a point made by J. T. Stevenson in Paper VI. Smart's view, roughly speaking, is that unless sensations are identical with brain processes they are 'nomological danglers'. Stevenson's retort is that by insisting that sensations are identical with brain processes we have not got rid of any nomological danglers. He says: 'Indeed, on Smart's thesis it turns out that brain processes are

philosopher regards a brain process as a *paradigm* of something wholly explicable in terms of physics.

A defender of these two positions might try to avoid this outcome by claiming that the circumstances required for the occurrence of a thought do themselves consist of configurations of ultimate particles (or of their statistical properties, or something of the sort). I doubt, however, that anyone knows what it would mean to say, for example, that the *rule* that milk bottles will not be collected unless placed outside the door is a configuration of ultimate particles. At the very least, this defence would have to assume a heavy burden of explanation.

III

There is a further point connected with the one just stated. At the foundation of Smart's monism there is, I believe, the desire for a homogeneous system of explanation. Everything in the world, he feels, should be capable of the same *kind* of explanation, namely, one in terms of the entities and laws of physics. He thinks we advance towards this goal when we see that sensations, thoughts, etc., are identical with brain processes.

Smart has rendered a service to the profession by warning us against a special type of fallacy. An illustration of this fallacy would be to argue that a sensation is not a brain process because a person can be talking about a sensation and yet not be talking about a brain process.[12] The verb 'to talk about' might be called an 'intentional' verb, and this fallacy committed with it might be called 'the intentional fallacy'. Other intentional verbs would be 'to mean', to intend', 'to know', 'to predict', to 'describe', 'to notice', and so on.

It is easy to commit the intentional fallacy, and I suspect that Smart himself has done so. The verb 'to explain' is also an intentional verb and one must beware of using it to produce a fallacy. Suppose that the Prime Minister of Ireland is the ugliest Irishman. A man might argue that this cannot be so, because someone might be explaining the presence of the Irish Prime Minister in New York and yet not be explaining the presence in New York of the ugliest

---

danglers, for now brain processes have all those properties that made sensations danglers.'

[12] P. 57, above.

Irishman. It would be equally fallacious to argue that since the Irish Prime Minister and the ugliest Irishman *are* one and the same person, therefore, to explain the presence of the Prime Minister *is* to explain the presence of the ugliest Irishman.

I wonder if Smart has not reasoned fallaciously, somewhat as follows: If a sudden thought *is* a certain brain process, then to *explain* the occurrence of the brain process *is* to explain the occurrence of the thought. Thus there will be just one kind of explanation for both thoughts and brain processes.

The intentional fallacy here is transparent. If a thought is identical with a brain process, it does not follow that to explain the occurrence of the brain process is to explain the occurrence of the thought. And in fact, an explanation of the one differs in *kind* from an explanation of the other. The explanation of why someone *thought* such and such involves different assumptions and principles and is guided by different interests than is an explanation of why this or that process occurred in his brain. These explanations belong to different *systems* of explanation.

I conclude that even if Smart were right in holding that thoughts are strictly identical with brain processes (a claim that I do not yet find intelligible) he would not have established that there is one and the same explanation for the occurrence of the thoughts and for the occurrence of the brain processes. If he were to appreciate this fact then, I suspect, he would no longer have any *motive* for espousing the identity theory. For this theory, even if true, would not advance us one whit towards the single, homogeneous system of explanation that is the goal of Smart's materialism.

IV

I shall close by taking note of Smart's conceptual experiment with a human brain kept alive *in vitro*.[18] What is supposed to be proved by this experiment? That for thinking, pain, and so-called 'mental experience' in general, what goes on in the brain is more 'important' or 'essential' than behaviour. How is this proved? By the supposed fact that the experimental brain has thoughts, illusions, pains, and so on, although separated from a human body.

Could this supposed fact be a fact? Could a *brain* have thoughts, illusions or pains? The senselessness of the supposition seems so

[18] Pp. 167–8, above.

obvious that I find it hard to take it seriously. No experiment could establish this result for a brain. Why not? The fundamental reason is that a brain does not sufficiently resemble a human being.[14]

What can have led Smart to suppose that a brain can have thoughts? The only explanation which occurs to me is that he thinks that if my thought is in my brain, then my brain has a thought. This would be like thinking that if my invitation to dinner is in my pocket, then my pocket has an invitation to dinner. One bad joke deserves another.

[14] Cf. Wittgenstein, *Investigations*, sections 281 and 283.

XVIII Professor Malcolm on 'Scientific materialism and the Identity Theory'

Ernest Sosa

Professor Norman Malcolm argues that even if the scientific materialist identity theorist (the materialist, for short) were right – and thoughts were brain processes – still this would not advance him towards his ultimate goal: a homogeneous and universal system of explanation in terms of the entities of physics.

As the first step in his argument Malcolm remarks that 'to explain' is an intentional verb, i.e. that even though in explaining the holding of a certain state of affairs S_1 we do not explain the holding of S_2; S_1 and S_2 might yet be the same state of affairs.[1]

To use Malcolm's example (with a slight modification), someone might explain the presence in New York of the Prime Minister of Ireland without explaining the presence in New York of the ugliest Irishman, even though the presence in New York of the Prime Minister of Ireland and the presence in New York of the ugliest Irishman be one and the same state of affairs.

Malcolm then wonders

> if Smart [or, generally, the materialist] has not reasoned fallaciously, somewhat as follows: If a sudden thought *is* a certain brain process, then to explain the occurrence of the brain process *is* to explain the occurrence of the thought. Thus, there will be just one kind of explanation for both thoughts and brain processes.

And we are thereupon told:

> The intentional fallacy here is transparent. If a thought is identical with a brain process, it does not follow that to explain the

[1] For an excellent discussion of the intentionality of explanation, see Israel Scheffler's *The Anatomy of Inquiry* (New York 1963) pp. 57–60.

occurrence of the brain process is to explain the occurrence of the thought . . .

I conclude that even if Smart [or, the materialist] were right in holding that thoughts are strictly identical with brain processes . . . he would not have established that there is one and the same explanation for the occurrence of the thoughts and for the occurrence of the brain processes. If he were to appreciate this fact then, I suspect, he would no longer have any *motive* for espousing the identity theory. For this theory, even if true, would not advance us one whit toward the single, homogeneous system of explanation that is the goal of Smart's [or, the materialist's] materialism.

Quite to the contrary, it seems to me that the truth of the identity theory would advance us a long way towards that 'single, homogeneous system of explanation'. And the point I wish to make in showing this is an extremely brief and simple one. To introduce it I shall again make use of his example.

Suppose we are furnished with an explanation why the Prime Minister of Ireland is in New York; say it consists of five propositions, p_1 through p_5. And suppose we are further told, p_6, that the Prime Minister of Ireland and the ugliest Irishman are one and the same person. Would not p_1 through p_5 *plus* p_6 then give us an explanation why the ugliest Irishman is in New York?

Now of course Malcolm is right in holding that an explanation for the occurrence of a certain brain process does not automatically afford us an explanation for the occurrence of any thought. *Given* that the identity theory is correct, however, and that we know with which thought that certain brain process is one and the same, then surely by adding this bit of knowledge to the explanation for the occurrence of the brain process we would as a result have an explanation for the occurrence of the thought.

The important point to grasp now is that in adding that bit of knowledge we would not – if the identity theorist is right – require the acknowledgement of any transcendent entities (entities beyond those existing in space and time, including the processes undergone by matter). For in speaking of 'the thought' we would simply be using a different expression to talk about the same thing as is indicated by 'the brain process', namely the process taking place in a certain chunk of matter at such and such a spatio-temporal location. And so, while not quite within arm's reach, that single homogeneous system of explanation would be as much closer to us as is the possible by contrast to the impossible.

XIX Rejoinder to Mr Sosa

Norman Malcolm

I believe that Mr Sosa is right about my example but wrong on the substantive issue; which shows that my example was poorly chosen. If the ugliest Irishman was so ugly that even the Irish were offended, they might form a committee to get rid of him. Suppose he was kidnapped and deposited in New York. If we were informed of all this and also knew that the ugliest Irishman is the Prime Minister, I agree that we should have been given an adequate explanation of why the Prime Minister is in New York.

But if a thought were a brain process (a hypothesis that I find unintelligible) a neurophysiological explanation of the occurrence of a certain brain process would not be an explanation of the occurrence of a thought, because an explanation of the occurrence of a thought is not a neurophysiological explanation. An explanation of the occurrence of a thought is an explanation of why the thought that p occurred to some person. How do such explanations go? 'The reason the thought occurred to him that John is jealous of his wife is that he noticed how John insisted on being at the front door with her whenever she said goodnight to a male guest.' 'As he looked out at the morning sky and saw there was no fog he realised it would be a hot day.' 'The reason it occurred to me, just then, that I wanted to go fishing, is that I saw a cloud that looked very like a whale, and that reminded me of fishing.' And so on. An explanation of the occurrence of a certain thought consists in mentioning a reminder, or an association, or some reasoning, or a desire, or a worry, or an observation, or an image, etc., that led to that thought, or provoked it. A neurophysiological explanation of the occurrence of a brain process cannot do *that*. It cannot do the job of giving the kind of explanation everyone has always understood an explanation of the occurrence of a thought to be. It might turn out that if all of us came to have the (unintelligible) belief that a thought is 'strictly identical' with a brain process, then we should lose interest in explaining the occurrence of thoughts. We might even start calling a neurophysiological explanation of the occurrence of a brain process an 'explanation' of the occurrence of a thought. Who knows?

One more point. I fear that Mr Sosa has committed a form of the intentional fallacy in his final paragraph. He says that if we came to believe the identity theory then 'in speaking of "the thought" we would simply be using a different expression to talk about the same thing as is indicated by "the brain process".' Professor Smart and I agree that it would be a fallacy to infer that a thought is *not* a brain process from the fact that a person can be talking about a thought and yet not be talking about a brain process.[1] It is also fallacious to argue that if a thought *is* a brain process, then if a person is talking about a thought he is talking about a brain process. And it is likewise a fallacy to argue, as Mr Sosa does, that if we *believed* that a thought is a brain process, then if we talked about a thought we should be talking about a brain process. Even if I believe that the President of France is the tallest Frenchman, it does not follow that in talking about (or criticising or eulogising or impeaching) the President of France I am talking about (or criticising or eulogising or impeaching) the tallest Frenchman.

[1] See p. 178, above.

PART FIVE

Further Contributions to the Controversy

XX Mind–body identity, privacy and categories
Richard Rorty

I. INTRODUCTORY

Current controversies about the Mind–Body Identity Theory form a case-study for the investigation of the methods practised by linguistic philosophers. Recent criticisms of these methods question that philosophers can discern lines of demarcation between 'categories' of entities, and thereby diagnose 'conceptual confusions' in 'reductionist' philosophical theories. Such doubts arise once we see that it is very difficult, and perhaps impossible, to draw a firm line between the 'conceptual' and the 'empirical' and thus to differentiate between a statement embodying a conceptual confusion and one that expresses a surprising empirical result. The proponent of the Identity Theory (by which I mean one who thinks it sensible to assert that empirical inquiry will discover that *sensations* (not thoughts) are identical with certain brain-processes)[1] holds that his opponents' arguments to the effect that empirical inquiry *could* not identify brain processes and sensations are admirable illustrations of this difficulty. For, he argues, the classifications of linguistic expressions that are the ground of his opponents' criticism are classifications of a language which is as it is because it is the language spoken at a given stage of empirical inquiry. But the sort of empirical results that would show brain processes and sensations to be identical would also bring about changes in our ways of speaking.

[1] A proponent of the Identity Theory is usually thought of as one who predicts that empirical inquiry *will* reach this result – but few philosophers in fact stick their necks out in this way. The issue is not the truth of the prediction, but whether such a prediction makes sense. Consequently, by 'Identity Theory' I shall mean the assertion that it does make sense.

I include only sensations within the scope of the theory because the inclusion of thoughts would raise a host of separate problems (about the reducibility of intentional and semantic discourse to statements about linguistic behaviour), and because the form of the Identity Theory which has been most discussed in the recent literature restricts itself to a consideration of sensations.

These changes would make these classifications out of date. To árgue against the Identity Theory on the basis of the way we talk now is like arguing against an assertion that supernatural phenomena are identical with certain natural phenomena on the basis of the way in which superstitious people talk. There is simply no such thing as a method of classifying linguistic expressions that has results guaranteed to remain intact despite the results of future empirical inquiry. Thus in this area (and perhaps in all areas) there is no method which will have the sort of magisterial neutrality of which linguistic philosophers fondly dream.

In this paper I wish to support this general line of argument. I shall begin by pressing the claims of the analogy between mental events and supernatural events. Then I shall try to rebut the objection which seems generally regarded as fatal to the claims of the Identity Theory – the objection that 'privacy' is of the essence of mental events, and thus that a theory which holds that mental events might *not* be 'private' is *ipso facto* confused. I shall conclude with some brief remarks on the implications of my arguments for the more general metaphilosophical issues at stake.

II. The Two Forms of the Identity Theory

The obvious objection to the Identity Theory is that 'identical' either means a relation such that

$$(x) \ (y) \ [(x = y) \supset (F) \ (Fx \equiv Fy)]$$

(the relation of 'strict identity') or it does not. If it does, then we find ourselves forced into

> saying truthfully that physical processes such as brain processes are dim or fading or nagging or false, and that mental phenomena such as after-images are publicly observable or physical or spatially located or swift,[2]

and thus using meaningless expressions, for

> we can say that the above expressions are meaningless in the sense that they commit a category mistake; i.e. in forming these expressions we have predicated predicates, appropriate to one logical category, of expressions that belong to a different logical category. This is surely a conceptual mistake.[3]

[2] Cornman, p. 127, above.   [3] P. 127, above.

But if by 'identical' the Identity Theory does *not* mean a relation of strict identity, then what relation *is* intended? How does it differ from the mere relation of 'correlation' which, it is admitted on all sides, might without confusion be said to hold between sensations and brain processes?

Given this dilemma, two forms of the Identity Theory may be distinguished. The first, which I shall call the *translation* form, grasps the first horn, and attempts to show that the odd-sounding expressions mentioned above do not involve category-mistakes, and that this can be shown by suitable translations into 'topic-neutral' language of the sentences in which these terms are originally used.[4] The second, which I shall call the *disappearance* form, grasps the second horn, and holds that the relation in question is not strict identity, but rather the sort of relation which obtains between, to put it crudely, existent entities and non-existent entities when reference to the latter once served (some of) the purposes presently served by reference to the former – the sort of relation that holds, for example, between 'quantity of caloric fluid' and 'mean kinetic energy of molecules'. There is an obvious sense of 'same' in which what used to be called 'a quantity of calorific fluid' is *the same thing* as what is now called a certain mean kinetic energy of molecules, but there is no reason to think that all features truly predicated of the one may be sensibly predicated of the other.[5] The translation form of the theory holds that if we really understood what we were saying when we said things like 'I am having a stabbing pain' we should see that since we are talking about 'topic-neutral' matters we might, for all we know, be talking about brain processes. The disappearance form holds that it is unnecessary to show that suitable translations (into 'topic-neutral' language) of our talk about sensations can be

[4] Cf. Smart, Paper III, esp. pp. 59–61, and especially the claim that 'When a person says "I see a yellowish-orange after-image" he is saying something like this: "There is something going on which is like what is going on when I have my eyes open, am awake, and there is an orange illuminated in good light in front of me, that is, when I really see an orange"' (p. 60). For criticisms of Smart's programme of translation, see Papers X, XI and XIII; also the articles cited in the first footnote to Smart's own article.

[5] No statement of the disappearance form of the theory with which I am acquainted is as clear and explicit as Smart's statement of the translation form. See, however, Feyerabend, Papers XIV and XV. See also Wilfrid Sellars, 'The Identity Approach to the Mind–Body Problem', *Review of Metaphysics*, 18 (1965) pp. 430–51. My indebtedness to this and other writings of Sellars will be obvious in what follows.

given – as unnecessary as to show that statements about quantities of calorific fluid, when properly understood, may be seen to be topic-neutral statements.[6]

From the point of view of this second form of the theory, it is a mistake to assume that 'X's are nothing but Y's' entails 'All attributes meaningfully predicable of X's are meaningfully predicated of Y's', for this assumption would forbid us ever to express the results of scientific inquiry in terms of (in Cornman's useful phrase) 'cross-category identity'.[7] It would seem that the verb in such statements as 'Zeus's thunderbolts are discharges of static electricity' and 'Demoniacal possession is a form of hallucinatory psychosis' is the 'is' of identity, yet it can hardly express *strict* identity. The disappearance form of the Identity Theory suggests that we view such statements as elliptical for e.g. 'What people used to call "demoniacal possession" is a form of hallucinatory psychosis,' where the relation in question *is* strict identity. Since there is no reason why 'what people call "X"' should be in the same 'category' (in the Rylean sense) as 'X', there is no need to claim, as the translation form of the theory must, that topic-neutral translations of statements using 'X' are possible.

In what follows, I shall confine myself to a discussion and defence of the disappearance form of the theory. My first reason for this is that I believe that the analysis of 'Sensations are identical with certain brain processes' proposed by the disappearance form (viz. 'What people now call "sensations" are identical with certain brain processes') accomplishes the same end as the translation form's programme of topic-neutral translation – namely, avoiding the charge of 'category-mistake', while preserving the full force of the traditional materialist position. My second reason is that I believe that an attempt to defend the translation form will inevitably get bogged down in controversy about the adequacy of proposed topic-neutral translations of statements about sensations. There is obviously a sense of 'adequate translation' in which the topic-neutrality of the purported translations *ipso facto* makes them inadequate. So the

[6] Both forms agree, however, on the requirements which would have to be satisfied if we are to claim that the empirical discovery in question has been made. Roughly, they are (1) that one–one or one–many correlations could be established between every type of sensation and some clearly demarcated kind(s) of brain processes; (2) that every known law which refers to sensations would be subsumed under laws about brain processes; (3) that new laws about sensations be discovered by deduction from laws about brain processes.

[7] P. 129, above.

proponent of the translation form of the theory will have to fall back on a weaker sense of 'adequate translation'. But the weaker this sense becomes, the less impressive is the claim being made, and the less difference between the Identity Theory and the non-controversial thesis that certain brain processes may be constantly correlated with certain sensations.

III. The Analogy between Demons and Sensations

At first glance, there seems to be a fatal weakness in the disappearance form of the Identity Theory. For normally when we say 'What people call "X's" are nothing but "Y's"' we are prepared to add that 'There are no X's.' Thus when, for example, we say that 'What people call "caloric fluid" is nothing but the motion of molecules' or 'What people call "witches" are nothing but psychotic women' we are prepared to say that there are no witches, and no such thing as caloric fluid. But it seems absurd to say that there might turn out to be no such things as sensations.

To see that this disanalogy is not fatal to the Identity Theory, let us consider the following situation. A certain primitive tribe holds the view that illnesses are caused by demons – a different demon for each sort of illness. When asked what more is known about these demons than that they cause illness, they reply that certain members of the tribe – the witch-doctors – can see, after a meal of sacred mushrooms, various (intangible) humanoid forms on or near the bodies of patients. The witch-doctors have noted, for example, that a blue demon with a long nose accompanies epileptics, a fat red one accompanies sufferers from pneumonia, etc. They know such further facts as that the fat red demon dislikes a certain sort of mould which the witch-doctors give people who have pneumonia. (There are various competing theories about what demons do when not causing diseases, but serious witch-doctors regard such speculations as unverifiable and profitless.)

If we encountered such a tribe, we would be inclined to tell them that there are no demons. We would tell them that diseases were caused by germs, viruses, and the like. We would add that the witch-doctors were not seeing demons, but merely having hallucinations. We would be quite right, but would we be right on *empirical* grounds? What empirical criteria, built into the demon-talk of the tribe, go unsatisfied? What predictions which the tribesmen make fail to come true? If there are none, a sophisticated witch-doctor may reply that all modern science can do is to show (1) that the

presence of demons is constantly correlated with that of germs,
viruses, and the like, and (2) that eating certain mushrooms sometimes makes people think they see things that aren't really there.
This is hardly sufficient to show that there are no demons. At best,
it shows that if we forget about demons, then (a) a simpler account
of the cause and cure of disease and (b) a simpler account of why
people make the perceptual reports they do, may be given.

What do we reply to such a sophisticated witch-doctor? I think
that all that we would have left to say is that the simplicity of the
accounts which can be offered if we forget about demons *is* an
excellent reason for saying that there are no demons. Demon-
discourse is one way of describing and predicting phenomena, but
there are better ways. We *could* (as the witch-doctor urges) tack
demon-discourse on to modern science by saying, first, that diseases
are caused by the compresence of demons and germs (each being a
necessary, but neither a sufficient, condition) and, second, that the
witch-doctors (unlike drunkards and psychotics) really do see intangible beings (about whom, alas, nothing is known save their visual
appearances). If we did so, we would retain all the predictive and
explanatory advantages of modern science. We would know as
much about the cause and cure of disease, and about hallucinations,
as we did before. We would, however, be burdened with problems
which we did not have before: the problem of why demons are
visible only to witch-doctors, and the problem of why germs cannot
cause diseases all by themselves. We avoid both problems by saying
that demons do not exist. The witch-doctor may remark that this
use of Occam's razor has the same advantage as that of theft ovei
honest toil. To such a remark, the only reply could be an account of
the practical advantages gained by the use of the razor in the past.

Now the Identity Theorist's claim is that sensations may be to
the future progress of psycho-physiology as demons are to modern
science. Just as we now want to deny that there are demons, future
science may want to deny that there are sensations. The only obstacle
to replacing sensation-discourse with brain-discourse seems to be
that sensation-statements have a reporting as well as an explanatory
function. But the demon case makes clear that the discovery of a
new way of explaining the phenomena previously explained by
reference to a certain sort of entity, *combined with a new account
of what is being reported by observation-statements about that sort
of entity*, may give good reason for saying that there are no entities
of that sort. The absurdity of saying 'Nobody has ever felt a pain'
is no greater than that of saying 'Nobody has ever seen a demon',

if we have a suitable answer to the question 'What *was* I reporting when I said I felt a pain?' To this question, the science of the future may reply 'You were reporting the occurrence of a certain brain process, and it would make life simpler for us if you would, in the future, *say* "My C-fibres are firing" instead of saying "I'm in pain".' In so saying, he has as good a prima facie case as the scientist who answers the witch-doctor's question 'What *was* I reporting when I reported a demon?' by saying 'You were reporting the content of your hallucination, and it would make life simpler if, in the future, you would describe your experiences in those terms.'

Given this prima facie analogy between demons and sensations, we can now attend to some disanalogies. We may note, first, that there is no simple way of filling in the blank in 'What people called "demons" are nothing but ———.' For neither 'hallucinatory contents' nor 'germs' will do. The observational and the explanatory roles of 'demon' must be distingushed. We need to say something like 'What people who reported seeing demons were reporting was simply the content of their hallucinations', and *also* something like 'What people explained by reference to demons can be explained better by reference to germs, viruses, etc.' Because of the need for a relatively complex account of how we are to get along without reference to demons, we cannot *identify* 'What we called "demons"' with anything. So, instead, we simply deny their existence. In the case of sensations, however, we can give a relatively simple account of how to get along in the future. Both the explanatory *and* the reporting functions of statements about sensations can be taken over by statements about brain processes. Therefore we are prepared to identify 'What we called "sensations"' with brain processes, and to say 'What we called "sensations" turn out to be nothing but brain processes.'

Thus this disanalogy does not have the importance which it appears to have at first. In both the demon case and the sensation case, the proposed reduction has the same pragmatic consequences: namely, that we should stop asking questions about the causal and/ or spatio-temporal relationships holding between the 'reduced' entities (demons, sensations) and the rest of the universe, and replace these with questions about the relationships holding between certain other entities (germs, hallucinatory experiences, brain processes) and the rest of the universe. It happens, for the reasons just sketched, that the proposed reduction is put in the form of a denial of existence in one case, and of an identification in another case. But 'There are no demons' and 'What people call "sensations" are nothing but brain processes' can both equally well be paraphrased as 'Elimination of the referring use of the expression in question ("demon", "sensation") from our language would leave our ability to describe and predict undiminished.'

Nevertheless, the claim that there might turn out to be no such thing as a 'sensation' seems scandalous. The fact that a witch-doctor might be scandalised by a similar claim about demons does not, in itself, do much to diminish our sense of shock. In what follows, I wish to account for this intuitive implausibility. I shall argue that it rests *solely* upon the fact that elimination of the referring use of 'sensation' from our language would be in the highest degree *impractical*. If this can be shown, then I think that the Identity Theorist will be cleared of the charge of 'conceptual confusion' usually levelled against him. Rather than proceeding directly to this argument, however, I shall first consider a line of argument which has often been used to show that he *is* guilty of this charge. Examining this line of argument will permit me to sketch in greater detail what the Identity Theorist is and is not saying.

IV. The Eliminability of Observation Terms

The usual move made by the opponents of the Identity Theory is to compare suggested reduction of sensations to brain processes to certain other cases in which we say that 'X's turn out to be nothing but Y's.' There are two significantly different classes of cases and it might seem that the Identity Theorist confuses them. First, there is the sort of case in which both 'X' and 'Y' are used to refer to observable entities, and the claim that 'what people called "X's" are nothing but Y's' backed up by pointing out that the statement 'This is an X' commits one to an empirically false proposition. For example, we say that 'What people called "unicorn horns" are nothing but narwhal horns', and urge that we cease to respond to a perceptual situation with 'This is a unicorn horn'. We do this because 'This is a unicorn horn' commits one to the existence of unicorns, and there are, it turns out, no unicorns. Let us call this sort of case *identification of observables with other observables*. Second, there is the sort of case in which 'X' is used to refer to an observable entity and 'Y' is used to refer to an unobservable entity. Here we do not (typically) back up the claim that 'What people called "X's" are nothing but Y's' by citing an empirically false proposition presupposed by 'This is an X'. For example, the statement that 'What people call "tables" are nothing but clouds of molecules' does not suggest, or require as a ground, that people who say 'This is a table' hold false beliefs. Rather, we are suggesting that something *more* has been found out about the sort of situation reported by 'This is a table'. Let us call this second sort of case *identification of observables with theoretical entities*.

It seems that we cannot assimilate the identification of sensations with brain processes to either of these cases. For, unlike the typical case of identification of observables with other observables, we do not wish to say that people who have reported sensations in the past have (necessarily) any empirically disconfirmed beliefs. People are not wrong about 'unicorn horns'. Again, unlike the typical case of the identification of observables with theoretical entities, we do not want to say that brain processes are 'theoretical' or unobservable. Furthermore, in cases in which we identify an observable X with an unobservable Y, we are usually willing to accept the remark that 'That does not show that there are no X's'. The existence of tables is not (it would seem) impugned by their identification with clouds of electrons, as the existence of unicorn horns is impugned by their identification with narwhal horns. But a defender of the disappearance form of the Identity Theory *does* want to impugn the existence of sensations.

Because the claim that 'what people call "sensations" may turn out to be nothing but brain processes' cannot be assimilated to either of these cases, it has been attacked as trivial or incoherent. The following dilemma is posed by those who attack it: either the Identity Theorist claims that talk about sensations presupposes some empirically disconfirmed belief (and what could it be?) or the 'identity' which he has in mind is the uninteresting sort of identity which holds between tables and clouds of molecules (mere 'theoretical replaceability').

The point at which the Identity Theorist should attack this dilemma is the premise invoked in stating the second horn – the premise that the identification of tables with clouds of molecules does not permit us to infer to the non-existence of tables. This premise is true, but *why* is it true? That there is room for reflection here is apparent when we place the case of tables side-by-side with the case of demons. If there is any point to saying that tables are nothing but clouds of molecules it is presumably to say that, in principle, we could stop making a referring use of 'table', and of any extensionally equivalent term, and still leave our ability to describe and predict undiminished. But this would seem just the point of (and the justification for) saying that there are no demons. Why does the realisation that nothing would be lost by the dropping of 'table' from our vocabulary still leave us with the conviction that there are tables, whereas the same realisation about demons leave us with the conviction that there are no demons? I suggest that the only answer to this question which will stand examination is that although we could *in principle* drop 'table', it would be monstrously inconvenient to do so, whereas it is both possible in principle and convenient in practice to drop 'demon'. The reason 'But there still are tables' sounds so plausible is that nobody would dream of suggesting that we stop reporting our experiences in table-talk and start reporting them in molecule-talk. The reason 'There are no demons' sounds so plausible is that we are quite willing to suggest that the witch-doctors stop reporting their experiences in demon-talk and start reporting them in hallucination-talk.

A conclusive argument that this practical difference is the *only* relevant difference would, obviously, canvass all the other differences which might be noted. I shall not attempt this. Instead, I shall try to make my claim plausible by sketching a general theory of the conditions under which a term may cease to have a referring use without those who made such a use being convicted of having held false beliefs.

Given the same sorts of correlations between X's and Y's, we are more likely to say 'X's are nothing but Y's' when reference to X's is habitually made in non-inferential reports, and more likely to say 'There are no X's' when such reference is never or rarely made. (By 'non-inferential report' I mean a statement in response to which questions like 'How did you know?' 'On what evidence do you say ... ?' and 'What leads you to think ... ?' are normally considered misplaced and unanswerable, but which is none the less capable of empirical confirmation.) Thus we do not say that the identification of temperature with the kinetic energy of molecules shows that there is no such thing as temperature, since 'temperature' originally (i.e. before the invention of thermometers) stood for something which was always reported non-inferentially, and still is frequently so reported. Similarly for all identifications of familiar macro-objects with unfamiliar micro-objects. But since in our culture-circle we do not *habitually* report non-inferentially the presence of caloric fluid, demons, etc., we do not feel unhappy at the bald suggestion that there are no such things.

Roughly speaking, then, the more accustomed we are to 'X' serving as an observation-term (by which I mean a term habitually used in non-inferential reports) the more we prefer, when inquiry shows the possibility of accounting for the phenomena explained by reference to X's without such reference, to 'identify' X's with some sort of Y's, rather than to deny existence to X's *tout court*. *But the more grounds we have for such identification, the more chance there is that we shall stop using 'X' in non-inferential reports*, and thus the greater chance of our eventually coming to accept the claim that 'there are no X's' with equanimity. This is why we find borderline cases, and gradual shifts from assimilations of X's to Y's to an assertion that X's do not exist. For example, most people do not report the presence of pink rats non-inferentially (nor inferentially, for that matter), but some do. The recognition that they are in the minority helps those who do so to admit that there are no pink rats. But suppose that the vast majority of us had always seen (intangible and uncatchable) pink rats, would it not then be likely that we should resist the bald assertion that there are no pink rats and insist on something of the form 'pink rats are nothing but ...'? It might be a very long time before we came to drop the habit of reporting pink rats and began reporting hallucinations instead.

The typical case-history of an observation-term ceasing to have a referring use runs the following course: (1) X's are the subjects of both inferential and non-inferential reports;[8] (2) empirical discoveries are made which enable us to subsume X-laws under Y-laws and to produce new X-laws by studying Y's; (3) inferential reports of X's cease to be made; (4) non-inferential reports of X's are reinterpreted either (4a) as reports of Y's, *or* (4b) as reports of mental entities (thoughts that one is seeing an X, hallucinatory images, etc.); (5) non-inferential reports of X's cease to be made (because their place is taken by non-inferential reports either of Y's or of thoughts, hallucinatory images, etc.); (6) we conclude that there simply are no such things as X's.

This breakdown of stages lets us pick out two crucial conditions that must be satisfied if we are to move from 'X's are nothing but Y's' (stage 2) to 'there are no X's' (stage 6). These conditions are:

(A) The Y-laws must be *better* at explaining the kinds of phenomena explained by the X-laws (not just equally good).

---

[8] Note that if X's are *only* referred to in inferential reports – as in the case of 'neutrons' and 'epicycles', no philosophically interesting reduction takes place. For in such cases there is no hope of getting rid of an explanandum; all we get rid of is a putative explanation.

Indeed, they must be sufficiently better so that *the inconvenience of changing one's linguistic habits by ceasing to
make reports about X's is less than the inconvenience of
going through the routine of translating one's X-reports into
Y-reports in order to get satisfactory explanations of the
phenomena in question.* If this condition is not satisfied, the
move from stage (2) to stage (3) will not be made, and thus
no later move will be made.

(B)   Either Y-reports may themselves be made non-inferentially,
or X-reports may be treated as reports of mental entities. For
we must be able to have some answer to the question 'What
am I reporting when I non-inferentially report about an
X?', and the only answers available are 'you're reporting on
a Y' or 'you're reporting on some merely mental entity.' If
neither answer is available, we can move neither to (4a) nor
to (4b), nor, therefore, on to (5) and (6).

Now the reason we move from stage (2) to stage (3) in the case of
demons is that (A) is obviously satisfied. The phenomena which we
explained by reference to the activity of demons are so much better
explained in other ways that it is simpler to stop inferring to the
existence of demons altogether than to continue making such in-
ferences, and then turning to laws about germs and the like for an
explanation of the behaviour of the demons. The reason why we
do *not* move from (2) to (3) – much less to (6) – in the case of temperature or tables is that explanations formulated in terms of temperatures are so good, on the ground which they were originally
intended to cover, that we feel no temptation to stop talking about
temperatures and tables merely because we can, in some cases, get
more precise predictions by going up a level to laws about molecules.
The reason why we move on from (3) to (4) in the case of demons
is that the alternative labelled (4b) is readily available – we can
easily consign experiences of demons to that great dumping-ground
of outdated entities, the Mind. There were no experiences of
demons, we say, but only experiences of mental images.

Now it seems obvious that, in the case of sensations, (A) will not
be satisfied. The inconvenience of ceasing to talk about sensations
would be so great that only a fanatical materialist would think it
worth the trouble to cease referring to sensations. If the Identity
Theorist is taken to be predicting that some day 'sensation', 'pain',
'mental image', and the like will drop out of our vocabulary, he is
almost certainly wrong. But if he is saying simply that, at no greater

cost than an inconvenient linguistic reform, we *could* drop such terms, he is entirely justified. And I take this latter claim to be all that traditional materialism has ever desired.

Before leaving the analogy between demons and sensations, I wish to note one further disanalogy which an opponent of the Identity Theory might pounce upon. Even if we set aside the fact that (A would not be satisfied in the case of sensations, such an opponent might say, we should note the difficulty in satisfying (B). It would seem that there is no satisfactory answer to the question 'What *was* I non-inferentially reporting when I reported on my sensations?' For neither (4a) nor (4b) seems an available option. The first does not seem to be available because it is counter-intuitive to think of, for example, 'I am having my C-fibres stimulated', as capable of being used to make a non-inferential report. The second alternative is simply silly – there is no point in saying that when we report a sensation we are reporting some 'merely mental' event. For sensations are *already* mental events. The last point is important for an understanding of the prima facie absurdity of the disappearance form of the Identity Theory. The reason why most statements of the form 'there might turn out to be no X's at all' can be accepted with more or less equanimity in the context of forecasts of scientific results is that we are confident we shall always be able to 'save the phenomena' by answering the question 'But what about all those X's we've been accustomed to observe?' with some reference to thoughts-of-X's, images-of-X's, and the like. Reference to mental entities provides non-inferential reports of X's with something to have been about. But when we want to say 'There might turn out to be no mental entities at all', we cannot use this device. This result makes clear that if the analogy between the past disappearance of supernatural beings and the possible future disappearance of sensations is to be pressed, we must claim that alternative (4a) is, appearances to the contrary, still open. That is, we must hold that the question 'What *was* I non-inferentially reporting when I non-inferentially reported a stabbing pain?' can be sensibly answered 'You were reporting a stimulation of your C-fibres.'

Now why should this *not* be a sensible answer? Let us begin by getting a bad objection to it out of the way. One can imagine someone arguing that this answer can only be given if a stimulation of C-fibres is strictly identical with a stabbing pain, and that such strict identification involves category-mistakes. But this objection presupposes that 'A report of an X is a report of a Y' entails that 'X's are Y's.' If we grant this presupposition we shall not be able to say that the question 'What was I reporting when I reported a demon?' is properly answered by 'You were reporting the content of a hallucination which you were having.' However, if we ask why this objection is plausible, we can see the grain of truth which it embodies and conceals. We are usually unwilling to accept 'You were reporting a Y' as an answer to the question 'What *was* I non-inferentially reporting when I non-inferentially reported an X?' unless (a) Y's are themselves the kind of thing we habitually report on non-inferentially, and (8) there does not exist already a habitual practice of reporting Y's non-inferentially. Thus we accept 'the content of a hallucination' as a sensible answer because we know that such contents, being 'mental images', are just the sort of thing which does get non-inferentially reported (once it is recognised for what it is) and because we are not accustomed to making non-inferential reports in the form 'I am having a hallucinatory image of. . . .'[9] To take an example of answers to this sort of question that are *not* sensible, we reject the claim that when we report on a table we are reporting on a mass of whirling particles, for either we think we know under what circumstances we should make such a report, and know that these circumstances do not obtain, or we believe that the presence of such particles can only be inferred and never observed.

The oddity of saying that when I think I am reporting on a stabbing pain I am actually reporting on a stimulation of my C-fibres is similar to these last two cases. We either imagine a situation in which we can envisage ourselves non-inferentially reporting such stimulation (periscope hitched up to a microscope so as to give us a view of our trepanned skull, overlying fibres folded out of the way, stimulation evident by change in colour, etc.), or else we regard 'stimulation of C-fibres' as not the sort of thing which *could* be the subject of a non-inferential report (but inherently a 'theoretical' state of affairs whose existence can only be inferred, and not observed). In either case, the assertion that we have been non-inferentially reporting on a brain process all our lives seems absurd. So the proponent of the disappearance form of the Identity Theory must show that reports of brain processes are neither incapable of being

[9] Note that people who *become* accustomed to making the latter sort of reports may no longer accept explanations of their erroneous non-inferential reports by reference to hallucinations. For they know what mental images are like, and they know that *this* pink rat was not a hallucinatory content. The more frequent case, fortunately, is that they just cease to report pink rats and begin reporting hallucinations, for their hallucinations no longer deceive them.

non-inferential nor, if non-inferential, necessarily made in the way just imagined (with the periscope–microscope gadget) or in some other peculiar way. But now we must ask who bears the burden of proof. Why, after all, should we think that brain processes are *not* a fit subject-matter for non-inferential reports? And why should it not be the case that the circumstances in which we make non-inferential reports about brain processes are just those circumstances in which we make non-inferential reports about sensations? For this will in fact be the case if, when we were trained to say, for example, 'I'm in pain' we were in fact being trained to respond to the occurrence within ourselves of a stimulation of C-fibres. If this is the case, the situation will be perfectly parallel to the case of demons and hallucinations. We *will*, indeed, have been making non-inferential reports about brain processes all our lives *sans le savoir*.

This latter suggestion can hardly be rejected *a priori*, unless we hold that we can only be taught to respond to the occurrence of A's with the utterance 'A!' if we were able, prior to this teaching, to be aware, when an A was present, that it was present. But this latter claim is plausible only if we assume that there is an activity which can reasonably be called 'awareness' prior to the learning of language. I do not wish to fight once again the battle which has been fought by Wittgenstein and many of his followers against such a notion of awareness. I wish rather to take it as having been won, and to take for granted that there is no *a priori* reason why a brain process is inherently unsuited to be the subject of a non-inferential report. The distinction between observation-terms and non-observation-terms is relative to linguistic practices (practices which may change as inquiry progresses), rather than capable of being marked out once and for all by distinguishing between the 'found' and the 'made' elements in our experience. I think that the recognition of this relativity is the first of the steps necessary for a proper appreciation of the claims of the Identity Theory. In what follows, I want to show that this first step leads naturally to a second: the recognition that the distinction between *private* and *public* subject-matters is as relative as that between items signified by observation-terms and items not so signified.

The importance of this second step is clear. For even if we grant that reports of brain processes may be non-inferential, we still need to get round the facts that reports of sensations have an epistemological peculiarity that leads us to call them reports of *private* entities, and that brain processes are intrinsically *public* entities. Unless we can overcome our intuitive conviction that a report of a private matter (with its attendant infallibility) cannot be identified with a report of a public matter (with its attendant fallibility), we shall not be able to take seriously the claim of the proponents of the disappearance form of the Identity Theory that alternative (4a) is open, and hence that nothing prevents sensations from disappearing from discourse in the same manner, and for the same reasons, as supernatural beings have disappeared from discourse. So far in this paper I have deliberately avoided the problem of the 'privacy' of sensations, because I wished to show that if this problem *can* be surmounted, the Identity Theorist may fairly throw the burden of proof on to his opponent by asking whether a criterion can be produced which would show that the identification of sensations and brain processes involves a conceptual confusion, while absolving the claim that demons do not exist because of such a confusion. Since I doubt that such a criterion *can* be produced, I am inclined to say that if the problem about 'privacy' is overcome, then the Identity Theorist has made out his case.

V. The 'Privacy' Objection

The problem that the privacy of first-person sensation reports presents for the Identity Theory has recently been formulated in considerable detail by Baier.[10] In this section, I shall confine myself to a discussion of his criticism of Smart's initial reply to this argument. Smart holds that the fact that 'the language of introspective reports has a different logic from the logic of material processes' is no objection to the Identity Theory, since we may expect that empirical inquiry can and will change this logic:

> It is obvious that until the brain-process theory is much improved and widely accepted there will be no *criteria* for saying 'Smith has an experience of such-and-such a sort' except Smith's introspective reports. So we have adopted a rule of language that (normally) what Smith says goes.[11]

Baier thinks that this reply 'is simply a confusion of the privacy of the subject-matter and the availability of external evidence'.[12] Baier's intuition is that the difference between a language-stratum in which the fact that a report is sincerely made is sufficient warrant for its truth, and one in which this situation does not obtain, seems so great as to call for an explanation – and that the only explanation

10 See Paper VIII.
11 Paper III, p. 63, above.
12 P. 100, above.

is that the two strata concern different subject-matters. Indeed Baier is content to let the mental–physical distinction stand or fall with the distinction between 'private' subject-matters and 'public' subject-matters, and he therefore assumes that to show that 'introspective reports are necessarily about something private, and that being about something private is *incompatible with* being about something public'[13] is to show, once and for all, that the Identity Theory involves a conceptual confusion. Baier, in short, is undertaking to show that 'once private, always private'.

He argues for his view as follows:

> To say that one day our physiological knowledge will increase to such an extent that we shall be able to make absolutely reliable encephalograph-based claims about people's experiences is only to say that, if carefully checked, our encephalograph-based claims about 'experiences' will always be *correct*, i.e. will make the *same claims* as *truthful* introspective reports. If correct encephalograph-based claims about Smith's experiences contradict Smith's introspective reports, we shall be entitled to infer that he is *lying*. In that sense, what Smith says will no longer go. But we cannot of course infer that he is making a mistake, for that is nonsense. . . . *However good the evidence may be, such a physiological theory can never be used to show to the sufferer that he was mistaken in thinking that he had a pain, for such a mistake is inconceivable.* The sufferer's epistemological authority must therefore be better than the best physiological theory can ever be. Physiology can therefore never provide a person with more than *evidence* that someone else is having an experience of one sort or another. It can never lay down independent and overriding *criteria* for saying that someone is having an experience of a certain sort. Talk about brain processes therefore must be about something other than talk about experiences. Hence, introspective reports and brain-process talk cannot be merely different ways of talking about the same thing.[14]

Smart's own reply to this line of argument is to admit that

> No physiological evidence, say from a gadget attached to my skull, could make me withdraw the statement that I have a pain when as a matter of fact I feel a pain. For example, the gadget might show no suitable similarities of cerebral processes on the various occasions on which I felt a pain. . . . I must, I think, agree with Baier that if the sort of situation which we have just invisaged did in fact come about, then I should have to reject the brain-process thesis, and would perhaps espouse dualism.[15]

[13] P. 97, above.
[14] Pp. 102–3, above; italics added.
[15] P. 107, above.

But this is not the interesting case. The interesting case is the one
in which suitable similarities are in fact found to occur – the same
similarities in all subjects – until one day (long after all empirical
generalisations about sensations *qua* sensations have been subsumed
under physiological laws, and long after direct manipulation of the
brain has become the exclusive method of relieving pain) somebody
(call him Jones) thinks he has no pain, but the encephalograph says
that the brain process correlated with pain did occur. (Let us
imagine that Jones himself is observing the gadget, and that the
problem about whether he might have made a mistake is a problem
for Jones; this eliminates the possibility of lying.) Now in most cases
in which one's observation throws doubt on a correlation which is
so central to current scientific explanations, one tries to eliminate
the possibility of observational error. But in Baier's view it would
be absurd for Jones to do this, for 'a mistake is inconceivable'.
Actually, however, it is fairly clear what Jones' first move would
be – he will begin to suspect that he does not know what pain is –
i.e. that he is not using the word 'pain' in the way in which his
fellows use it.[16]

So now Jones looks about for independent verification of the
hypothesis that he does not use 'I am in pain' incorrectly. But here
he runs up against the familiar difficulty about the vocabulary used
in making introspective reports – the difficulty of distinguishing
between 'misuse of language' and 'mistake in judgement', between
(a) recognising the state of affairs which obtains for what it is, but
describing it wrongly because the words used in the description are
not the right words, and (b) being able to describe it rightly once it
is recognised for what it is, but not in fact recognising it for what
it is (in the way in which one deceived by an illusion does not
recognise the situation for what it is). If we do not have a way of
determining which of these situations obtains, we do not have a
genuine contrast between misnaming and misjudging. To see that
there is no genuine contrast in this case, suppose that Jones was not
burned prior to the time that he hitches on the encephalograph, but
now he is. When he is, the encephalograph says that the brain process constantly correlated with pain reports occurs in Jones' brain.
However, although he exhibits pain-behaviour, Jones thinks that he
does not feel pain. (But, now as in the past, he both exhibits pain-
behaviour and thinks that he feels pain when he is frozen, stuck,
struck, racked, etc.) How is it that he does not know that *pain* covers

[16] This problem will remain, of course, even if Jones merely *thinks* about
whether he is in pain, but does not say anything.

what you feel when you are burned as well as what you feel when you are stuck, struck, etc.? Or is it that he really does not feel pain when he is burned? Suppose we tell Jones that what he feels when he is burned is *also* called 'pain'. Suppose he then admits that he does feel *something*, but insists that what he feels is quite *different* from what he feels when he is stuck, struck, etc. Where does Jones go from here? Has he failed to learn the language properly, or is he correctly (indeed infallibly) reporting that he has different sensations from these normally had in the situation in question? (Compare the parallel question in the case of a man who uses 'blue' in all the usual ways except that he refuses to grant that blue is a colour – on the ground that it is so different from red, yellow, orange, violet, etc.)

The only device which would decide this question would be to establish a convention that anyone who sincerely denied that he felt a pain while exhibiting pain-behaviour and being burned *ipso facto* did not understand how to use 'pain'. This denial would *prove* that he lacked an understanding. But this would be a dangerous path to follow. For not to understand when to use the word 'pain' in non-inferential reports is presumably to be unable to know which of one's sensations to call a 'pain'. And the denial that one felt pain in the circumstances mentioned would only prove such inability if one indeed *had* the sensation normally called a pain. So now we would have a public criterion, satisfaction of which would count as showing that the subject had such a sensation – i.e. that he felt a pain even though he did not think that he did. But if such a criterion exists, its application overrides any contradictory report that he may make – for such a report will be automatically disallowed by the fact that it constitutes a demonstration that he does not know what he is talking about. The dilemma is that either a report about one's sensations which violates a certain public criterion is a sufficient condition for saying that the reporter does not know how to use 'pain' in the correct way, or there is no such criterion. If there is, the fact that one cannot be mistaken about pains does not entail that sincere reports of pain cannot be overridden. If there is not, then there is no way to answer the question formulated at the end of the last paragraph, and hence no way to eliminate the possibility that Jones may not know what pain is. Now since the *a priori* probability that he does not is a good deal higher than the *a priori* probability that the psycho-physiological theory of Jones' era is mistaken, this theory has little to fear from Jones. (Although it would have a great deal to fear from a sizable accumulation of cases like Jones'.)

To sum up this point, we may look back at the italicised sentence in the above quotation from Baier. We now see that the claim that 'such a mistake is inconceivable' is an ellipsis for the claim that a mistake, made *by one who knows what pain is*, is inconceivable, for only this expanded form will entail that when Jones and the encephalograph disagree, Jones is always right. But when formulated in this way our infallibility about our pains can be seen to be empty. Being infallible about something would be useful only if we could draw the usual distinction between misnaming and misjudging, and, having ascertained that we were not misnaming, know that we were not misjudging. But where there are no criteria for misjudging (or to put it more accurately, where in the crucial cases the criteria for misjudging turn out to be the same as the criteria for misnaming) then to say that we are infallible is to pay ourselves an empty compliment. Our neighbours will not hesitate to ride roughshod over our reports of our sensations unless they are assured that we know our way around among them, and we cannot satisfy them on this point unless, up to a certain point, we tell the same sort of story about them as they do. The limits of permissible stories are flexible enough for us to be able to convince them occasionally that we have odd sensations, but not flexible enough for us to use these surprising sensations to break down, at one blow, well-confirmed scientific theories. As in the case of other infallible pronouncements, the price of retaining one's epistemological authority is a decent respect for the opinions of mankind.

Thus the common-sense remark that first-person reports always will be a better source of information about the occurrence of pains than any other source borrows its plausibility from the fact that we normally do not raise questions about a man's ability to use the word 'pain' correctly. Once we *do* raise such questions seriously (as in the case of Jones), we realise that the question (1) 'Does he know which sensations are called "pains"?' and (2) 'Is he a good judge of whether he is in pain or not?' are simply two ways of asking the same question, viz. 'Can we fit his pain reports into our scheme for explaining and predicting pains?' or, more bluntly, 'Shall we disregard his pain reports or not?' And once we see this we realise that if 'always be a better source of information' means 'will never be overridden on the sort of grounds on which presumed observational errors are overridden elsewhere in science', then our common-sense remark is probably false. If 'always be a better source of information' means merely 'can only be overridden on the basis of a charge of misnaming, and never on the basis of a charge of misjudging', then our common-sense remark turns out to depend upon a distinction that is not there.

This Wittgensteinian point that sensation reports must conform to public criteria or else be disallowed may also be brought out in the following way. We determine whether to take a surprising first-person report of pain or its absence seriously (that is, whether to say that the sensation reported is something that science must try to explain) by seeing whether the reporters' overall pattern of pain-reporting is, by the usual behavioural and environmental criteria, normal. Now suppose that these public criteria (for 'knowing how to use "pain"') change as physiology and technology progress. Suppose, in particular, that we find it convenient to speed up the learning of contrastive observation predicates (such as 'painful', 'tickling', etc.) by supplying children with portable encephalo-graphs-cum-teaching-machines which, whenever the appropriate brain process occurs, murmur the appropriate term in their ears. Now 'appropriate brain process' will start out by meaning 'brain process constantly correlated with sincere utterances of "I'm in pain" by people taught the use of "pain" in the old rough-and-ready way'. But soon it will come to mean 'the brain process which we have always programmed the machine to respond to with a murmur of "pain".' (A metre is [now, but was not always] what matches the Standard Metre; intelligence is [now, but was not always] what intelligence tests test ; pains will be [but are not now] what the Standard 'Pain'-Training Programme calls 'Pain'.) Given this situation, it would make sense to say things like 'You say you are in pain, and I'm sure you are sincere, but you can see for yourself that your brain is not in the state to which you were trained to respond with "Pain", so apparently the training did not work, and you do not yet understand what pain is.' In such a situation, our 'inability to be mistaken' about our pains would remain, but our 'final epistemo-logical authority' on the subject would be gone, for there would be a standard procedure for overriding our reports. Our inability to be mistaken, is after all, no more than our ability to have such hypo-thetical statements as 'If you admit that I'm sincere and that I know the language, you have to accept what I say' accepted by our fel-lows. But this asset can only be converted into final epistemological authority if we can secure both admissions. Where a clear-cut public criterion *does* exist for 'knowing the language', inability to be mis-taken does not entail inability to be overridden.

Now Baier might say that if such criteria did exist, then we should no longer be talking about what we currently mean by 'pains'. I

do not think that this needs to be conceded,[17] but suppose that it is.
Would this mean that there was now a subject-matter which was not
being discussed – viz. the private subject-matter the existence of
which Baier's argument was intended to demonstrate? That we once
had contact with such a subject-matter, but lost it? These rhetorical
questions are meant to suggest that Baier's explanation of the final
epistemological authority of first-person reports of pains by the
fact that this 'logic' is 'a function of this type of subject-matter'
rather than, as Smart thinks, a convention is an explanation of the
obscure by the more obscure. More precisely, it will not be an
explanation of the epistemological authority in question – but only
an unenlightening redescription of it – unless Baier can give a meaning to the term 'private subject-matter' other than 'kind of thing
which is reported in reports which cannot be overridden'. These
considerations show the need for stepping back from Baier's argument and considering the criteria which he is using to demarcate
distinct subject-matters.

VI. 'PRIVACY' AS A CRITERION OR CATEGORICAL DEMARCATION

The closest Baier comes to giving a definition of 'private subject-
matter' is to say that

> We must say that 'I have a pain' is about 'something private',
> because in making this remark we report something which is (1)
> *necessarily owned* ... (2) *necessarily exclusive or unsharable*
> ... (3) *necessarily imperceptible by the senses* ... (4) *necessarily
> asymmetrical*, for whereas it makes no sense to say 'I could see
> (or hear) that *I* had a pain', it makes quite good sense to say 'I
> could see (or hear) that *he* had a pain'; (5) something about the
> possession of which the person who claims to possess it could not
> possibly examine, consider, or weigh any evidence, although other
> people could ... and lastly (6) it is something about which the per-
> son whose private state it is has final epistemological authority for it
> does not make sense to say 'I have a pain unless I am mistaken.'[18]

Now this definition of 'something private' entails that nothing could

[17] My reasons for thinking this concession unnecessary are the same as
those presented in some recent articles by Hilary Putnam: cf. 'Minds and
Machines', *Dimensions of Mind*, pp. 148–79, esp. pp. 166–75; 'The
Analytic and the Synthetic', *Minnesota Studies in the Philosophy of
Science*, III, ed. H. Feigl and G. Maxwell (Minneapolis 1962) pp. 358–97;
'Brains and Behaviour' in *Analytical Philosophy*, II, ed. R. J. Butler (Oxford
1965) pp. 1–19.
[18] P. 98, above; the numbers in parenthesis have been added.

be private except a state of a person, and is constructed to delimit all and only those states of a person which we call his 'mental' states. To say that mental states are private is to say simply that mental states are described in the way in which mental states are described. But it is not hard to take *any* Rylean category of terms (call it *C*), list all the types of sentence-frames which do and do not make sense when their gaps are filled with terms belonging to this category, and say that 'something *C*' is distinguished by the fact that it is 'necessarily X', 'necessarily Y', etc. where 'X' and 'Y' are labels for the fact that certain sentence-frames will or will not receive these terms as gap-fillers. For example, consider the thesis that:

> We must say that 'The devil is in that corner' is about 'something supernatural' because in making this report we report something which is *necessarily intangible*, since it makes no sense to ask about the texture of his skin, not *necessarily simply located*, since it does not follow from the fact that a supernatural being is in the corner that the same supernatural being is not simultaneously at the other side of the globe, *necessarily immortal*, since it does not make sense to say that a supernatural being has died, *necessarily perceptible to exorcists*, since it would not make sense to say that a man was an exorcist and did not perceive the devil when he was present. . . .

Are devils hallucinations? No, because when one reports a hallucination one reports something which, though intangible, is simply located, is neither mortal nor immortal, and is not always perceptible to exorcists. Are reports of devils reports of hallucinations? No, because reports of devils are reports of something supernatural and reports of hallucinations are reports of something private. Is it simply because we lack further information about devils that we take exorcists' sincere reports as the best possible source for information about them? No, for this suggestion confuses the supernatural character of the subject-matter with the availability of external evidence. Those without the supernatural powers with which the exorcist is gifted may find ways of gathering *evidence* for the presence of supernatural beings, but they can never formulate an overriding and independent *criterion* for saying that such a being is present. Their theories might become so good that we might sometimes say that a given exorcist was *lying*, but we could never say that he was *mistaken*.

If this pastiche of Baier's argument seems beside the point, it is presumably either (1) because the language-game I have described is not in fact played, or else (2) because 'necessarily intangible, not necessarily simply located, necessarily immortal, and necessarily perceptible to exorcists' does not delimit a subject-matter in the way in which 'necessarily owned, exclusive, imperceptible by the senses, asymmetrical, etc.' does. In (1) one has to ask 'what if it *had* been played?' After all, if the technique of detecting distinct subject-matters which Baier uses is a generally applicable technique, and not just constructed *ad hoc* to suit our Cartesian intuitions, then it ought to work on imaginary as well as real language-games. But if it is, we ought to be able to formulate rules for applying it which would tell us *why* (2) is the case. For if we cannot, and if the language-game described once was played, then Baier's objection to the Identity Theory is an objection to the theory that reports of visible supernatural beings are reports of hallucinations.

Baier gives no more help in seeing what these rules would be. But I think that the root of Baier's conviction that 'something private' is a suitable candidate for being a 'distinct subject-matter' is the thesis that certain terms are *intrinsically* observation predicates, and signify, so to speak, 'natural explananda'. When in quest of such predicates we look to the 'foundations' of empirical knowledge, we tend to rapidly identify 'observation predicate' with 'predicate occurring in report having final epistemological authority' with 'predicate occurring in report about something private'. This chain of identifications leaves us with the suspicion that if there were no longer a private subject-matter to be infallible about, the whole fabric of empirical inquiry about public matters would be left up in the air, unsupported by any absolute epistemological authority. The suggestion that the distinction between items reportable in infallible reports and items not so reportable is 'ultimate', or 'irreducible', or 'categorical', owes its intuitive force to the difficulty of imagining a stage in the progress of inquiry in which there was not *some* situation in which absolute epistemological authority about *something* would be granted to *somebody*.

There probably could *not* be such a stage, for inquiry cannot proceed if everything is to be doubted at once, and if inquiry is even to get off the ground we need to get straight about what is to be questioned and what not. These practical dictates show the kernel of truth in the notion that inquiry cannot proceed without a foundation. Where we slide from truth into error is in assuming that certain items are *naturally* reportable in infallible reports, and thus assume that the items presently so reportable always were and always will be reportable (and conversely for items not presently so reportable). A pain looks like the paradigm of such an item, with the situation described by 'seems to me as if I were seeing something red' almost as well-qualified. But in both cases, we can imagine situations in which we should feel justified in overriding sincere reports using these predicates. More important, we see that the device which we should use to justify ourselves in such situations – viz. 'The reporter may not know how to use the word . . .' – is one which can apply in *all* proposed cases. Because this escape-hatch is always available, and because the question of whether the reporter does know how to use the word or not is probably not itself a question which could ever be settled by recourse to any absolute epistemological authority, the situation envisaged by Baier – namely, the body of current scientific theory foundering upon the rock of a single overriding report – can probably never arise. Baier sees a difference in kind between the weight of evidence produced by such a theory and the single, authoritative *criterion* provided by such a report. But since there can be no overriding report until the ability of the speaker to use the words used in the report is established, and since this is to be established only by the weight of the evidence and not by recourse to any single criterion, this difference in kind (even though it may indeed be 'firmly embedded in the way we talk' for millennia) is always capable of being softened into a difference of degree by further empirical inquiry.

VII. Reductionist Philosophical Theories and Categorical Distinctions

In the preceding sections of this paper I have constantly invoked the fact that language changes as empirical discoveries are made, in order to argue that the thesis that 'What people now call "sensations" might be discovered to be brain processes' is sensible and unconfused. The 'deviance' of a statement of this thesis should not, I have been urging, blind us to the facts that (a) entities referred to by expressions in one Rylean category may also be referred to by expressions in another, (b) expressions in the first category may drop out of the language once this identity of reference is realised, and (c) the thesis in question is a natural way of expressing the result of this realisation in the case of 'sensation' and 'brain process'. Now a critic might object that this strategy is subject to a *reductio ad absurdum*. For the same fact about linguistic change would seem to justify the claim that *any* statement of the form (S) 'What people call "X's" may be discovered to be Y's' is *always* sensible and unconfused. Yet this seems paradoxical, for consider the result of substituting, say 'neutrino' for 'X' and 'mushroom' for 'Y'. If the resulting statement is not conceptually confused, what statement is?

In answer to this objection, I should argue that it is a mistake to attribute 'conceptual confusions' to *statements*. No statement can be known to express a conceptual confusion simply by virtue of an acquaintance with the meanings of its component terms. Confusion is a property of people. Deviance is a property of utterances. Deviant utterances made by using sentences of the form (S) *may* betoken confusion on the part of the speaker about the meaning of words, but it may simply indicate a vivid (but unconfused) imagination, or perhaps (as in the neutrino–mushroom case) merely idle fancy. Although the making of such statements may be prima facie evidence of conceptual confusion – i.e. of the fact that the speaker is insufficiently familiar with the language to find a non-deviant way of making his point – this evidence is only prima facie, and questioning may bring out evidence pointing the other way. Such questioning may show that the speaker actually has some detailed suggestions about possible empirical results which would point to the discovery in question, or that he has no such suggestions, but is nevertheless not inclined to use the relevant words in any *other* deviant utterances, and to cheerfully admit the deviance of his original utterance. The possibility of such evidence, pointing to imagination or to fancy rather than to confusion, shows that from the fact that certain questions are typically asked, and certain statements typically made, by victims of conceptual confusion, it does not follow that all those who use the sentences used to ask these questions or to make these statements are thus victimised.

This confusion about confusion is due to the fact that philosophers who propound 'reductionist' theories (such as 'There is no insensate matter', 'There are no minds', 'There are no physical objects', etc.) often *have* been conceptually confused. Such theories are often advocated as solutions to pseudo-problems whose very formulation involves deviant uses of words – uses which in fact result from a confusion between the uses of two or more senses of the same term, or between two or more related terms (e.g. 'name' and 'word') or between the kind of questions appropriately asked of entities referred to by one set of terms and the kind appropriately asked of entities referred to by another. (That these deviant uses *are* the result of such confusion, it should be noticed, is only capable of being determined by questioning of those who use them – and we only feel *completely* safe in making this diagnosis when the original user has, in the light of the linguistic facts drawn to his attention, admitted that his putative 'problem' has been dissolved.) Because reductionist theories may often be choked off at the source by an examination of uses of language, anti-reductionist philosophers have lately become prone to use 'conceptual confusion' or 'category-mistake' as an all-purpose diagnosis for any deviant utterance in the mouth of a philosopher. But this is a mistake. Predictions of the sort illustrated by (S) may be turned to confused purposes, and they may be made by confused people. But we could only infer with certainty from the deviance of the utterance of a sentence of the form (S) to the conceptual confusion of the speaker if we had a map of the categories which are exhibited in all possible languages, and were thus in a position to say that the cross-category identification envisaged by the statement was eternally impossible. In other words, we should only be in a position to make this inference with certainty if we knew that empirical inquiry could *never* bring about the sort of linguistic change which permits the non-deviant use of 'There are no X's' in the case of the 'X's' to which the statement in question refers. But philosophers are in no position to say that such change is impossible. The hunt for categorial confusions at the source of reductionist philosophical theories is an extremely valuable enterprise. But their successes in this enterprise should not lead linguistic philosophers to think that they can do better what metaphysicians did badly – namely, prove the irreducibility of entities. Traditional materialism embodied many confusions, but at its heart was the unconfused prediction about future empirical inquiry which is the Identity Theory. The confusions may be eradicated without affecting the plausibility or interest of the prediction.[19]

[19] I have been greatly helped in preparing this paper by the comments of Richard Bernstein, Keith Gunderson, Amélie Rorty, and Richard Schmitt.

XXI Physicalism

Thomas Nagel

I

It is the purpose of this paper to examine the reasons for believing that physicalism cannot possibly be true.[1] I mean by physicalism the thesis that a person, with all his psychological attributes, is nothing over and above his body, with all its physical attributes. The various theories which make this claim may be classified according to the identities which they allege between the mental and the physical.[2] These identities may be illustrated by the standard example of a quart of water which is identical with a collection of molecules, each containing two atoms of hydrogen and one of oxygen.

All states of the water are states of that collection of molecules: for the water to be in a particular bottle is for those molecules to be arranged in that bottle; for the water to be frozen is for the molecules to be arranged in a space lattice, with strong intermolecular attractive force and relatively weak individual vibratory motion; for the water to be boiling is for the molecules to have a kinetic energy sufficient to produce a vapour pressure equal to the atmospheric pressure; and so forth. In addition to general identities like these, there will be particular ones.[3] One such is the identity between an individual splash of the water and a particular sudden displacement of certain of the molecules – an identity which does not imply that a splash is always identical with that particular type of displacement. In all of these cases we can say something like the following: that the water's splashing is not anything over and above the displacement of those molecules; they are the same occurrence.

[1] An earlier version of this paper was read at the Pacific Division American Philosophical Association meetings in Seattle, 5 September 1964.

[2] I shall not consider behaviourism or reductionism of any kind.

[3] Any identity both of whose terms are universal in form will be called general, even if their specification involves reference to particulars. Thus, 'Water is H_2O', 'For water to be frozen is for its molecules to be in condition F', and 'For *this* water to be frozen is for its molecules to be in condition F' are all general identities. On the other hand, 'This water's (now) being frozen is its molecules' being in condition F' is a particular identity.

It is not clear whether every physicalist theory must assert the identity of each person with his body, nor is the connection between this identity and that of psychological with physical states easy to describe. Still, we can specify a range of possible views in terms of the latter relation alone. (1) An implausibly strong physicalism might assert the existence of a general identity between each psychological condition and a physical counterpart. (2) A weaker view would assert some general identities, particularly on the level of sensation, and particular identities for everything that remains. (3) A still weaker view might not require that a physical condition be found identical even in the particular case with every psychological condition, especially if it were an intensional one. (4) The weakest conceivable view would not even assert any particular identities, but of course it is unclear what other assertion by such a theory about the relation between mental and physical conditions might amount to a contention of physicalism.

I am inclined to believe that some weak physicalist theory of the third type is true, and that any plausible physicalism will include some state and event identities, both particular and general. Even a weak view, therefore, must be defended against objections to the possibility of identifying *any* psychological condition with a physical one. It is with such general objections that we shall be occupied.

I shall contend that they fail as objections to physicalism, but I shall also contend that they fail to express properly the real source of unhappiness with that position. This conclusion is drawn largely from my own case. I have always found physicalism extremely repellent. Despite my current belief that the thesis is true, this reaction persists, having survived the refutation of those common objections to physicalism which I once thought expressed it. Its source must therefore lie elsewhere, and I shall make a suggestion about that later.[4] First, however, it will be necessary to show why the standard objections fail, and what kind of identity can hold between mental and physical phenomena.

II

Since Smart refuted them, it has presumably become unnecessary to discuss those objections which rest on the confusion between

---

[4] In sec. v; of the other sections, II attempts to rebut some standard objections, and III contains a general discussion of identity whose results are applied to physicalism in IV.

identity of meaning and identity in fact.[5] We may concentrate rather on two types of objection which seem still to be current.

The first is that physicalism violates Leibniz's law, which requires that if two things are identical they have all their non-intensional and non-modal properties in common. It is objected that sensory impressions, pains, thoughts, and so forth have various properties which brain states lack, and vice versa. I shall eventually propose a modification of Leibniz's law, since I do not believe that in its strict form it governs the relation asserted by the identity thesis. At this point, however, the thesis may be defended without resorting to such methods, through a somewhat altered version of a device employed by Smart, and earlier by U. T. Place.[6]

Instead of identifying thoughts, sensations, after-images, and so forth with brain processes, I propose to identify a person's having the sensation with his body's being in a physical state or undergoing a physical process. Notice that both terms of this identity are of the same logical type, namely (to put it in neutral terminology) a subject's possessing a certain attribute. The subjects are the person and his body (not his brain), and the attributes are psychological conditions, happenings, and so forth, and physical ones. The psychological term of the identity must be the person's having a pain in his shin rather than the pain itself, because although it is undeniable that pains exist and people have them, it is also clear that this describes a condition of one entity, the person, rather than a relation between two entities, a person and a pain. For pains to exist *is* for people to have them. This seems to me perfectly obvious, despite the innocent suggestions of our language to the contrary.

So we may regard the ascription of properties to a sensation simply as part of the specification of a psychological state's being ascribed to the person. When we assert that a person has a sensation of a certain description *B*, this is not to be taken as asserting that there exist an *x* and a *y* such that *x* is a person and *y* is a sensation and *B(y)*, and *x has y*. Rather we are to take it as asserting the existence of only one thing, *x*, such that *x* is a person, and moreover *C(x)*, where *C* is the attribute 'has a sensation of description *B*'. The specification of this attribute is accomplished in part by the ascription of properties to the sensation; but this is merely part of

---

[5] See Paper III; also Paper XVI, and his book *Philosophy and Scientific Realism* (London 1963), for fuller discussion of the identity thesis.

[6] Place, pp. 49–50, above; for Smart, see p. 61, above. My formulation of the identity differs from Smart's, and I do not accept his psychological reductionism.

the ascription of that psychological state to the person. This position seems to me attractive independently of physicalism, and it can be extended to psychological states and events other than sensations. Any ascription of properties to them is to be taken simply as part of the ascription of other attributes to the person who has them – as *specifying* those attributes.

I deviate from Smart in making the physical side of the identity a condition of the body rather than a condition of the brain,[7] because it seems to me doubtful that anything without a body of some conventional sort could be the subject of psychological states.[8] I do not mean to imply that the presence of a particular sensation need depend on the condition of any part of one's body outside of the brain. Making the physical term of the identity a bodily rather than a brain state merely implies that the brain is *in* a body. To identify the person's having a pain with the brain's being in state X rather than with the body's containing a brain in state X would imply, on the other hand, that if the individual's brain could have been in that state while the rest of his body was destroyed, he would still have been in the corresponding psychological state.

Given that the terms of the identity are as specified, nothing obliges us to identify a sensation or a pain or a thought with anything physical, and this disposes of numerous objections. For although I may have a visual sense impression whose attributes of form and colour correspond closely to those which characterise the 'Mona Lisa', my *having* the sense impression does not possess those attributes, and it is therefore no cause for worry that nothing in my brain looks like the 'Mona Lisa'. Given our specification of the psychological side of the identity, the demands on the physical side are considerably lessened. The physical equivalents of auditory impressions may be silent, those of olfactory impressions odourless, and so forth.

Most important, we can be rid of the stubbornest objection of this type, that having to do with location.[9] Brain processes are located in the brain, but a pain may be located in the shin and a thought has

[7] One might alternatively make it a physical condition of the *person,* so that the two identified attributes would be guaranteed the same subject. I cannot say how such a change would affect the argument.

[8] Cf. Malcolm, pp. 179–80, above.

[9] Malcolm, pp. 174–5, above. See also Shaffer, Paper X. Shaffer thinks the difficulty can be got over, but that this depends on the possibility of a *change* in our concept of mental states, which would make it meaningful to assign them locations.

no location at all. But if the two sides of the identity are not a
sensation and a brain process, but my *having* a certain sensation or
thought and my body's *being* in a certain physical state, then they
will both be going on in the same place – namely, wherever I (and
my body) happen to be. It is important that the physical side of the
identity is not a brain process, but rather my *body's* being in that
state which may be specified as 'having the relevant process going
on in its brain'. *That* state is not located in the brain; it has been
located as precisely as it can be when we have been told the precise
location of that of which it is a state – namely, my body. The same
is true of my having a sensation: that is going on wherever I happen
to be at the time, and its location cannot be specified more precisely
than mine can. (That is, even if a pain is located in my right shin,
I am *having* that pain in my office at the university.) The location
of bodily sensations is a very different thing from the location of
warts. It is phenomenal location, and is best regarded as one feature
of a psychological attribute possessed by the *whole* person rather
than as the spatial location of an event going on in a part of him.

The other type of objection which I shall discuss is that physicalism fails to account for the privacy or subjectivity of mental phenomena. This complaint, while very important, is difficult to state
precisely.

There is a trivial sense in which a psychological state is private
to its possessor, namely, that since it is his, it cannot be anyone
else's. This is just as true of haircuts or, for that matter, of physiological conditions. Its triviality becomes clear when we regard
thoughts and sensations as conditions of the person rather than as
things to which the person is related. When we see that what is
described as though it were a relation between two things is really a
condition of one thing, it is not surprising that only one person can
stand in the said relation to a given sensation or feeling. In this
sense, bodily states are just as private to their possessor as the
mental states with which they may be equated.

The private-access objection is sometimes expressed epistemo-
logically. The privacy of haircuts is uninteresting because there is
lacking in that case a special connection between possession and
knowledge which is felt to be present in the case of pains. Consider
the following statement of the privacy objection.[10] 'When I am in a

10 See Baier, Paper VIII, and Smart, Paper IX. This is regarded as a
serious difficulty by Smart and other defenders of physicalism. See Armstrong, 'Is Introspective Knowledge Incorrigible?', *Philosophical Review*,
LXXII (1963) pp. 418–19. On the other hand, Hilary Putnam has argued

psychological state – for example, when I have a certain sensation –
it is logically impossible that I should fail to know that I am in that
state. This, however, is not true of any bodily state. Therefore no
psychological state is identical with any bodily state.' As it happens,
I believe that the first clause of this objection – namely, the incorrigibility thesis – is false, but I do not have to base my attack on that
contention, for even if the incorrigibility thesis were true it would
not rule out physicalism.

If state x is identical with state y it does not follow by Leibniz's
law that if I know I am in state x then I know I am in state y,
since the context is intensional. Therefore neither does it follow
from 'If I am in state x then I know I am in state x' that if I am
in state y I know I am in state y. All that follows is that if I am in
state y I know I am in state x. Moreover, this connection will not
be a necessary one, since only one of the premises – the incorrigibility thesis – is necessary. The other premise – that x is identical
with y – is contingent, making the consequence contingent.[11]

There may be more to the special-access objection than this, but
I have not yet encountered a version of it which succeeds. We shall
later discuss a somewhat different interpretation of the claim that
mental states are subjective.

III

Let us now consider the nature of the identity which physicalism
asserts. Events, states of affairs, conditions, psychological and otherwise, may be identical in a perfectly straightforward sense which
conforms to Leibniz's law as strictly as does the identity between,

---

that all the problems about privacy and special access which can be raised
about persons can be raised about machines as well. See his paper 'Minds
and Machines', *Dimensions of Mind*, pp. 148–79.

[11] It is worth noting that if two mental states are necessarily connected,
this connection must be mirrored on the level of the physical states with
which we identify them. Although the connection between the physical
states need not be a logically necessary one, that would be a desirable
feature in a physicalistic theory, and it seems in fact to be present in the
example of water and molecules: the water's being frozen necessarily
includes its being cold, and the specification of the molecular state which
is its being frozen entails that the molecules will have a low average kinetic
energy — which is in fact the same thing as the water's being cold.

say, the only horse in Berkeley and the largest mammal in Berkeley. Such identities between events may be due to the identity of two things referred to in their descriptions – for example, my being kicked by the only horse in Berkeley and my being kicked by the largest mammal in Berkeley – or they may not – for example, the sinking of the *Titanic* and the largest marine disaster ever to occur in peacetime. Whether they hold between things, events, or conditions, I shall refer to them as *strict* identities.

We are interested, however, in identities of a different type – between psychological and physical events, or between the boiling of water and the activity of molecules. I shall call these theoretical identities[12] and shall concentrate for the moment on their application to events and attributes rather than to things, although they hold between things as well. It is a weaker relation than strict identity, and common possession of causal and conditional attributes is crucial for its establishment.[13] Strict identities are likely to be established in other ways, and we can infer the sameness of all causal and conditional attributes. Thus, if being kicked by the only horse in Berkeley gave me a broken leg, then being kicked by the largest mammal in Berkeley had the same effect, given that they are the same creature; and if it is the case that I should not have been kicked by the only horse in Berkeley if I had stayed in my office that afternoon, then it follows that if I had stayed in my office I should not have been kicked by the largest mammal in Berkeley.

But if we lack grounds such as these, we must establish sameness of conditional attributes independently, and this depends on the discovery of general laws from which the particular conditionals follow. Our grounds for believing that a particular quart of water's

---

[12] Following Hilary Putnam, in *Dimensions of Mind,* who says that the 'is' in question is that of theoretical identification. The word 'identity' by itself is actually too strong for such cases, but I shall adopt it for the sake of convenience.

[13] An attribute, for our purposes, is signified by any sentence-frame containing one free variable (in however many occurrences) where this may be a variable ranging over objects, events, and so forth. (One gets a particular instance of an attribute by plugging in an appropriate particular for the variable and converting to gerundival form.) Thus all three of the following are attributes: ' . . . is boiling', '∴ . . . will stop boiling if the kettle is taken off the fire', and ' . . . will stop if the kettle is taken off the fire'. A particular quart of water has the second of these attributes if and only if that water's boiling has the third, where this can be described as the possession of the third attribute by a particular instance of the first.

boiling is the same event as a collection of molecules' behaving in a certain way are whatever grounds we may have for believing that all the causes and effects of one event are also causes and effects of the other, and that all true statements about conditions under which the one event would not have occurred, or about what would have happened if it had not, or about what would happen if it continued, and so forth, are also true of the other.

This is clearly more than mere constant conjunction; it is a fairly strong requirement for identity. Nevertheless it is weaker than the standard version of Leibniz's law in that it does not require possession by each term of *all* the attributes of the other. It does not require that the complex molecular event which we may identify with my being kicked by the only horse in Berkeley be independently characterisable as ridiculous – for example, on the grounds that the latter event was ridiculous and if the former cannot be said to be ridiculous, it lacks an attribute which the latter possesses. There are some attributes from the common possession of which the identity follows, and others which either do not matter or which we cannot decide whether to ascribe to one of the terms without first deciding whether the identity in question holds.

To make this precise, I shall introduce the notion of independent ascribability. There are certain attributes such as being hot or cold, or boiling or offensive, which cannot significantly be ascribed to a collection of molecules *per se*. It may be that such attributes *can* be ascribed to a collection of molecules, but such ascription is dependent for its significance on their primary ascription to something of a different kind, like a body of water or a person, with which the molecules are identical. Such attributes, I shall say, are not independently ascribable to the molecules, though they may be dependently ascribable. Similarly, the property of having eighty-three trillion members is not independently ascribable to a quantity of water, though it may be possessed by a collection of H_2O molecules. Nevertheless, there is in such cases a class of attributes which are independently ascribable to both terms, and the condition for theoretical identity may be stated as follows: that the two terms should possess or lack in common all those attributes which can be independently ascribed to each of them individually – with the qualification that nothing is by this criterion to be identical with two things which are by the same criterion distinct.[14] Actually this

[14] The qualification takes care of such possibly problematic claims as that I am the square root of 2, for although it may be that we share all attributes which can be independently ascribed to each of us, I also share those

will serve as a condition for identity in general; a strict identity will simply be one between terms sufficiently similar in type to allow independent ascription to both terms of *all* the same attributes, and will include such cases as the sinking of the *Titanic* being the largest marine disaster ever to occur in peacetime, or the Morning Star being the Evening Star. The identities I have characterised as theoretical hold across categories of description sufficiently different to prohibit independent ascription to both terms of all the same attributes, although, as I have observed, such ascriptions may be meaningful as *consequences* of the identity.

The question naturally arises, to what extent do particular theoretical identities depend on corresponding general ones? In the examples I have given concerning the case of water, the dependence is obvious. There the particular identities have simply been instances of general ones, which are consequences of the same theory that accounts for the common possession of relevant attributes in the particular cases. Now there is a technical sense in which every particular theoretical identity must be an instance of a general identity, but not all cases need be like that of water. Although it is essential that particular identities must follow from general laws or a general theory, this does not prevent us from distinguishing between cases in which, for example, the molecular counterpart of a macroscopic phenomenon is always the same, and those in which it varies from instance to instance. The common possession of conditional attributes can follow for a particular case from general laws, without its being true that there is a general correlation between macroscopic and microscopic phenomena of that type. For example, it may at the same time follow from general laws that types of microscopic phenomena other than the one present in this case would also share the requisite conditional properties.

The technical sense in which even in such cases the particular identity must be an instance of a general one is that it must be regarded as an instance of the identity between the macroscopic phenomenon and the disjunction of all those microscopic phenomena which are associated with it in the manner described, via general laws. For suppose we have a type of macroscopic phenomenon *A* and two types of microscopic phenomena *B* and *C* so associated with it. Suppose on one occasion particular cases of *A* and *B* are occurring at the same place and time, and so forth, and suppose it

---

attributes with the square root of 3, whose attributes clearly contradict those of the square root of 2.

is asserted that since it follows from general laws that they also have all their conditional attributes in common, A is in this case identical in the specified sense with B. They do not, however, have in common the conditional attribute $F(X)$, defined as follows: 'If C and not B, then X.' That is, $F(A)$ but not $F(B)$. Therefore, we must identify the occurrence of A even in this case with the occurrence of the disjunction B or C. This does not prevent us, however, from introducing as a subsidiary sense of identity for particular cases that in which A is B because the disjunction B or C which is properly identical with A is in fact satisfied by B. There is of course a range of cases between the two kinds described, cases in which the disjuncts in the general identity consist of conjunctions which overlap to a greater or lesser degree, and this complicates the matter considerably.[15] Nevertheless we can, despite the technicality, differentiate roughly between particular identities which are in a narrow sense instances of general identities and those which are not – that is, which are instances only of radically disjunctive general identities. Henceforth when I refer to general identities I shall be excluding the latter.

I have concentrated on identities between states, events, and attributes because it is in such terms that physicalism is usually conceived, but if it is also part of physicalism to hold that people are their bodies it becomes appropriate to inquire into the relation between the theoretical identity of things and the theoretical identity of their attributes. Unfortunately, I do not have a general answer to this question. The case of strict identity presents no problem, for there every attribute of one term is strictly identical with the corresponding attribute of the other; and in our standard example of theoretical identity, each attribute of the water seems to be theoreti-

---

[15] A fuller treatment would have to include a discussion of the non-symmetrical relation '... consists of ...' which is distinct from identity. A macroscopic event (the freezing of some water, for example) may be identical with a microscopic event A described in general terms (average kinetic energy, spatial ordering, and the like) while at the same time consisting of a very specific collection B of microscopic events with which it is not identical, since if one of them (the motion of a particular molecule) had been different, that particular complex of microscopic events would not have occurred though both A and the macroscopic event would have. (Presumably in such cases the occurrence of B entails the occurrence of A, but more than that needs to be said about the relation between the two.) The same concept applies to the relation between World War II and the immense collection of actions and events of which it consisted, or that between the Eiffel Tower and the girders and rivets which make it up.

cally identical with some attribute of the molecules, but not vice versa. This may be one (asymmetrical) condition for the theoretical identity of things. It is not clear, however, whether the identity of things must always be so closely tied to the identity of their attributes. For example, it might be that everything we could explain in terms of the water and its attributes could be explained in terms of the batch of molecules and their attributes, but that the two systems of explanation were so different in structure that it would be impossible to find a single attribute of the molecules which explained all and only those things explained by a particular attribute of the water.

Whether or not this is true of water, the possibility has obvious relevance to physicalism. One might be able to define a weak criterion of theoretical identity which would be satisfied in such a case, and this might in turn give sense to an identification of persons with their bodies which did not depend on the discovery of a single physical counterpart for every psychological event or condition. I shall, however, forgo an investigation of the subject; this general discussion of identity must remain somewhat programmatic.

IV

It provides us with some things to say, however, about the thesis of physicalism. First, the grounds for accepting it will come from increased knowledge of (a) the explanation of mental events and (b) the physiological explanation of happenings which those mental events in turn explain. Second, in view of the condition of independent ascribability, physicalism need not be threatened by the difficulty that although anger may be, for example, justified, it makes no sense to say this of a physical state with which we may identify it. Third, it does not require general identities at every level: that is, there need not be, either for all persons or even for each individual, a specific physical state of the body which is *in general* identical with intending to vote Republican at the next election, or having a stomach-ache, in order that physicalism be true. It seems likely that there will be general identities of a rough kind for non-intensional states, such as having particular sensations or sensory impressions, since the physical causes of these are fairly uniform. But one can be practically certain that intensional mental states, even if in each particular case they are identical with some physical state, will not have general physical counterparts, because both the causes and the effects of a given belief or desire or intention are extremely various on different occasions even for the same individual, let alone for different persons. One might as easily hope to find a general equivalent, in molecular terms, of a building's collapsing or a bridge's being unsafe – yet each instance of such an event or circumstance is identical with some microscopic phenomenon.

The relation of intensional mental states to physical states may be even more involved than this. For one thing, if it should be the case that they are dispositional in a classical sense, then physicalism requires only that the events and states to which they are the dispositions be identical with physical events and states. It does not require that they be identical with any additional independent physical state, existing even when the disposition is not being exercised. (In fact, I do not believe that dispositions operate according to the classical Rylean model, and this will affect still further the way in which the identity thesis applies to dispositional mental states; but this is not the place for a discussion of that issue.)

There is still another point: many intensional predicates do not just ascribe a condition to the person himself but have implications about the rest of the world and his relation to it. Physicalism will of course not require that these be identical simply with states of the person's body, narrowly conceived. An obvious case is that of knowledge, which implies not only the truth of what is known but also a special relation between this and the knower. Intentions, thoughts, and desires may also imply a context, a relation with things outside the person. The thesis that all states of a person are states of his body therefore requires a liberal conception of what constitutes a state – one which will admit relational attributes. This is not peculiar to mental states: it is characteristic of intensional attributes wherever they occur. That a sign says that fishing is forbidden does not consist simply in its having a certain geometrically describable distribution of black paint on its surface; yet we are not tempted here to deny that the sign is a piece of wood with paint on it, or to postulate a non-corporeal substance which is the subject of the sign's intensional attributes.

Even with all these qualifications, however, it may be too much to expect a specific physical counterpart for each particular psychological phenomenon. Thus, although it may be the case that what explains and is explained by a particular sensation can also explain and be explained by a particular neurological condition, it may also be that this is not precisely true of an intention, but rather that the various connections which we draw between causes and effects via the intention can be accounted for in terms of many different physical conditions, some of which also account for connections which in psychological discourse we draw via states other than the intention, and no subset of which, proper or improper, accounts for all and only those connections which the intention explains. For this reason a thorough-going physicalism might have to fall back on a criterion for identity between things not dependent on the identity of their attributes – a criterion of the sort envisaged at the end of the previous section.

Obviously any physicalistic *theory*, as opposed to the bare philosophical thesis of physicalism, will be exceedingly complex. We are nowhere near a physical theory of how human beings work, and I do not know whether the empirical evidence currently available indicates that we may expect with the advance of neurology to uncover one. My concern here has been only to refute the philosophical position that mental–physical identity is *impossible*, and that *no* amount of further information could constitute evidence for it.

V

Even if what might be called the standard objections have been answered, however, I believe that there remains another source for the philosophical conviction that physicalism is impossible. It expresses itself crudely as the feeling that there is a fundamental distinction between the subjective and the objective which cannot be bridged. Objections having to do with privacy and special access represent attempts to express it, but they fail to do so, for it remains when they have been defeated. The feeling is that I (and hence any 'I') cannot be a mere physical object, because I possess my mental states: I am their *subject*, in a way in which no physical object can possibly be the subject of its attributes. I have a type of internality which physical things lack; so in addition to the connection which all my mental states do admittedly have with my body, they are also mine – that is, they have a particular *self* as subject, rather than merely being attributes of an object. Since any mental state must have a self as subject, it cannot be identical with a mere attribute of some object like a body, and the self which is its subject cannot therefore be a body.

Why should it be thought that for *me* to have a certain sensation

– to be in a certain mental state – cannot consist merely in a physical object's being in some state, having some attribute? One might put it as follows. States of my body, physical states, are, admittedly, physical states of me, but this is not simply because they are states of that body but because in addition it is my body. And its being my body consists in its having a certain relation, perhaps a causal one, to the subject of my mental states. This leads naturally to the conclusion that I, the subject of my mental states, am something else – perhaps a mental substance. My physical states are only derivatively mine, since they are states of a body which is mine in virtue of being related in the appropriate way to my psychological states. But this is possible only if those psychological states are mine in an original, and not merely derivative, sense; therefore *their* subject cannot be the body which is derivatively mine. The feeling that physicalism leaves out of account the essential subjectivity of psychological states is the feeling that nowhere in the description of the state of a human body could there be room for a physical equivalent of the fact that *I* (or any self), and not just that body, am the subject of those states.

This, so far as I can see, is the source of my uneasiness about physicalism. Unfortunately, whatever its merits, it is no more an argument against physicalism than against most other theories of mind, including dualism, and it therefore provides us with no more reason for rejecting the former in favour of the latter than do the standard objections already discussed. It can be shown that if we follow out this type of argument, it will provide us with equally strong reasons for rejecting any view which identifies the subject of psychological states with a substance and construes the states as attributes of that substance. A non-corporeal substance seems safe only because, in retreating from the physical substance as a candidate for the self, we are so much occupied with finding a subject whose states are originally, and not just derivatively, mine – one to which the physical body can be related in a way which explains how *it* can be mine – that we simply postulate such a subject without asking ourselves whether the same objections will not apply to it as well: whether indeed any substance can possibly meet the requirement that its states be *underivatively* mine.

The problem can be shown to be general in the following way: consider everything that can be said about the world without employing any token-reflexive expressions.[16] This will include the

---

[16] I.e. expression *functioning* as token reflexives. Such words of course lose this function in quotation and in certain cases of *oratio* (or *cogitatio*) *obliqua*: e.g. 'John Smith thinks that he is Napoleon.'

description of all its physical contents and their states, activities, and attributes. It will also include a description of all the persons in the world and their histories, memories, thoughts, sensations, perceptions, intentions, and so forth. I can thus describe without token reflexives the entire world and everything that is happening in it – and this will include a description of Thomas Nagel and what he is thinking and feeling. But there seems to remain one thing which I cannot say in this fashion – namely, which of the various persons in the world *I* am. Even when everything that can be said in the specified manner has been said, and the world has in a sense been completely described, there seems to remain one fact which has not been expressed, and that is the fact that I am Thomas Nagel. This is not, of course, the fact ordinarily conveyed by those words, when they are used to inform someone else who the *speaker* is – for that could easily be expressed otherwise. It is rather the fact that *I* am the subject of *these* experiences; this body is my body; the subject or centre of my world is this person, Thomas Nagel.

Now it follows from this not only that a sensation's being mine cannot consist simply in its being an attribute of a particular body; it follows also that it cannot consist in the sensation's being an attribute of a particular soul which is joined to that body; for nothing in the specification of that soul will determine that *it* is mine, that I am *that* person. So long as we construe psychological states as attributes of a substance, no matter what substance we pick, it can be thrown, along with the body, into the 'objective' world; its states and its relation to a particular body can be described completely without touching upon the fact that I am that person.[17] It turns out therefore that, given the requirements which led us to reject physicalism, the quest for the self, for a substance which *is* me and whose possession of a psychological attribute will *be* its being mine, is a quest for something which could not exist. The only possible conclusion is that the self is not a substance, and that the special kind of possession which characterises the relation between me and my psychological states cannot be represented as the possession of certain attributes by a subject, no matter what that subject may be. The subjectivity of the true psychological subject is of a different kind from that of the mere subject of attributes. And if I am to extend this to cases other than my own, I must conclude that for no person is it the case that his having a particular sensation consists in some occupant of the world having a particular attribute or being in a certain state.

[17] Cf. Wittgenstein, *Tractatus*, 5.64. (London 1922).

I shall not discuss the reasons for rejecting this position. My attitude towards it is precisely the reverse of my attitude toward physicalism, which repels me although I am persuaded of its truth. The two are of course related, since what bothers me about physicalism is the thought that I cannot be a mere physical object, cannot in fact be anything *in* the world at all, and that my sensations and so forth cannot be simply the attributes of some substance.

But if we reject this view (as it seems likely that we must) and accept the alternative that a person is something in the world and that his mental states are states of that thing, then there is no *a priori* reason why it should not turn out to be a physical body and those states physical states. We are thus freed to investigate the possibility, and to seek the kind of understanding, of psychological states which will enable us to formulate specific physicalistic theories as neurology progresses.

POSTSCRIPT 1968

I now believe that theoretical identity is not distinct from strict identity, and that the device by which I formerly defined theoretical identity can be used to explain how Leibniz's law is satisfied by identities whose terms are of disparate types.

Suppose boiling is independently ascribable to a quart of water but not to the molecules which compose it. Nevertheless we can say that the molecules are boiling if they bear a certain relation to the water, and the water is boiling. The relation in question, call it R, is simply that which I formerly described as theoretical identity. It holds between a and b if (i) they possess or lack in common all those attributes which can be independently ascribed to each of them individually (call this relation S), and (ii) neither a nor b bears relation S to any third term which does not bear relation S to the other.[18] Let F range over non-intensional and non-modal attributes, and let us symbolise the modal statement 'F is independently ascribable (truly or falsely) to a' as $I(F,a)$. Then

(1) $S(a,b) \equiv df\ (F)(I(F,a).I(F,b). \supset .F(a) \equiv F(b))$

(2) $R(a,b) \equiv df$ (i) $S(a,b)$ & (ii) a true statement results whenever a name or definite description is substituted for 'x' in the schema $S(a,x) \equiv S(b,x)$

[18] Condition (ii) is added for the reason cited in footnote 14 of my 1965 paper.

I claim that a true statement results whenever names or definite descriptions are substituted for 'x' and 'y' in the following schema:

(3) $(F)(I(F,x).F(x).R(x,y). \supset F(y))$

If this is correct, then when a and b are related by R they will share all the attributes independently ascribed to either of them. By Leibniz's law, therefore,

(4) $R(a,b) \equiv a = b$.

XXII Mind–body identity, a side issue?

Charles Taylor

In recent years, a number of philosophers have argued in favour of materialism in the form of an identity thesis – that is, a thesis to the effect that mental events are identical with certain physiological events.[1] Some have argued directly in favour of a thesis of this kind;[2] others have tried to show that it at least escapes the charge of logical incoherence which has been levelled against it;[3] the implication is that, if this charge can be set aside, the thesis is quite plausible.

It is more rarely questioned, however, just how plausible the ground is on which the thesis rests, and whether it really amounts to an affirmation of materialism. I should like to raise both these questions.

The attempt is made by identity theorists to show that an event considered typical of the mental, like a sensation or the having of an after-image, can be considered without contradiction or incoherence to be identical with a process in the brain or some physiological process in the body as a whole, and that, if further research in neurophysiology, biochemistry, and so on turns out as it is plausible to expect it will, then the identity thesis will impose itself as beyond further objection.

The argument therefore turns on the question whether, granted certain results expected from physiology, biochemistry, and so forth, we can speak of an identity between, say, the having of after-images and the occurrence of brain processes, or the having of sensations and the occurrence of physiological processes in the body as a whole. The argument therefore turns on whether these results will permit us to say that, according to the generally accepted criterion of

---

[1] Cf., among others, Place, Paper II; Feigl, 'The "Mental" and the "Physical" ', *Minnesota Studies in the Philosophy of Science*, II, pp 370–497; Smart, *Philosophy and Scientific Realism* (London 1963).

[2] E.g Smart, *Philosophy and Scientific Realism* and Place, Paper II.

[3] E.g. Rorty, Paper XX; and Nagel, Paper XXI.

identity, the having of after-images and brain processes, say, have
all their non-intensional and non-modal properties in common, or,
if not, whether there is not a more refined concept of identity, more
appropriate in the context of scientific theoretical explanation, which
will still permit the identification.

What are the results, plausibly expected, which form the basis
of this discussion? They are what we would normally describe as a
set of correlations between – to use the above examples – the having
of after-images, and so forth, and brain processes. To speak of
'correlations' here is not to beg any questions. Not even the most
convinced identity theorist would want to deny that the identity in
question is far from open to common observation, and would constitute a hard-won discovery of science. The evidence which would
legitimate it would be the discovery that correlations held between
types of events previously identifiable (and by most people thought
of) as distinct – in this case, the 'raw feel' or the after-image and
the process in the brain. Hence, without prejudice to our eventual
ontological option, we can speak here of the discovery of 'correlations'.

Correlations of this kind can be called the 'ground' of identity
theories, since their protagonists' argument starts from the supposition that such correlations can be established.[4] And it is easy to
see why this is so: unless a given mental event is invariably accompanied by a given, say, brain process, there is no ground for even
mooting a general identity between the two. And since one of the
grounds for affirming an identity which is present in the cases cited
by identity theorists as analogues – for example, lightning and the
electric discharge – namely, sameness of location, is not applicable
here, since mental events cannot be given as precise a location as
physiological events, all the more weight reposes on our ability to
correlate events of the two kinds.[5]

[4] Cf. Feigl, in *Minnesota Studies in the Philosophy of Science,* II, pp.
438–65; Smart, *Philosophy and Scientific Realism,* p. 68; Place, Paper II.

[5] Cf. the argument of Jerome Shaffer in Paper X. Rorty (Paper XX)
also stresses the importance of correlations of this type in view of other
difficulties which the identity thesis encounters. Nagel (Paper XXI) holds
that the difficulty about location can be overcome, but requires the common possession by mental and physical events of causal and conditional
attributes (p. 220, above).

Of course, the failure of correlations of this type would still allow us to
look for *particular* identities, holding not between, say, a yellow after-
image and a certain type of brain process in general, but between a par-

But is the discovery of correlations of this kind after all that plausible? It has appeared so to many materialists, because the only alternative to an outcome of this kind would seem to be the establishing of some sort of 'interactionist' view. A view of this kind is one which takes mental and physical events to be happenings of fundamentally different kinds which are in causal interaction with each other. The difference between this view and its negation is not so easy to define as is sometimes thought. We have to distinguish the interaction of mental events, identified, say, by introspection (such as the having of an after-image) and physical events, identified, say, by the planting of electrodes in the cortex, on one hand, and the kinds of correlations between these events which form the basis of the identity theory on the other.

There are two ways of stating the difference, which seem to be commonly implied, if not stated directly, in the literature.

(1) On the non-interactionist view, we can account for human behaviour having recourse only to laws and conditions governing events on the physical level.[6] The correlations between physical and mental events – for example, brain states and states of consciousness – are 'nomological danglers', which play no role in the explanation of behaviour; whereas on the 'interactionist' view, *ex hypothesi*, mental events are sometimes causes of physical events, and when this is so, reference must be made to them in explaining these events and therefore behaviour.

(2) On the interactionist view, it is possible for there to be mental happenings, quite unlinked with any physical happening, even if this should in fact never come about. The term 'possible' here requires clarification, of course. If we speak of logical possibility, then we cannot deny it even on the non-interactionist view, without prejudging the identity thesis. Indeed, it is one of the arguments deployed against this thesis that there could (logically) be feeling and thought even if there were no body. But on the non-interactionist view the ontological possibility of mental happenings unlinked with physical happenings – that is, of disembodied thinking or feeling – is denied; or, if this possibility is not denied for all being, it is as far as human thinking and feeling are concerned. Whereas on

---

ticular occurrence of this yellow after-image and a particular occurrence of a brain process. This possibility, which does not receive much attention from identity theorists who are usually intent on establishing general identities, will be touched on below.

[6] Cf. Feigl, in *Minnesota Studies in the Philosophy of Science*, II, ibid., esp. pp. 374–87.

the interactionist view, this possibility is affirmed; for if the mental and the physical are seen as two types of event in causal interaction, then there is a stronger than logical possibility that an event of one range could occur without an event of the other range occurring.

To put the point in another way: on both views, disembodied thought or feeling is logically possible, if we apply this term to any state of affairs which can be described without logical contradiction. But only interactionism allows the real possibility, in that by envisaging mental and physical events as causes of each other, it allows that it makes sense to inquire whether after all a given mental event does not have physical causes or consequences, even if a case of this kind is never discovered; whereas, on a materialist view, where the mental can only be some reflection of the physical, it makes sense to inquire *which* physical events are linked with a given mental event, but not *whether* there are any which are linked at all.

Now interactionism in both these senses lacks plausibility for today's *Zeitgeist*. Very few philosophers, be they from positivist, phenomenological, or Hegelian traditions, find the idea of disembodied thought very credible, so interactionists tend to lose out on point (2), the 'ontological' one. And on (1), the 'methodological' point, the widespread acceptance of the view that mental events are unobservable, except to the subject himself, seems to rule out any explanations which have recourse to mental states as unreceivable according to the canons of intersubjective, public scientific inquiry.[7]

But if there is no disembodied thought or feeling, and if all behaviour can be explained in physiological terms, then, surely, the thoughts and feelings which we have and which seem part of the conditions explaining our behaviour must reveal themselves to be, on careful scrutiny, the by-products of those physiological conditions to which the adequate scientific explanation of our behaviour refers. For causes, they cannot be considered *simpliciter*, since we will have an adequate explanation in physiological terms, and they cannot be independent events; they must therefore be linked to those physiological events which provide the explanation of the behaviour we used to invoke them to explain.

We must therefore be able to discover correlations linking these thoughts and feelings to physiological happenings, and the question can then arise whether we will consider them as dependent variables, the tail end of a set of 'dangling' correlations, or whether we will consider them as identical with the physiological conditions with

[7] Cf. Feigl, ibid. esp. pp. 382–7 and 428.

which they are linked. In this latter case we can rehabilitate them as causes of behaviour, on the ground that thought- and feeling-descriptions will now designate the same things as the real causes.

Thus the thesis of mind–body identity is launched, as it were, from the platform of expectation that the progress of physiology will yield an explanation of behaviour in physiological terms, and a set of correlations between mental and physical events which will be in the position of 'nomological danglers' relative to the main science of behaviour.[8] This expectation is in turn given weight by the implausibility of interactionism.

Against this view, I should like to maintain (*a*) that, even granting the case of materialism against interactionism on both (1) and (2), it by no means follows that correlations between certain mental happenings and the holding of certain physiological conditions can be discovered, and (*b*) that we can grant the case of materialism on (2) without granting it on (1), where indeed its position is much less plausible, and that if its case falls here, the identity question is, to say the least, transformed out of all recognition.

(*a*) Even granting that we may be able to account for behaviour by laws and conditions expressed exclusively in physiological terms, it does not follow that we can discover correlations between, say, after-images and brain states, or physical sensations and states of the body. For there is nothing that guarantees that a given after-image, judged the same on repeated occurrences in virtue of its phenomenal properties, will always be accompanied by the same brain state, or even finite disjunction of brain states, whenever it occurs, even in the biography of one person, let alone in all human beings. And the same could be said of the occurrence of any mental conditions, sensation, thought, or feeling.

For if human behaviour exhibits lawlike regularity, on the physiological level, of the sort which enables prediction and control, and a rougher regularity of a less all embracing kind on the psychological level, it does not follow that we can discover one–one or even one–many correspondences between the terms which figure in the first regularities and those which figure in the second. For we can talk usefully about a given set of phenomena in concepts of different ranges, belonging to different modes of classification, between which there may be no exact correspondence, without denying that one range yields laws which are far richer in explanatory force than the others. Thus at one level we may talk about a highway's being dan-

[8] Cf. Smart, *Philosophy and Scientific Realism*, pp. 68 and 90; and H. Feigl, in *Minnesota Studies in the Philosophy of Science*, II, p. 382.

gerous, while at another we talk about the angle of turns, the friction on wet surfaces, the visibility at certain points given normal eyesight, the psychological effect of certain regular patterns on drivers' wakefulness, and so on; or we may talk at one level of a building's being unsafe, while at another we will speak of structural faults, sinking foundations, and so forth. There is no correspondence between the terms at these two levels, because there is no finite set of reasons why a highway may be dangerous or a bridge unsafe. But there is no doubt which level is more fruitful from an explanatory point of view; there is no doubt, that is, that we can explain any case of a highway's being dangerous or a building unsafe in terms of the concepts and laws at the other level.[9]

Thus, even granting the case of materialism in both (1) and (2), granting thus that we can discover a complete explanation for behaviour on the physiological level, and that mental events are not independent of the physiological but susceptible of explanation themselves in physiological terms, it still may be that we can discover no correlations linking given mental events to the occurrence of even a finite disjunction of physiological states. Whether this is so or not is a matter for detailed empirical discovery, even granting the validity of the materialist framework. What is known about cerebral localisation would rather incline us to doubt on this score. And even if it turns out that correlates can be found for such mental events as the occurrence of yellow after-images and toothaches, they may be lacking when we come to the experiencing of oceanic feelings, or the certainty that one has the solution to a problem. Indeed, the more 'global' the mental event, the less plausible it is to suppose a correlation; which is undoubtedly one of the reasons why the examples chosen by identity theorists are usually situated in the sensation–after-image range.

For, if there are no such correlations, then the identity thesis must at least undergo a change. General identities between classes of mental and physiological events will no longer be tenable. But, since in each case a given mental event will be mediated by some physiological happening, particular identities could perhaps be established.[10] We could perhaps say things like: 'The particular yellow after-image that I am now experiencing is the same thing as a brain process with description xyz, now taking place.' But if all we can establish are particular links of this kind, some of the temptation to speak of identity will abate. For the possibility of a systematic

[9] A similar point is made by Nagel, pp. 224–6, above.
[10] Cf. Nagel, Paper XXI.

replacement of phenomenal vocabulary by physiological terms[11] would no longer exist, and this is one of the strongest props of the identity thesis.

(*b*) But supposing materialism, while being right about (2), is wrong about (1)? This is perfectly possible. The position of materialism on (2) is that there can be no mental events which are not linked with physical happenings, because the mental can be only some reflection or aspect of physical reality. Mental events can occur only if mediated by the physical events of which they are the reflection, or on which they are dependent in some way. If we describe this relation between the mental event and the physical event on which it depends in terms of the concept of 'embodiment', we can say that no mental event can occur without the corresponding physical embodiment: for example, there cannot be thinking without a corresponding pattern of excitation in the brain, pain without some corresponding pattern of excitation in nerves and brain, and so on. Of course, as we have seen above, this embodiment may differ from case to case, but it must always be present.

Now conceding the materialist case here (which as we shall see is a position held by other than 'materialists') does not in any way prejudge the answer to question (1). For that all mental events have their physiological embodiments does not mean that the most fruitful set of explanatory laws must be couched in the terms we use to describe these physiological embodiments. The materialist thesis on (2) simply means that the human (and presumably also animal) organism is a complex being where, for the entire range of events which can be described in psychological terms, there are embodiments which must be described in physiological terms. But this does not mean that the explanation, or the most fruitful explanation, of these events must be found in laws governing the embodiments – that, in other words, we can explain what happens at the psychological level by what goes on at the physiological level, or that the regularities observable in mental life will receive a fuller and more wide-reaching explanation in laws of physiology.

For a range of phenomena which can be described at more than one level and in more than one mode of classification, it cannot be determined *a priori* which level will yield explanations of the phenomena which will enable us to predict and control them, or which level will yield the most fruitful explanations. Indeed, a large part of the slow and difficult progress of science in all domains has con-

[11] Cf. Feigl, in *Minnesota Studies in the Philosophy of Science*, ii, pp. 469–70.

sisted in the discovery of the key concepts in which explanatory laws
can be couched. To leap over this stage of inquiry by *a priori* fiat
is no more possible in the sciences of behaviour than it is
in natural science. There is no more reason *a priori* why the
series of 'mental events' which consist of my weighing two courses
of action and then taking a decision should be accounted for in
terms of the series of events which constitute their embodiment,
than there is for the converse relation, where we account for the
occurrence of the series of embodiments in terms of the deliberation
and decision.

Nor does the knowledge that we possess at the moment incline in
the first direction rather than the second. There are some aspects of
human behaviour, using this word in a broad sense, notably in the
case of certain pathological conditions, where the most fruitful
explanation seems to lie on a physiological or biochemical level, but
there are many other ranges of behaviour where this is far from
being the case. It may be that these latter will be accounted for
more fruitfully by laws couched in psychological terms, like those,
for example, of psycho-analysis – that is to say, by explanations
some of which are of teleological form and which refer to intentional properties, that is, properties of the way in which things (self
or situation) appear to the agent (even unconsciously).

Thus, supposing that I decide to vote for candidate A against
candidate B in an election; supposing that the choice is difficult, and
I first weigh their party's platform, the merits of the two candidates, the type of campaign they waged, the possible results of elect-
ing one or the other on the course of future elections, and so on. If
we take the materialist side on question (2), all these 'mental' happenings will be embodied in physiological processes (here largely
located in the brain). I and others are perhaps able to explain my
choice in terms of my long-term aims, my short-term pique, my
(conscious or unconscious) fears, certain images which have a profound (perhaps unconscious) attraction or repulsion for me, my
'identification' with candidate A, or other factors of this type. The
explanation may not show the action to have been a 'rational' one,
but accounts of this type are what I have called psychological, in
that they have (very often) a teleological form, and they refer to
intentional properties.

The materialist thesis on question (1) is that we can discover an
explanation couched in terms of the properties of the physiological
embodiment of these mental happenings, and that, moreover, this
account will be richer than our psychological one, in the sense that

it will enable us to explain the regularities on which our psychological account is based, and much more.

But why should this be so? There is a widespread tendency, among many philosophers of the logical empiricist tradition and among behaviour theorists, to assume that it is, because the only alternative seems to them to be some form of interactionism. Even some philosophers who do not side with materialism, such as J. Shaffer,[12] seem to assume that the only alternative to a 'complete neurophysiological account . . . of brain phenomena,'[18] and hence to epiphenomenalism (if not the identity theory) is interactionism, in which there are 'gaps in the sequence of brain events which are inexplicable physiologically but explainable on an interactionist hypothesis'.[14] It is the conceiving of the alternative to materialism in terms of 'gaps' into which mental events are fitted which, together with the belief about the unobservability of mental events, seems to justify its rejection in the name of science.

But it is premature to assume that regularities will be discovered on the physiological level which mental events might from time to time 'interrupt'. Indeed, in making this assumption we will have already decided the important issue at stake. We need not assume that no regularities will ever be discovered by means of which we can predict or explain physiological events such as those which constitute the embodiment of the above deliberation and decision. But may it not be that the only regularities discoverable will be those which emerge when we characterise these events as *embodiments* of the corresponding thoughts and feelings? In other words, no regularities may come to light as long as we characterise the embodiments in terms of physiological properties, but only when we see them as vehicles of the thoughts and feelings concerned. In this case we would have to say that the most fruitful – indeed the only – explanation of these events was psychological.

This third possibility is usually hidden from those whose attention is riveted by Cartesian (and, it might also be added, empiricist) dualism, either to espouse it or refute it. But it cannot be set aside *a priori*. Our only choice is not between a machine with and one without a ghost. And so we must separate question (2) from question (1) – that is, the question of embodiment from that of the language in which our most fruitful explanations will be couched. The

---

[12] Cf. his 'Recent Work on the Mind–Body Problem', *American Philosophical Quarterly*, 2 (1965) pp. 81–104.

[18] Ibid., p. 100.

[14] Ibid., p. 99.

more so in that, once we have set aside the bogyman of Cartesian dualism, there is no reason to hold that the emotions, feelings, or beliefs of a person are any less observable than the chemical condition of his hypothalamus.

But once we accept that there is more than one answer to question (1), then much of the interest of the identity thesis is lost. True, we can maintain some kind of identity thesis, even if it turns out that some of the most fruitful explanations are psychological, for we can hold the identity of mental states and their embodiments. This manner of speaking may be defensible; it may even be a good way of putting the point that all mental states are embodied. But it will no longer be linked with a reductionist thesis concerning the relation of the mental to the physical, which is, after all, the soul of materialism. The centre of debate about materialism shifts to question (1), whether or not the most fruitful explanations are in physiological terms, or whether some of them are not psychological.

Thus there are good reasons for raising the two questions mentioned at the beginning of this paper. First, the ground of the identity thesis, as this is generally conceived – that is, in terms of general identities – is not as secure as it is taken to be. Even granting the materialist case all along the line, general correlations of the kind required and usually supposed to hold may not be found, at least not across the board.

But the identity thesis could survive this setback; it could be resurrected as a thesis about particular identities. Indeed, the identity thesis could even survive, in a sense, the refutation of the materialist answer to question (1). For interpreted as asserting particular identities between mental events and physiological happenings, it could be seen as identical with the thesis of universal embodiment (to give this high-sounding name to the materialist answer to (2)). But this raises the second question mentioned at the outset: is the identity thesis really an affirmation of materialism? Once one takes seriously the possibility of a non-interactionist alternative to materialism on question (1), it would appear that the major question in dispute between materialists and their opponents is no longer the validity of the identity thesis, which can, indeed, be accepted by either side (not, indeed, by unrepentant dualists, but by phenomenologists, Hegelians, some Marxists, and so forth), but the (ultimately empirical) question of the most fruitful forms of explanation of behaviour.

At this point one may ask what the relevance is of the question whether yellow after-images,[15] or 'raw feels',[16] or sensations[17] are identical with brain processes or physiological processes in the body. The choice of examples in this range shows the preoccupation of philosophers of the tradition of logical empiricism with Cartesian (and empiricist) dualism. For it is after-images, raw feels, and so on which are the best candidates for disembodied mental events accessible only to the subject's self-observation. It is these, therefore, which must be 'reduced' by being shown to depend on, and ultimately to be identical with, brain states or whatever. Other mental conditions, such as being angry, suspicious, and so on, we are accustomed to observing in people's behaviour. It is more tempting to 'reduce' these states along the lines of logical behaviourism.[18]

But the choice of these examples also serves to hide from view certain of the difficulties discussed above. An after-image or a toothache is more likely to have a general neural correlate than the condition of being suspicious of communists, or desiring a promotion, so that the possibilities discussed in (a) are hidden from view. At the same time, we have little difficulty in envisaging an explanation of toothache in terms of tissue damage, nerve excitations, and so forth, or of after-images in terms of neural function. The case is not so clear when we come to events like, for example, becoming angry with a friend who tells us an unpalatable truth we have been hiding from ourselves, or deciding to dodge the draft. So the choice of these examples also serves to hide the possibilities discussed in (b). To focus on such examples is to lend plausibility to a picture in which simple correlations are established with the mental event as dependent variable. This then forms a good platform for the identity thesis, which also becomes the expression of the basic thesis of materialism. But when the two sets of considerations which have been raised above are given their due weight, it may well be that the question whether, say, after-images are identical with brain processes will be thought to be relatively uninteresting.

[15] Smart, *Philosophy and Scientific Realism*, ch. v.
[16] Feigl, in *Minnesota Studies in the Philosophy of Science*, ii.
[17] Rorty, Paper XX.
[18] Cf. Smart, *Philosophy and Scientific Realism*, pp. 88–9; Place, Paper II.

XXIII Illusions and identity[1]

J. M. Hinton

A 'phosphene' is an illusion of a flash of light, which you get when
an electric current is passed through your brain in a certain way.
I shall assume that for every particular phosphene anyone has, there
is such a thing as the (one and only) physiologically describable event
with which the phosphene could be identified if it could be identified with any such event. For if you could equally well identify
something with this or that thing, then you could by no means
identify it with either.[2]

On the assumption that there is such a sole physicalistic identity-
candidate, ϕ, for a given phosphene, some philosophers would argue
as follows: 'ϕ is an actual event and the phosphene is an actual
event; and there is no good reason to hold that two (different) actual
events have been mentioned here. Therefore there is good reason,
on grounds of economy, to hold that one, and only one, actual event
has been mentioned: namely ϕ, or the phosphene.' (Cf. J. J. C.
Smart, 'Sensations and brain processes' (Paper III).)

---

[1] Revised by the author, February 1969.

[2] What would have to be the case for the assumption that every particular
phosphene has such an identity-candidate to be true? It would be enough if
there were at least and at most one physiological statement P – counting
equivalents as one – of a kind to which you could attach a time clause and
a reference to a subject, and such that whenever P was true for any subject,
that subject had a phosphene, and vice versa. (P might be of the form
'Some A-neurons are X-ing', to which you could add 'in s' and 'at t'.)
If these conditions were satisfied there would be a sole physicalistic identity-
candidate for the phosphene that a particular subject, s, had at a particular
time, t; namely, the event described by the statement 'in s, P at t' or 'sPt'.
I do not think, though, that there need be such a statement as P for there
to be such an identity-candidate. Suppose we had a well-attested generalisation. 'Whenever sQ, s has a phosphene', whose antecedent 'sQ' described
what was, of the conditions actually satisfied at t, the most complex condition sufficient for s's having a phosphene that could be stated as a conjunction of economically sufficient conditions for this. In that case I should
have thought there would be a sole physicalistic identity-candidate for the
phosphene s had at t: namely the event described by 'sQt'.

Others would reply that they do not understand the contention that φ and the phosphene are one and the same event; and that they lack a 'criterion of identity' for the case. This not understanding, and this request for a criterion of identity, could themselves do with some explaining. What is a criterion of identity? When someone produces the criterion of identity that he is using in a given context, does this involve his giving proof, or conclusive evidence, of identity? If so, no philosopher who agreed that one must always have a criterion of identity would have offered the economy argument in the first place. The economy argument is a substitute for proof or conclusive evidence: someone who brings it is trying to show that the identity thesis may or should be asserted, instead of trying to show that it is true. Perhaps one could be said to have produced one's criterion of identity if one tried to show the assertibility, the meet-to-be-asserted-ness, of something that would in itself be proof or conclusive evidence of identity; something that itself presented no problem as to the absent conditions in which it might truly be said to have been conclusively ascertained. But is that procedure the only proper alternative to offering proof or conclusive evidence of identity? Perhaps the demand for a criterion of identity is to be interpreted in an even less stringent way, so that indiscernibility, the having all properties in common, would fill the bill. But must the identity thesis be supported by an argument which actually makes some use of this criterion – as distinct from an argument which, by showing that identity is assertible, shows that indiscernibility is equally assertible if it follows from identity?

An objection, however, to the economy argument – an objection which does seem to me to have great force – arises from a reductive analysis of the grammatical predicate 'x is an event'. The analysis is in line with views advanced by Geach (*Procs. Brit. Acad.*, 1965) – and, I should have thought, with the views of Carnap, Wittgenstein and Ryle on categorical or 'categorial' predications.[8]

---

[8] That such analyses of grammatical predicates like '... is an event', '... is a state', etc., obstruct without actually refuting psycho-physical identity theses may be obvious to some: it was brought home to me in correspondence by Geach – who is not to be held responsible for my attempt to spell out the way in which the obstruction occurs in this instance.

The economy argument can, not unfairly it seems, be set up like this:

(1) φ at time t was an actual event.
(2) Bill's phosphene at time t was an actual event.
(3) There is no good reason to hold that two (different) actual events have been mentioned above.
(4) So let us assert that just one actual event has been mentioned.

This way of putting the economy argument corresponds to an always available, and sometimes useful, way of paraphrasing the statement that x is one and the same N as y (where N is a common noun). You can always take such a statement as saying three things: that x is an N; that y is an N; and that the number of N's mentioned in saying so is exactly one.

The trouble is that this economy argument is shattered if its first two premises reduce to, say,

(1r) Bill 'φ-ed' at time t
(2r) Bill 'phosphened' at time t,

where these are verbs introduced to say that Bill underwent the relevant neural change and that he had a phosphene. For now no 'actual events' whatever are 'mentioned above'. Nothing is mentioned but Bill. Nor would it make any difference if we made Bill's brain, or a part of it, the logical subject of (1r) and (2r) rather than Bill himself; or if we got rid of a logical subject altogether, so that 'it φ-ed and phosphened' as it rains and snows.

'Nonsense', someone will say. 'An event is mentioned in (1r) and also in (2r). Admittedly, neither of these statements mentions an event in exactly the way in which it mentions Bill, by making an event its logical subject. Still, each may be said to 'mention' an event in a broader sense of the verb.'

No doubt each statement may be said to 'mention an event', in some sense of the *phrase*. That each mentions an event is true, but what does it mean? Suppose it means merely that each statement is an event-statement, a syntactically proper answer to the question 'What happened at t?' Or suppose it means this and, moreover, that the statements are true: that Bill did indeed φ and phosphene at t. If this is all it means then, contrary to appearances, it no more entails that the number of events is at least one, than do the two statements themselves. And *is* this all it means? Someone who reduces (1) and (2) to (1r) and (2r) will hardly shrink from saying that it is.

On the reductionist view, then, the statement '(1r) mentions an actual event' no more entails that the number of actual events is at least one, than does (1r) itself; nor will it help to put them together. And similarly with (2r). But if the economy argument does not establish that the number of actual events is at least one, then it can hardly establish that the number of actual events mentioned in its first two premises is at least and at most one.

To put it another way; suppose that, in the course of some philosophical discussion, in which we are using fantasy-examples, I have occasion to say: '(The point is that) a prince's being turned into a toad is a happening (whereas his being in the shape of a toad is a state).' I shall probably be receptive to the suggestion that, in making this general, 'categorical' assertion, I was only making a second-order statement, to the effect that statements like 'A prince was turned into a toad', 'The prince was turned into a toad', and so forth, belong in the syntactical box or category labelled 'Statements that answer the question "What happened?".' This box collects statements that 'answer that question' in the sense in which 'Two' does, and 'Brown' does not, answer the question 'How many?'; the sense in which 'Brown' does, and 'Two' does not, answer the question 'What sort of a one?' It is a logico-grammatical fact that statements like 'The prince was turned into a toad' answer that question; and this logico-grammatical fact is surely the only fact I stated when I said: '. . . a prince's being turned into a toad is a happening' – or '. . . is an event'.

If now I say, still speaking generally, 'Someone's reflecting is an actual happening' or 'Someone's after-imaging is an actual happening', then I have at least given the same sort of second-order, logico-grammatical information. And if to this I have added the information that after-imaging or reflecting actually occur – then I have merely added this information. I have added that people reflect or after-image; or that 'it reflects' or 'it after-images' humanly. I have not given some mysterious sort of mother-information, from whose womb the logico-grammatical and the psycho-biological pieces of information issue like offspring that have nothing in common. I have just given those two bits of information: my statement analyses into those components. By saying with a peculiar emphasis that after-imagery actually *occurs*, I may confuse but cannot logically fuse such disparate contents.

There will be no change in this basic situation if I try to apply the general statement that 'Someone's after-imaging is an actual event' to a particular case, by saying that Bill's after-imaging at this very moment is an actual event. In this statement Bill is classified: as a present after-imager. (Or you can say so if you like, though it does some violence to the notion of classification.) And this act of classifying, or what is stated in it, is classified in its turn; as an answer to the question 'What happened?' And that is all the classifying there really is, in the apparent, the so-called, 'classifying of Bill's present after-imaging as an actual event'. Similarly with the so-called classifying of Bill's ϕ-ing as an actual event. So if I ask whether, in this pair of so-called classifications, the case is really that two different things have each been classified as an actual event, or whether it is really that one and the same thing has twice been classified as an actual event; then the answer is a simple if unexpected 'No'. Which obviously precludes me from arguing, from the impermissibility of answering 'Two different things', to the permissibility of answering 'One and the same thing'.

This reductionist objection shows only that the argument from economy will not do,[4] and not that the numerical identity of ϕ with the phosphene cannot be established in some other way. (For instance, by trying to show that ϕ falls into every genuine, as distinct from merely so-called, classification into which the phosphene falls, and vice versa; so that they have all genuine properties in common.) The objection does, however, throw light on the demand for a criterion of identity in so far – though only in so far – as this comes from those who accept the reduction. This demand, from that quarter, can be seen as a demand for proof of the identity-thesis. Proof or demonstration in a broad sense is demanded by the reductionist, not just because he would like to think that proof was necessary, but because his reduction – if accepted – destroys the argument from economy; and because the idea of an empirical substantiation of the identity thesis seems inapplicable.

An objector's avowal of event-reductionism would also throw some light on his claim not to understand the identity-thesis. He, though not necessarily another, has some right to demand a clarification, since for him the event-identity thesis cannot simply be taken as meaning what it says: that one is the number of a certain set of events identified by a two-member list of names or other designations. He cannot be content to paraphrase the thesis as 'The phosphene is an event; the after-imaging is an event; and the num-

---

[4] Indeed, all the objection shows is that the economy argument will not do unless it can be restated in terms of some common noun that can be relied upon not to do the same sort of disappearing trick as the noun 'event' does. But I do not think it is easy to find a suitable noun.

ber of events mentioned in saying so is one'; so he needs an account of what the thesis really means.

Not all those who would block 'physicalism' with a call for a criterion of identity are reductionistic analysts of the predicate '... is an event'. But when they are not, the exact nature of the difficulty they see in the economy argument is something they should surely explain.

Perhaps this may not be too hard a task, however. Perhaps the economy argument would still fail, even if the common noun that was applied to both the brain processes and the after-imaging did not get lost in the process of clarification.[5] Assuming a case in which, in all strictness of speech and even in the last analysis, at least one N has indeed been mentioned in 'x is an N and y is an N'; the difficulty now concerns the next premise: that there is 'no good reason' to assert that two different N's have been mentioned there. This cannot, of course, mean merely that no good reason for 'two' has yet been found. That would be a very inadequate ground for the final recommendation that we assert 'Exactly one'. The right course, in that case, would clearly be just to go on asserting 'At least one'. Nor, I think, can it mean merely that no good reason for 'two' will ever be found. Why would that make it reasonable to assert 'Exactly one', rather than to stick with 'At least one'? It must mean that there is no discovered or undiscovered reason, though a reason is needed. The trouble with this, I now think, is that it would yield a straight deductive argument for 'Exactly one'.

We are given 'At least one', and also of course 'At most two' (N's mentioned in the statement 'x is an N and y is an N'). If we are given, further, that the answer 'Two' could not be known to be true without a ground; and also that no true proposition, discovered or undiscovered, is a ground for it; then it follows that even one who knew, with respect to every proposition, whether it was true or not, would not know that the answer 'Two' was true. But from this it seems to follow that he would know that it was not true; and from this, that it is not true; and from this, together with what we were

---

[5] I did not think so, when I wrote the unrevised version of this article: I then saw no way of justifying a rejection of the economy argument except the reductionist way. Still, even if we ought to say that the economy argument will not do no matter what noun is used, and that we therefore need something like a proof of the identity thesis, and that this will automatically give us what you might call a criterion of identity; this is different from saying that the economy argument will not do because we need a criterion of identity.

given, it seems to follow that the answer 'One' is true. But if this does indeed follow from the premises of the 'economy' argument, then not only is the argument ill-named but we cannot expect anyone who is inclined towards the answer 'Two' to accept its premises.

Tentatively accepting the limited reductionism and its consequence, the breakdown of the economy argument; and supposing for the moment that there is no better way (discovered or undiscovered) of getting to the identity thesis than the way of economy; it would seem to follow that there is – in the strong sense – no good reason to assert identity. Would this mean that there was good reason to assert duality: to assert that ϕ and the phosphene were two different events? Even on the assumption that there is no discovered or undiscovered ground, independent of the reductionism, for the rejection of duality, could we pass from there being – in the strong sense – no good reason to assert identity, to there being good reason to assert duality? I should have thought not; for such a step would surely assume that some number of actual events, not zero, is listed in the statement 'ϕ is an actual event and the phosphene is an actual event'; and our reductionism will not allow us to assume this.

It may now seem as if our reductionism will not allow us to assert event-identity and event-duality at all. I am led, with some misgivings, to the view that this is so in a way; but that we should distinguish here between oneness and sameness, duality and difference.

What I mean is this. We can, surely, say that the beheading of Charles I and his execution were the same event, because that was how he was executed. But it would seem strange to admit, on this ground, that the class of events has at least one member, if we are unwilling to admit it on the ground that Charles I was executed. 'The events', then, 'are the same'; but not 'That makes one'. Similarly, we can surely say that Mrs Jones' party and the party in honour of Professor Smith were different parties, and so different events, because Mrs Jones' party was not in honour of Professor Smith. But it would seem strange to admit, on this ground, that the class of events has at least two members, if we are not willing to admit that it has at least one member on the ground that Mrs Jones gave a party. So it seems that 'the events are different', but not that 'that makes two'. We might well adopt a similar view, with less reluctance, where sameness and difference of *qualities* is concerned. However, my distinction between oneness and sameness, duality and difference, is not offered too solemnly. A 'sameness statement' is just a numerical identity statement that cannot simply be taken as meaning what it says. And similarly a 'difference statement' is just a numerical duality statement that cannot be taken in that way.

Where does this leave the supposed law that where x and y are actual events, they must either be one and the same actual event or two different actual events? It surely destroys it, if these statements imply 'That makes one' and 'That makes two' respectively. The general principle, that if x is an N and y is an N then either x and y are one (the same) N or they are two (different) N's, cannot possibly hold good *a priori*, where 'x is an N' and 'y is an N' reduce in such a way that no statement as to the number of N's is formulable in the last analysis. And as for the law 'Where x and y are actual events, they must either be the same or be different' (where this does not imply there being any number of actual events) I do not think we have to accept that either. It is clearly not the case that x and y must either be capable of being shown to be the same or capable of being shown to be different: and if no statements as to their number can be made, it would seem odd to insist that what is true of them, and what is capable of being shown to be true of them, are two quite different things. If we have no ontology of events, we need fear no confusion between the orders of being and of knowing, where events are concerned.[6]

[6] More to the point, perhaps: we have already said that 'x is (one and) the same event as y' has got to be given some non-face-value meaning if the reductive analysis of '... is an event' is accepted. Failing some such clarification applicable to the particular case, someone who agrees with the reductive analysis can hardly be expected to accept as significant the alleged *a priori* statement 'Either these events are one and the same, or they are not'.

In the first version of this article I used a common but misleading metaphor: I represented the reductive analysis of '... is an event' as implying that the number of events was or might be zero. The point is rather that, in the last analysis, no statement as to the number of events, or the number of events which (for example) were mentioned in a given remark, can be made. The analysis of '... is an event' is a 'new-level' one, in the demythologised sense of 'new-level'; that is to say, when we express ourselves about events in clearer terms we just do not have the predicate '... is an event', or any equivalent predicate, in our vocabulary. Not having it, we can hardly attach it to a quantifier. Not having 'Hx', 'x is a happenment',

Objections to the economy argument which, unlike the reductionist objection, strike me as lacking any force, include the following:

(i) All those which are based on the assumption that the economy argument requires us to obey the absurd order to say how many events occurred at a certain time. In what way does it require us to do so? The old Scottish nursery rhyme is, after all,

> The laverock and the lark,
> How many birds is that?

and not, say, 'The laverock and the lark, how many birds are there in the Kingdom of Fife?' We are not invited to count unlisted birds – or events. So what is the relevance of the fact that we cannot count the events, or the after-imagings, that occurred between time one and time two? This fact has, it seems to me, no relevance at all.

---

we do not have '... Hx...'. So we do not have $\sim\exists x{:}Hx$', i.e. '$0x{:}Hx$', any more than we have '$\exists x{:}Hx$'; or have '$!\exists x{:}Hx$', i.e. '$1x{:}hx$'; or have '$1x{:}Hx\&Mx$' or '$2x{:}Hx\&Mx$', where 'Mx' means 'x is mentioned in such and such a statement'.

True, the grammatical predicate '... happened' occurs in our utterance when we say that a certain statement answers the question 'What happened?' And it will be objected that this predicate is a synonym of '... was a happening'; so that a predicate equivalent to this does seem to figure in our clarified vocabulary, after all. (R. G. Swinburne drew my attention to the difficulty.) It is not a satisfactory reply to the objection to say that we mention rather than use the word 'happened' when we say that a certain statement answers the question 'What happened?' For in mentioning the question we do seem to imply that we have it, and therefore also the predicate, in our vocabulary. However, a statement like 'He after-imaged' can be a *complete* answer to the question 'What happened?'; it can tell the questioner *all* he wants to know. In a context in which it does so, we must do one of two things. We must either regard 'He after-imaged' as a less perspicuous form of 'His after-imaging was a happening', which strikes me as all wrong; or else we must accept that the question 'What happened?' can be completely answered without classifying anything as a happening. In that case, the appearance of requiring that something be so classified, which a philosophical eye can see in the question, must be an illusion. And so our reference to, and use of, this question does not bring into our vocabulary a predicate equivalent to the so-called classificatory predicate '... is a happening'.

The reduction relates solely to the given predicate, of course. From the fact that '... is an event' is reductively, eliminatively analysed, is excluded from the language in the process of clarification, it in no way follows that '... is a tea-party' is to be treated in the same way, for all that 'a tea-party is an event'. It may be, that '... is a tea-party' is to be treated in that way, but not for that reason. The point was often stressed in the older Philosophy of Logical Analysis.

Certainly, if all birds are composed of birds, then this is unfortunate for all statements about 'the bird in my hand', irrespective of whether they state it to be identical with something, or just to sing, say. But even under these conditions, if I speak of 'the largest' or of 'the ringed' bird in my hand, then I can say that it is singing, and is identical with such-and-such a thing; and all those smaller, unringed birds will be of no further interest. Similarly with Bill's *whole* after-imaging between time one and time two: any events, or even after-images, of which this may be composed, or which it may help to compose, have nothing to do with the case, as they have not been mentioned. The question is, how many N's were mentioned in 'x is an N and y is an N', not how many are to be found in some spatial or temporal context. It is false that this last question must always be a sensible one if 'x is one and the same N as y' is to make sense. The bit of ground now covered by Tom's garage is the very same bit of ground as the bit of ground he marked out with pegs and string a week ago, even though the question 'How many bits of ground are there in Tom's garden?' is far from being a sensible one.

(ii) Objections based on the assumption that an economy argument must invite us to count 'listeds' in some other way than what is involved in merely saying '1' because '0' has been ruled out and '2' is unreasonable.

(iii) Objections based on the assumption that identity is always established by re-identification; almost as if, in the phrase 'It's that man again!', it were not 'It's that man' but 'again!' that related to the man's identity. Identity, after all, is not a kind of 'again-ness', and does not consist in re-presentation to a subject, whatever the etymology may suggest.

In J. J. C. Smart's article, already cited, there are what might be regarded as two other ways of getting to the identity thesis, apart from the argument from economy. These might be called the way of specification and the way of assimilation. According to the first, φ and the phosphene are one and the same event in the way in which the doctor's telephoning and somebody's telephoning are, when it is the doctor who telephones.

This way of specification (transposed from Smart's case of an after-image to the case of a phosphene) involves two steps. The first is meaning-analytical, and consists in claiming that a subject's report of his phosphene has roughly the sense: 'Something is happening that is similar to what happens when I see a flash of actual light, a photic flash.' The second step is to claim that, when such a report is true, ϕ is in fact happening and is in fact similar to what happens when the subject sees a photic flash; so that ϕ stands to the subject's report as the doctor stands to the report 'Someone telephoned'.

Unfortunately the first step here, the meaning-analytical one, seems to me to get its plausibility from a confusion between the two very different statements that are set out as (a) and (b) below. (a), the less intrinsically certain of the two, is of the sort that is required for the second step in the way of specification, but it cannot plausibly be claimed to be what a subject's report of his phosphene means. Of (b) this claim can plausibly be made, but (b) is not the sort of statement needed for the second step:

(a) 'Something or other must be happening which actually has properties in common with whatever it is that happens when I see a flash of light.'

(b) '(You can take it from me that) something is happening which I find like seeing a flash of light.'

Statement (a) seems to be a conjecture or hypothesis, however rational, as distinct from a report on one's present experience. That is why (a) can be verified by the discovery of ϕ, and of ϕ's similarity to what happens when the subject sees a flash of light. In (b) on the other hand, if we could add a 'namely-rider' at all, we could not add 'namely ϕ' but only 'namely a phosphene'. When I find that a particular sensation or experience is like going up in a high-speed lift or when to me it is like this, what 'is to me like' this or 'is found by me like' this, is not a neural process; even if the sensation or experience is identical with a neural process. 'x is to me like y' is non-extensional. And if the very idea of a namely-rider to 'Something is happening that is to me like seeing a flash of light' should prove misleading; if this statement should prove indistinguishable from 'It is to me as if I were seeing a flash of light'; then the gap between (a) and (b) would open wider still. (It would, by the way, be most unwise in my view to try to use this distinction between two statements to prove that ϕ and the phosphene are two. What is established is only a difference between two statements, but I think the 'way of specification' depends on our failing to see this difference.)

So it seems as if the 'way of specification will not do, even as a way to the sort of reducible, non-serious identity-statement which I am calling a 'sameness' statement: this is all we are looking for, now.

The way of assimilation, in Smart's article and its predecessor

(U. T. Place, 'Is consciousness a brain process?' (Paper II)) consists in representing the case of the phosphene as not relevantly different from other scientific cases which, it is assumed, we shall be willing to think of as involving alternative descriptions of the same event: for instance the case of a flash of lightning, or electric discharge exciting the atoms of the air. One might, perhaps, add such cases as the sun's rising over Samoa, or the earth's rotation bringing Samoa into the sunlight: where as in the case of the phosphene and of the after-image, we would not happily speak of Place's ' "is" of composition'.

At present I feel that in the light of our reductionism this line of argument is inconclusive; if only because it is not clear that we ought to speak of the 'same' event, as distinct from not speaking seriously of two different events, in the cases to which appeal is made. The only cases of this scientific kind that seem quite clear to me are those literally of composition, e.g. a body of water's boiling and the water molecules' reaching critical velocity.

There occurs to me a fourth way of trying to get to the 'sameness' thesis. I can only call it the way of identification; not identification in the sense of saying or finding that this and that are the same, which would hardly be what I mean by 'a way of getting to' the thesis that they are the same; but identification in the sense of saying exactly what something is. In outline the argument goes like this.

'The statement that ϕ occurred – or that the subject ϕ-ed – states exactly the actual nature, the identity, of the event that we describe colloquially as the illusion of a flash of light. In that sense it identifies this event. Identification-statements may not always entail the corresponding identity-statements, but they entail them unless there is some good reason to deny this.'

When stated more fully, this 'fourth way' argument requires you to take three steps. I can only take the first two, and so I have to reject the argument.

The first step is simply to accept, as a meaningful part of our language, a certain kind of conjunction. I mean a 'conjunction' in the logical sense; an 'and'-statement, albeit one in which the 'and' may have further implications pinned to it, as it has in 'p although q', 'p, moreover q' and 'p, therefore q'. The relevant kind of conjunction is: 'Apparently p, but in reality q'. Here the force of the 'but' with its implication of contrast, gives 'apparently' the sense 'in *mere* appearance' or 'in illusion'. 'In reality q' or 'actually q' differs hardly at all from 'q' *tout court*: the adverbial expression only indicates that 'q' is occurring as a conjunct in a conjunction of the relevant kind. The other conjunct is not, of course, 'p' but 'In mere appearance p'; this is incompatible with 'p'.

The second step is to assert that only our ignorance prevents us from stating a conjunction of the form 'Apparently s saw a flash of light, but in reality he φ-ed', which would be true in a natural interpretation. (φ-ing has the meaning already explained.)

The third step, which seems to me probably wrong, is to claim that the conjunction just mentioned would identify, in its second clause, an event which in its first clause it merely described, as a preliminary to identification. What makes me think that this step is probably wrong is that it seems to require an assumption that is probably wrong: namely that of the two formulations

(i) s had the illusion of seeing a flash of light

and

(ii) In mere appearance (in illusion) s saw a flash of light

this last is the more perspicuous. This seems to be assumed, for (i) has the appearance of an identifying description of the event in question. It is therefore important to the 'fourth way' argument at its third step that (i) means (ii), rather than the other way round. Yet is seems to me that the other way round is the right way round: for 'In mere appearance p' surely means different things in different contexts, and needs to be clarified in this context by saying that (ii) means (i). (Or else by clarifying both still further, say as: 's was illuded that s saw a flash of light'.)

What account, after all, could one give of the operator 'In illusion p' or 'In mere appearance p', except one that went something like this?

'When "p" is a statement of the form "x saw o", "x heard o" etc., the statement "In illusion p" means "x had the illusion of seeing o" or "... of hearing o"; but when "p" is a statement like "A flying saucer descended in Regent's Park", then "In illusion p" means something like "Somebody had the (visual) illusion of a flying saucer descending in Regent's Park"; and perhaps in other contexts it means something else again. For instance "In illusion he produced the card out of thin air", said of a conjuror rehearsing without a mirror, possibly means or is like saying that if there had been an attentive audience, some of them would have had the visual illusion of his producing the card out of thin air.'

The operator 'In illusion p', or 'p in appearance only' seems to be a bit unidiomatic and a bit ambiguous: you can't regard it as speaking for itself. But when you translate it in the phosphene context into 'x had the illusion of seeing a flash of light', you no longer ap-

pear to have one member of an 'Only apparently p; in reality q'
conjunction which can plausibly be regarded as an identification. I
do not say that you no longer appear to have an 'Only apparently p,
in reality q' conjunction. I still accept step two of the 'fourth way'
argument. How, then, is the conjunction 'In mere appearance s
saw a flash of light; in reality he φ-ed' to be interpreted, if not as
an identification?

I think that this conjunction, and what I feel forced to regard
as its more perspicuous equivalent, 's had the illusion of seeing a flash
of light; actually he φ-ed', should be interpreted not as an identification but as what I will call 'a statement as to the fact of the matter'.
I can best explain what I mean by turning to the sort of case in
which we are told that x had, not the illusion, but the mistaken idea
that something or other was happening; say that he was being
chaired in triumph; and in which we reply by asking what was in
fact happening: were they taking him to the horsepond, or what?
We do not mean: What did his having that mistaken idea consist
in? We mean: What idea would he have had to have, in order to
have the right idea; or in other words, what was the fact of the
matter? (To ask this seems in general not unlike asking from what
fact or facts the falsity of the mistaken idea follows: though there
is also at least sometimes a selection among these facts, according to
what question the false idea was thought of as answering. If someone
has the idea that Lima is the capital of Bolivia, then the 'fact of the
matter' is either that Lima is the capital of Peru; or that La Paz is
the capital of Bolivia; or that both these things are so; according to
what the question was.)

Having an illusion is admittedly not the same thing as having a
mistaken idea – except in an irrelevant, transferred sense of 'illusion'
– but in the case of any illusion of sense there is a mistaken idea that
you would have if you 'believed the evidence of your senses': an
idea that you are tempted to have. It is open to us to ask, alluding
to this false idea, what was the fact of the matter: and it seems to me
that this may well be what we are doing when, apropos of the statement 'x had the illusion of seeing a flash of light', we ask what
actually or really happened.

If the statement apropos of which we ask this question were 'x
believed that he saw a flash of light', then the fact of the matter
could be said simply to be that he did not see one, or that no such
flash occurred. But if the statement we are given is that x had the
illusion of seeing a flash of light, then we have already been told that
much; and when we ask what actually, or in fact, happened our

interlocutor has to cast about for some more information to give us. ϕ's occurring is something he will most naturally mention if he thinks of it as a cause of the illusion; and he will not be any the less inclined to cite it if he thinks of cause and effect here as different, simultaneous events. So his statement as to what 'actually happened' cannot, it seems, be thought of as identification.[7]

Nor, I take it, can we interpret as an identification the scientific statement 'What (actually) happens, when you have a phosphene, is that 'p' (where 'p' is neurophysiological). This statement can be intended in various ways: as the neutral generalisation that a certain physiological statement with explanatory force of one kind or another, is true of a subject when it is true that he has a phosphene; or as an approach towards a physiological redefinition of a phosphene, a redefinition that is useful because it correlates with subjects' reportings; or as a mere correlating of those reports with the physiological process – a correlation in a spirit of methodical, as distinct from philosophical behaviourism. None of these three things is, or entails, a *contingent* identity-statement.

My tentative, and rather reluctant, conclusion, then, is that unless the other arguments for difference – other, that is, than the argument from the unprovability of sameness – are stronger than I think them to be, those of us who are inclined to accept a reductive analysis of 'x is an event' should refuse to say either that ϕ and the phosphene

---

[7] A variant of the 'fourth way' would be to argue that a phosphene, a false flash-sighting, must be a true something else, since nothing can be a false everything; and that there is nothing for the false flash-sighting to be but a true ϕ-ing, since a 'true phosphene' would just be a 'true false flash-sighting'.
But I said when discussing the way of specification that a ϕ-ing, which is a kind of electrical or electrochemical process, is not 'to the sentient subject like' a flash-sighting; in which case it can hardly be classified as a false one. It might still be identifiable in some way or other with some false flash-sighting or other; but not by way of being classified in its own right as a false flash-sighting, and consequently having to be identical with some false flash-sighting if anything is. And if there is nothing that can be classified in its own right as a true ϕ-ing and false flash-sighting, then how can there be anything that can be classified in its own right as a false flash-sighting and true ϕ-ing? The conclusion, that each false flash-sighting is identical with some ϕ-ing, cannot it seems, be reached by that way of identificatory classification.
So the phosphene, the false flash-sighting, is a true what? A true nothing? This would only mean that the 'Something is happening which...' construction was a misleading form of 'It is to me as if —'; as I implied it might be, when I was discussing the way of specification.

are the same event, or that they are different events. Also that when philosophers who do not accept such an analysis of 'x is an event' concur in this refusal, they should be asked why. I do not at present see how *they* can avoid accepting the *a priori* statement that one or the other of these things must be the case, though of course they are fully entitled to say that they do not know which of them it is.

Bibliography

Articles in this volume are not included. The following abbreviations have been used:

A – Analysis
AJP – Australasian Journal of Philosophy
APQ – American Philosophical Quarterly
D – Dialogue
JP – Journal of Philosophy
M – Mind
P – Philosophy
PPR – Philosophy and Phenomenological Research
PQ – Philosophical Quarterly
PR – Philosophical Review
PS – Philosophical Studies
RM – Review of Metaphysics
T – Theoria

BOOKS

S. Hook (ed.), *Dimensions of Mind* (New York: New York University Press 1960; Collier Books 1961).
J. J. C. Smart, *Philosophy and Scientific Realism* (London: Routledge & Kegan Paul 1963; New York: The Humanities Press 1963).
P. K. Feyerabend, G. Maxwell (eds), *Mind, Matter, and Method*, Essays in honour of Herbert Feigl (Minneapolis: University of Minnesota Press 1966).
C. F. Presley (ed.), *The Identity Theory of Mind* (Brisbane: University of Queensland Press 1967).
H. Feigl, *The "Mental" and the "Physical" – The Essay and a Postscript* (Minneapolis: University of Minnesota Press 1967). The essay first appeared in vol. II of *Minnesota Studies in the Philosophy of Science: Concepts, Theories and the Mind–Body Problem*, ed. H. Feigl, M. Scriven, G. Maxwell (Minneapolis: University of Minnesota Press 1958): references are to this publication. Feigl's book contains two very useful bibliographies comprising 565 items.

D. M. Armstrong, *A Materialist Theory of the Mind* (London: Routledge & Kegan Paul 1968; New York: Humanities Press 1968).

ARTICLES

D. M. Armstrong, 'Is Introspective Knowledge Incorrigible?', *PR*, LXXII (1963) pp. 417–32.
—— 'The Headless Woman Illusion and the Defence of Materialism', *A*, 29 (1968) pp. 48–9.
J. Beloff, 'The Identity Hypothesis: A Critique', in J. R. Smythies, (ed.) *Brain and Mind* (London: Routledge & Kegan Paul 1965; New York: The Humanities Press 1965).
M. C. Bradley, 'Sensations, Brain-processes and Colours', *AJP*, XLI (1963) pp. 385–93.
—— 'Critical Notice of Smart's *Philosophy and Scientific Realism*', *AJP*, XLII (1964) pp. 262–83.
R. B. Brandt and J. Kim, 'The Logic of the Identity Theory', *JP*, LXIV (1967) pp. 515–37.
K. Campbell, 'Critical Notice of *The Identity Theory of Mind*, ed. Presley', *AJP*, XLVI (1968) pp. 127–45.
J. W. Cornman, 'Mental Terms, Theoretical Terms, and Materialism', *Philosophy of Science*, 35 (1968) pp. 45–63.
—— 'On the Elimination of "Sensations" and Sensations', *RM*, XXII (1968) pp. 15–35.
A. C. Garnett, 'Body and Mind – The Identity Thesis', *AJP*, XLIII (1965) pp. 77–81.
D. F. Gustafson, 'On the Identity Theory' *A*, 24 (1963) pp. 30–2.
R. J. Hirst, 'Mind and Brain: The Identity Hypothesis', in *The Human Agent*, Royal Institute of Philosophy Lectures, 1, 1966–7 (London: Macmillan & Co. 1968; New York: St. Martin's Press 1968).
M. Hockutt, 'In Defence of Materialism', *PPR*, XXVII (1967) pp. 366–85.
R. Hoffman, 'Malcolm and Smart on Brain–Mind Identity', *P*, XLII (1967) pp. 128–36.
W. D. Joske, 'Sensations and Brain Processes: A Reply to Professor Smart', *AJP*, XXXVIII (1960) *pp.* 157–60.
J. Kim, 'On the Psycho-physical Identity Theory', *APQ*, 3 (1966) pp. 227–35.
—— 'Psychophysical Laws and Theories of Mind', *T*, XXXIII 1967) pp. 198–210.

W. Kneale, 'Critical Notice of *A Materialist Theory of the Mind*', *M*, LXXVIII (1969) pp. 292–301.

D. K. Lewis, 'An Argument for the Identity Theory', *JP*, LXIII (1966) pp. 17–25.

D. R. Luce, 'Mind–Body Identity and Psycho-Physical Correlation', *PS*, XVII (1966) pp. 1–7.

J. Margolis, 'Brain Processes and Sensations', *T*, XXXI (1965) pp. 133–8.

N. Maxwell, 'Understanding Sensations', *AJP*, XLVI (1968) pp. 127–45.

B. Medlin, 'Materialism and the Argument from Distinct Existences', in J. J. MacIntosh and S. C. Coval (eds), *The Business of Reason* (London: Routledge 1969).

R. Norton, 'On the Identity of Identity Theories', *A*, 25 (1964) pp. 14–16.

G. Pitcher, 'Sensations and Brain Processes: a Reply to Professor Smart', *AJP*, XXXVIII (1960) pp. 150–7.

R. Routley and V. Macrae, 'On the Identity of Sensations and Physiological Occurrences', *APQ*, 3 (1966) pp. 87–110.

W. S. Sellars, 'The Identity Approach to the Mind–Body Problem', *RM*, XVIII (1965) pp. 430–51.

J. Shaffer, 'Recent Work on the Mind–Body Problem', *APQ* 2 (1965) pp. 81–104.

G. Sheridan, 'The Electroencephalogram Argument against Incorrigibility', *APQ*, 6 (1969) pp. 62–70.

J. J. C. Smart, 'Sensations and Brain Processes: A Rejoinder to Dr Pitcher and Mr Joske', *AJP*, XXXVIII (1960) pp. 252–4.

—— 'The Identity Thesis: A Reply to Professor Garnett', *AJP*, XLIII (1965) pp. 82–3.

F. Stoutland, 'Ontological Simplicity and the Identity Hypothesis', *PPR* (forthcoming).

C. Taylor, 'Critical Study of Armstrong's *A Materialist Theory of the Mind*', *PQ*, 19 (1969) pp. 73–9.

J. Teichmann, 'The Contingent Identity of Minds and Brains', *M*, LXXVI (1967) pp. 404–15.

J. E. Tomberlin, 'About the Identity Theory', *AJP*, XLIII (1965) pp. 295–9.

G. N. A. Vesey, 'Agent and Spectator: The Double-Aspect Theory', in *The Human Agent*, pp. 295–9.

D. Weissman, 'A Note on the Identity Thesis', *M*, LXXIV (1965) pp. 571–7.

J. Wolfe and G. J. Nathan, 'The Identity Theory as a Scientific Hypothesis', *D*, VII (1968) pp. 469–72.